State Religious Education
and the State of Religious Life

State Religious Education
and the State of Religious Life

LIAM GEARON
and JOSEPH PRUD'HOMME

PICKWICK *Publications* · Eugene, Oregon

STATE RELIGIOUS EDUCATION AND THE STATE OF RELIGIOUS LIFE

Pickwick Publications
An Imprint of Wipf and Stock Publishers
199 W. 8th Ave., Suite 3
Eugene, OR 97401

www.wipfandstock.com

PAPERBACK ISBN: 978-1-62564-726-9
HARDCOVER ISBN: 978-1-4982-8776-0
EBOOK ISBN: 978-1-5326-4691-1

Cataloguing-in-Publication data:

Names: Gearon, Liam, author. | Prud'homme, Joseph, author.

Title: State religious education and the state of the religious life / Liam Gearon and Joseph Prud'homme.

Description: Eugene, OR: Pickwick Publications, 2018 | Includes bibliographical references and index.

Identifiers: ISBN 978-1-62564-726-9 (paperback) | ISBN 978-1-4982-8776-0 (hardcover) | ISBN 978-1-5326-4691-1 (ebook)

Subjects: LCSH: Religion and state | Religious education | Bible | Religion and civil society

Classification: LC111 G85 2018 (paperback) | BV1471.3 (ebook)

Manufactured in the U.S.A.   04/03/18

Contents

Acknowledgments, Dedications, Permissions, and Copyrights

WE WOULD LIKE TO acknowledge the superb work of the members of Blackfriars Hall, University of Oxford, at whose workshop on religious education we were fortunate to meet.

We are delighted to dedicate this work to our wives, for proving so clearly the wisdom of the Apostle Paul: love, indeed, is patient, love indeed is kind.

Sections of this work are drawn with permission from the following works/volumes:

1. Liam Gearon, "The King James Bible and the Politics of Religious Education: Secular State and Sacred Scripture," *Religious Education* 108 (2013) 9–27.

2. Liam Gearon, "European Religious Education and European Civil Religion," *British Journal of Educational Studies* 60 (2012) 51–169.

Taylor and Francis graciously extended permission to use substantial sections of these two essays. For more on the press, see www.tandfonline.com.

3. "Conclusion," by Joseph Prud'homme, in *Curriculum and the Culture Wars: Debating the Bible's Place in Public Schools*, edited by Melissa Deckman and Joseph Prud'homme, 177–203, Washington College Studies in Religion Politics and Culture 3 (New York: Lang, 2014).

For more information on the press or the series, please see www.peterlang.com.

4. We have drawn with permission from the following biblical versions:

   a. King James Version

Introduction

ACROSS THE UNITED STATES, a growing number of policy advocates, educational theorists, and social and political reformers argue that America's public secondary schools need much greater attention to the Bible to ensure adequate understanding by students of basic topics involving American and world history, literature, and the arts. Specifically, advocates have called for public schools to offer elective courses exclusively exploring the Bible and its influence on history, literature and culture, or to add to existing courses significant new sections studying the Bible and its cultural and historical legacy. This movement has also received what potentially could be significant financial and curricular support from *Hobby Lobby* magnate and billionaire philanthropist Steve Green through an ambitious development of a four-year sequence of Bible courses tied to the major new biblical museum that Green is funding in Washington, DC—a program he hopes eventually will find adoption in public schools across the country. What is more, in 2016, a national political party adopted as a core component of its platform a call to have local school boards nationwide adopt Bible courses in public secondary schools.

This movement has received its strongest endorsement by groups best identified as traditionally conservative, and, indeed, it is the Republican Party that incorporated this plank in its recent platform.[1] In turn, progress in incorporating a greater focus on biblical religion in public education has most strikingly been made in states commonly called "red states," that is, states in which a sizable percentage of citizens identify with traditional

---

1. Brown, *GOP Platform Encourages Teaching about the Bible in Public Schools.* What is more, Emmy award-winning producer and actress Roma Downey, a devout Christian whose highly popular movies and television shows have been watched and admired by millions and who will soon launch a new, twenty-four-hour Christian cable network (Light TV), is an impassioned proponent of non-devotional Bible courses in public schools. See Downey and Burnett, *Why Public Schools Should Teach the Bible.*

social and religious values. In 2007, the state legislature in Texas passed a law expanding biblical instruction on the cultural contributions of the Bible in American and Western civilization in the form of a requirement that high schools work to offer optional elective Bible courses, or to include major new sections on the Bible in existing elective coursework. In the past two decades, the legislatures in Florida (1996), Georgia (2006), South Carolina (2006), Tennessee (2008), Oklahoma (2010), South Dakota (2012), Arizona (2012), and Arkansas (2013) have each passed legislation promoting greater instruction of the Bible in their public high schools, with legislation also recently passed, after a period of delay, in Kentucky (2016). Further, proponents of enhanced instruction of the Bible in public schools have suffered only quite narrow defeats in the legislatures of Indiana, Alabama, Missouri, New Mexico, and Idaho, with advocates pledging to renew their efforts in the years ahead. In 2016, the Idaho legislature passed a bill permitting Bible courses, only for the bill to be vetoed by Governor C. L. "Butch" Otter. Given that the bill passed with overwhelming support, and given the passion on this issue of its sponsor, Senator Sheryl Nuxoll, the issue will almost certainly reemerge in the years ahead in the Gem State—as well as in states across the country.[2]

Such proposals are often spearheaded by organizations with strong affiliations with religious conservatives, including the National Council on Bible Curriculum in Public Schools, Wallbuilders, and the less conspicuously conservative Bible Literacy Project. As noted, the movement recently received the endorsement of Steve Green, the billionaire founder of the successful Hobby Lobby chain, through an educational initiative connected with his founding of a truly word-class museum on the Bible—the Museum of the Bible—located only blocks from the National Mall in Washington, D.C. Despite an initial setback, Green is committed to an eventual national campaign involving public school curricula.[3]

In this work, we first document the calls for a heightened appreciation of the Bible in public school curricula. Compelling arguments, we contend, support this movement. To underscore our point, in addition to documenting the calls for greater Bible courses, we also develop a sympathetic account

---

2. Haake, *GOP Idaho Governor Vetoes "Unconstitutional" Bill to Teach Bible in Public Schools.*

3. *Christianity Today,* "Hobby Lobby's Bible Course Cancelled by Oklahoma School District." In a recent, strongly critical, and at times uncharitable review of Green's efforts to date, Candida Moss and Joel Baden note, we think accurately, that Green "has not given up [his] dream of seeing the Bible taught across America." Moss and Baden, *Bible Nation: The United States of Hobby Lobby,* 136. We agree that his curriculum is "precisely the curriculum they would like to place in a public school, should another one be willing to give them the opportunity." Ibid., 119.

of the justifications advanced to support this cause, paying particular attention to the striking rise in biblical illiteracy in the United States; the cogent reasons for a curricular change to focus primarily on the Bible; and the constitutionality of the reform proposals. This last point—the constitutionality of the reform—holds notwithstanding the fact that curricular reform is often strongly advocated by religious conservatives and, in part, may involve a motive of advancing biblical religion.

Indeed, it may well be the case that there are advocates who promote these courses out of a variety of motives including that of advancing the cultural and social influence of the Bible. This does not disbar the effort. It is our contention that the presence of a motive of advancing religion cannot be barred when simultaneously a sufficient non-religious argument is advanced by the actor on behalf of the policy prescription. This is so for a number of reasons. We hold that the Constitution's prohibition on an established religion at most requires that policy have an articulable secular rationale, that is, a rationale that the agent genuinely believes and asserts is based on arguments accessible to reason unaided by religious tradition or divine inspiration. When agents advance such a claim, we speak of their being a sufficient secular argument. The actor does not need to have a secular motive for advancing secular arguments of this sort. To require anything more than a secular rationale—that is, to require the actual presence of a secular motive—is both an impermissible intrusion on the free exercise of religion, and might involve the state in epistemic difficulties for which it has no need to enter. We establish these points by imaging two types of motive: explicitly stated motives, and motives grounded only on inference. As to the former, we argue that the right of religious conscience to inform an individual's voting behavior and approach to public life is a key component of the constitutionally protected right of the free exercise of religion and, thus, any requirement for an exclusively secular motive in relation to public policy is indefensible.

As to the latter, our position is an argument *a fortiori*: not only is it constitutionally improper to search out unstated or imperfectly stated motives, but doing this—that is, divining unstated motives as a precondition to permitting the enjoyment of the constitutionally protected right of religious free exercise—establishes a dangerous principle, as it makes the enjoyment of rights conditional on a task for which the state is not well suited. Within this framework, our argument for the constitutionality of greater curricular attention to the Bible in public schools is supported by our recognition of a sufficient secular rationale for educating students about the Bible, namely, the proper pedagogical purpose of educating students about the country's cultural and literary heritage.

After developing our constitutional argument, we turn our attention to a further question, one that has not been asked in the literature on biblical instruction: Is it permissible for political debate to address issues from the perspective not of the positive impact of biblical instruction on the religious culture of a community, but on the *negative* impact of such educational programs on a community's religious vitality?

To this question, we argue that the very same reasons that justify the constitutionality of increased biblical instruction necessitate an affirmative response. Just as with the advancement of religion, so with its erosion or degradation, we maintain that when a sufficient secular rationale is articulated against a policy proposal, the state cannot further demand that the actors have no motives that relate to religious preservation or protection. This position, we argue, is equally grounded on the right of religious conscience to inform an individual's voting behavior and approach to political life and public affairs.

Lastly, we develop the crux of our assessment of calls to increase biblical instruction in public schools. We argue first for a sufficient secular argument against investing resources in biblical education in public schools, namely, the need to allocate scarce resources to meet other challenges, including the appropriate focus schools must place on scientific, technological, and mathematical coursework. However, we explicitly define as one of our motives for endorsing this position the suspicion that the inclusion of greater curricular attention to the Bible would serve over time to *undermine* biblical religious culture in various and important ways.

As part of this argument, we address the development of a desire among a growing number of educational elites for a globalized civil religion—a conception of religion that displaces traditional Christian orthodoxy—and the relationship this development bears to calls for state religious education in the United States, that is, calls for state-sponsored instruction on the contents and legacy of the Jewish and Christian scriptures. In all, our argument is, if only in part, a conservative theological argument but one directed *against* enhanced biblical instruction in public schools.

Our approach is novel in the literature addressing biblical instruction for at least four reasons. First is the sympathy with which we approach calls for greater biblical instruction while rejecting that call ourselves. A range of legal challenges have been developed by advocacy groups and a number of scholars, generally representing the cultural left, against calls for expanded biblical coursework. This body of literature argues that enhanced biblical instruction represents an unconstitutional change in educational policy. At the forefront of this charge has been Mark A. Chancey, a progressive religious studies professor at Southern Methodist University.[4] His influential essay "Sectarian Elements in Public School Bible Courses: Lessons from the Lone Star State,"[5] as well as his piece "Bible Bills, Bible Curricula, and Controversies of Biblical Proportions: Legislative Efforts to Promote Bible Courses in Public Schools,"[6] and other works challenge the constitutionality of calls for enhanced instruction of the Bible. In 2013, he engaged once more in a vigorous review—amounting, perhaps, to a spirited crusade—against elective Bible courses in Texas, with special focus on how too often he sees "a political agenda" at odds with strict separationism.[7] Also prominent has been the work of Stephen Webb, starting with his essay "The Supreme Court and the Pedagogy of Religious Studies: Constitutional Parameters for the Teaching of Religion in Public Schools."[8] Shorter pieces developed by the advocacy organization, Americans United for Separation of Church and State, and affiliated organizations, have echoed this sentiment, including sharply critical reports by the Texas Freedom Network[9] as well as independent scholarship by the director of Americans United, Barry Linn. We reject these arguments yet also reject increased biblical instruction, advancing thereby a unique claim in the field.

---

4. Apart from monitoring Bible courses, Professor Chancey specializes in the so-called historical Jesus hermeneutic of biblical scholarship. The historical Jesus hermeneutic has at times become clearly un-Orthodox. Catholic theologian John Peter Meier of the University of Notre Dame notes, "the historical Jesus" is quite different from what orthodox faith holds to be the "real Jesus." The historical Jesus is a "theoretical, modern construct." When it is treated as more than that, the hermeneutic—which refuses to consider any points about the resurrection and much about the early church—is outside any cognizable sense of Christian orthodoxy. See Meier, "Why Get to Know the Historical Jesus?"

5. Chancey, "Sectarian Elements in Public School Bible Courses: Lessons from the Lone Star State," 719–42. See also Osborne, "Study: Belton ISD's Bible Literature Course Breaks Federal Commandments."

6. Chancey, "Bible Bills, Bible Curricula, and Controversies of Biblical Proportions: Legislative Efforts to Promote Bible Courses in Public Schools," 1–20.

7. As co-chair of the Society of Biblical Literature's Working Group on the Bible and Public Education, Chancey has conducted a number of studies on this topic. In 2013, he updated his earlier study conducted for the liberal advocacy group, The Texas Freedom Network, under the title "Writing & Religion II: Texas Public School Bible Courses in 2011–2012." As to the Texas Freedom Network, its website states that "The Texas Freedom Network fights the powerful influence of the Religious Right . . . and has been instrumental in defeating initiatives backed by the Religious Right in Texas.."

8. Webb, "The Supreme Court and the Pedagogy of Religious Studies: Constitutional Parameters for the Teaching of Religion in Public Schools," 135–57.

9. For additional information on the views of the Texas Freedom Network, see *The Bible and Public Schools: Report on the National Council on Bible Curriculum in Public Schools.*

Second, our argument is unique because we do not address the issue from the perspective of a multicultural educational approach. A number of scholars have argued for enhanced biblical instruction but only as part of a broader multicultural and multi-confessional educational philosophy. Best-selling author Stephen Prothero in his work, *Religious Literacy: What Every American Needs to Know—And Doesn't*[10] argues for a broad-gauged instruction in religious traditions as a way to improve school children's understanding of cultural differences in a diverse and pluralistic society. This call is developed also by the American Academy of Religion and to a somewhat lesser extent by the Society of Biblical Literature.[11]

Especially important in this regard is the work of Diane Moore, chair of the American Academy of Religion's Religion in the Schools Taskforce, and her 2007 book *Overcoming Religious Illiteracy: A Cultural Studies Approach to the Study of Religion in Secondary Schools*.[12] Also important are works by Suzanne Rosenblith and Beatrice Bailey, including Bailey's 2008 piece "Cultivating a Religiously Literate Society: Challenges and Possibilities for America's Public Schools,"[13] as well as the earlier work of James W. Fraser, including his book *Between Church and State: Religion and Public Education in a Multicultural America*.[14] This position has also been defended with considerable passion in numerous works by the educational theorist Nell Noddings.[15]

We do not defend this multiculturalist position but instead argue—from a perspective that rejects the call for more religious education by public schools—that if there *were* to be enhanced instruction on a sacred text in public school curricula, it would be entirely appropriate for it to based primarily on the Bible, and not equally on alternative religious canons or sacred traditions. As such, our position is additionally unique in the existing literature.

---

10. Prothero, *Religious Literacy: What Every American Needs to Know—And Doesn't*.

11. See the American Academy of Religion's "Guidelines for Teaching about Religion in K–12 Public Schools in the United States, 2010." For additional resources from the Society of Biblical Literature, see "Bible Electives."

12. Moore, *Overcoming Religious Illiteracy: A Cultural Studies Approach to the Study of Religion in Secondary Schools*.

13. Rosenblith and Bailey, "Cultivating a Religiously Literate Society: Challenges and Possibilities for America's Public Schools," 145–61.

14. Fraser, *Between Church and State: Religion and Public Education in a Multicultural America*.

15. See, for example, Noddings, *Educating for Intelligent Belief or Unbelief*; and *Critical Lessons: What Our Schools Should Teach*.

Third, our argument is unique due to the kinds of arguments we do raise against enhanced biblical instruction. We develop a range of arguments that situates this debate within real world political and cultural forces marked by increasing ignorance of, and even hostility to, religion, and the growing multicultural values orientation, as well as the intransigent problem of radical Islam and the responses to this problem by state elites in the form of their defining a particular expression of Islam as legitimate, and the real possibility that such a movement would color the state's treatment of the Christian faith. By doing so, we take the issue out of the ethereal realm of pedagogical theory and desires for an ideal curriculum—where so much of the debate thus far has been located—and assess the call from the perspective of a realism about contemporary social and political trends. Such real world pressures, we argue, will inevitably infect the way biblical religion would be taught—and this would operate to the detriment of biblical religion's positive influence on contemporary culture.

Additionally, we supplement this argument about possible negative effects on biblical religion of public schools' instruction of the Bible by a distinctive trans-Atlantic assessment, exploring firstly the development of religious education in England and the lessons this experience holds for the United States. We argue that the experience in England with religious education in state-supported schools is highly pertinent to contemporary education policy in the United States. Our assessment starts with the Education Act of 1870 that made religious instruction compulsory in England, and then surveys the development of religious education in English state-supported schools from 1870 to the present. In doing so, we argue that religious education has been turned into a force that has in fact undermined English religious culture. Secondly, we explore the recent developments in state religious education by broadening our focus to include continental Europe, and by introducing the concept of a globalized civil religion—or a state-supported religion serving the state's objectives without regard to claims of traditional religion—and show it to be an aspiration of an increasingly influential segment of educational leaders, and we note the potential for similar developments to take place in the United States. Of course, in formulating this analysis, we take pains to develop the relevant similarities between the English and Continental European contexts and that of the United States, and develop a trans-Atlantic comparative account that is informed by the differing histories of these regions. In doing so, we establish an additionally distinct element in debates over the Bible's role in public schools.

Fourth, our view is unique because we develop an alternative model for addressing the genuine and pressing problems that advocates of biblical instruction are seeking, in part or in whole, to repair. We argue that the position we defend can itself supply tools and perspectives that can assist those seeking to redress the problems of religious illiteracy and rising religious hostility. This is so because a focus on the state's incapacity to address religion adequately is an often underappreciated aspect of church/state separationism, an account of the relationship between church and state that shifts the locus of concern from religious tenets and organizations to actions of the state. By locating the animating spirit of church/state separationism in skepticism concerning the state's involvement in religion, we are better able to appreciate the cogency of calls to empower state schools to permit out-of-class instruction on the Bible for academic credit in the public school system—a model recently adopted by the state of South Carolina. Hence, we aspire to be comprehensive in our assessment and to advance many of the same goals of educational reformers, even as we reject the use of state religious education to achieve these objectives.

In all, therefore, our claims are unique among much in the contemporary literature. Our work strives to ring a loud but we hope helpful tocsin: school boards in the United States should be cautious about heightened instruction of the Bible, and should learn from a Trans-Atlantic perspective. In sum, we provide a cautionary account that reformers seeking to enhance religious instruction in public schools would do well to heed, while also providing an approach that can help to advance the legitimate aspirations of biblical instruction advocates.

We do so specifically by addressing in chapter one the call for greater Bible instruction in public schools. In chapter two, we examine the relationship between the non-establishment clause of the First Amendment and the existence of religious motivations for legislative enactments, and then extend our discussion of religion in public affairs by defending the constitutionality of religiously informed legislation as long as a sufficient secular objective is also present. In chapter three, we advance a defense of curricular reform based on expanding course offerings addressing the historical, literary, and cultural value of the Bible. In chapter four, we then develop a secular objection to the Bible courses we sympathetically assessed in the preceding chapter—an argument based on the need to allocate scarce educational resources to STEM coursework. We then move in chapter five to set forth an additional, explicitly religiously grounded objection to Bible-focused curricular reform—the claim that Bible courses will undermine religious vitality due to a variety of likely and existing problems with the manner in which these courses are, or would be taught in the United States public schools. In chapter six, we supplement this argument with a set of objections against Bible coursework in public schools grounded on the concern that the state will "securitize" the Bible to serve real or perceived security interests. Chapter seven broadens our discussion to a review of state religious education in England, and ways we believe it has undermined the vitality of religious life. In chapter eight, we move to a discussion of the utilization of religion in state schools in Europe to serve state objectives—the specter of what we call global civil religion. In chapter nine, we move in a more positive direction by outlining an alternative to state religious education, focusing on the promise of for-credit public school courses on the historical and cultural importance of the Bible taught in private venues, including in private schools. Such a way forward opens the possibility of resisting the perils of state religious education, and especially its enervation of religious life, while responding to the national educational scandal of biblical illiteracy, as well as a culture of rising biblical hostility.

Chapter 1

State Religious Education
The Bible in Public Schools in the United States

IN THIS CHAPTER, WE survey the movement that seeks to have public educational agencies add or expand elective courses on the Bible, or add major new sections to existing elective courses.[1] These courses or modules, which almost always are at the high school level, are not designed to address a diversity of global religions but rather are directed only or overwhelmingly on the Bible; that is, on the Hebrew scripture and the New Testament (or what Christians usually call the Old and New Testaments). We shall refer to this as Bible-centered educational reform, to differentiate it from proposals for multicultural curricular change that situates increased biblical instruction in the context of greater teaching on a variety of religious traditions.

Surveying the Call

The call for enhancing biblical instruction can be seen as falling generally into three categories: 1) a call to adopt the pedagogical model advanced by The Bible Literacy Project (BLP), 2) a call to adopt the curriculum advanced by the National Council on Bible Curriculum in Public Schools (NCBCPS), and 3) a proposal advanced by businessman Steve Green, known as the Green Scholars Initiative. As to the first, in 2001, Charles Haynes, director

1. Melissa Deckman has done some of the most extensive work documenting the recent calls for Bible-centered curricular reform, and our analysis is shaped by her detailed work. See Deckman, "Religious Literacy in Public Schools: Teaching the Bible in America's Classrooms," 31–47.

of the First Amendment Center, joined with investors Chuck Stetson and Richard Scurry to establish the BLP.[2] The BLP has produced a well-received textbook, *The Bible and Its Influence,* written with assistance from more than 40 scholars from a range of disciplines and a wide variety of religious and ideological backgrounds. The work has also garnered national attention and has been featured heavily in the media.[3] In addition, the BLP offers a rich curriculum for teachers with an online website for teacher training, a teacher's edition of their text, test banks, and an online partnership with Concordia University of Portland Oregon. The BLP's advisory board includes many eminent leaders in religious and cultural studies, such as Professor Mary Anne Glendon of the Harvard Law School, prolific author Os Guiness, and the late Jean Bethke Elshtain of the University of Chicago. It is supported by a range of advocacy organizations including the Coalition of African American Pastors.

However, the call for Bible-centered instruction in public schools is also advanced by other organizations, the most prominent alternative being, until recently, the National Council on Bible Curriculum in Public Schools (NCBCPS). Founded by Elizabeth Ridenour, the NCBCPS provides interested parents and school boards a range of material it has developed on biblical instruction, including proposed curricula, lesson plans, and advice for implementing its suggested courses. The NCBCPS endorses the use of the Bible itself as the main reading in its curriculum although it also publishes a textbook titled *The Bible in History and Literature*.[4] A key factor behind the growth of the NCBCPS has been the conviction that the BLP is not doing enough to ensure that the Bible's prominence in American and Western literature is acknowledged as the cornerstone of this curricular reform. In fact, the NCBCPS has on its homepage a section devoted to commentary critical of the BLP, writings drawn mainly from Christian theologians such as the late D. James Kennedy and John Hagee.[5] Many NCBCPS supporters argue that the textbook published by the BLP has been influenced, if at times only subtly, by an ethos of political correctness, an argument it underscores by indicating how several prominent contributors to the BLP's work, including

2. Deckman, "Religious Literacy in Public Schools," 35. See also van Biema, "The Case for Teaching the Bible."

3. For a generally favorable analysis of the book, see, for example, Johnson, "Textbook Case: A Bible Curriculum for Public Schools," 34–37; and McKenzie, Review of *The Bible and its Influence, Society of Biblical Literature Forum.*

4. See National Council on Bible Curriculum in Public Schools.

5. Deckman, "Religious Literacy in Public Schools," 36. For criticism of the BLP's signature textbook, see Conn, "Church Stetson's Trojan Horse?"; and Hagee, "Letter to Representative Scott Benson and the Alabama State Legislature."

Charles Haynes, have ties to liberal interest groups prone to endorsing what it calls an overly multicultural educational ethic.[6]

The leadership of NCBCPS includes well known writers such as David Barton, and over 30 notable educational activists and scholars. Moreover, prominent organizations such as the American Family Association, the American Center for Law and Justice, the Eagle Forum, Concerned Women for America, and the Family Research Council have endorsed its curriculum.[7] Indeed, its work has earned the endorsement of Robert P. George, the McCormack Professor of Jurisprudence at Princeton University, and one of the leading figures in American constitutional and political studies. Although many on its advisory board might best be called members of the "Christian right," its leadership also includes prominent Jewish writers such as David Lapin and other prominent scholars such as Professor Gerard Bradley, whose work argues firmly against any state promotion of specifically or uniquely Christian claims.[8]

The Green Scholars Initiative is connected with the monumental enterprise funded by businessman Steve Green to construct a state-of-the-art museum containing leading materials relating to the Bible and its history. The scholars affiliated with the museum are preparing a detailed curriculum for a four-year elective sequence of courses, which they hope will be adopted across the country, and eventually in public as well as in private schools. Led by Michael Holmes, PhD and Jerry Pattengale, PhD—both scholars at well regarded institutions in the United States—the team assembled by Mr. Green includes over 60 eminent scholars including David Trobisch, Th.D., formerly of Yale University and Bangor Theological Seminary.[9]

We can now turn to the current status of Bible-centered instruction in public schools. Some school districts, for example in Alabama, have a long history of teaching elective courses on the Bible in public secondary schools without having adopted legislation addressing increased biblical instruction.[10] Indeed, teaching about the Bible—even through a course entirely on the Bible—is permissible under United States constitutional law:

6. Deckman, "Religious Literacy in Public Schools," 36.

7. Ibid., 53. See also National Council on Bible Curriculum in Public Schools.

8. See National Council on Bible Curriculum in Public Schools. Representative expressions of Bradley's view can be found in "Dueling Clios: Stevens and Scalia on the Original Meaning of the Establishment Clause," in Bradley, ed. *Challenges to Religious Liberty in the Twenty-First Century.*

9. Museum of the Bible, *The Scholars Initiative.*

10. Despite the lack of any state level legislative encouragement of Bible instruction, according to the Bible Literacy Project, anywhere from thirty to thirty-nine public schools in Alabama are teaching currently an elective Bible course.

non-devotional instruction about the Bible has not been construed by the Supreme Court as a violation of the Constitution's prohibition on laws respecting an establishment of religion, a point the Court underscored in the case of *School District of Abington Township v. Schempp*.[11] For this reason, it should not be surprising that elective courses on the Bible for purposes of historical, literary, and cultural education have not been unknown in United States' public education. Nevertheless, in 2004, a Gallup poll indicated that only eight percent of high school students reported that their school offered an elective Bible course.[12]

However, in the past ten years, a pronounced effort has been undertaken to increase curricular attention to the Bible in public schools. Ten state legislatures have recently passed laws which either mandate instruction on the Bible as an elective option in public schools, promote and encourage optional offerings on the Bible, or encourage the inclusion of significant new modules addressing the Bible in existing elective courses. Those states are as follows: Georgia, South Carolina, Texas, Tennessee, Oklahoma, Arkansas, South Dakota, Florida, Arizona, and Kentucky.[13] The South Carolina law has a distinction, which we explore in considerable depth. In the last decade, at least four other state legislatures have unsuccessfully attempted to pass similar legislation: Indiana (2000, 2001, and 2006), Alabama (2006), Missouri (2006), New Mexico (2007), and Idaho (2016).[14] In these states, however, advocates remain committed to securing eventual passage. In all states in the United States, other than the ten mentioned, there is no state-level legislation mandating, or encouraging biblical instruction. However, in a great many of the remaining states, as Nathan Black has documented, data indicates that elective Bible courses and new modules on the Bible in current elective classes are also increasing, due in significant part to the activism of the BLP and the NCBCPS.[15]

In sum, the concentrated work of the BLP and the NCBCPS along with the major new initiative of Steve Green and the Museum of the Bible, complemented by the inclusion of a strong endorsement of Bible courses

11. *School District of Abington v. Schempp* 374 U.S. 203 (1963).

12. Black, "Report: Over 350 Public Schools Teaching Bible."

13. Deckman, "Religious Literacy in Public Schools," 36; See also "Arizona Bible Course Bill to Teach Elective in Public Schools Becomes Law"; and "Kentucky Public Schools Create Bible Course as an Elective."

14. Deckman, "Religious Literacy in Public Schools," 37.

15. The BLP reports over 43 states currently using its curricula. Notable perhaps is California, where the BLP's curriculum is receiving increased adoption despite the absence of any state-level statute addressing Biblical instruction. Black, "Report: Over 350 Public Schools Teaching Bible," 29.

in a national political party's platform, indicate that tremendous energy is being dedicated to the cause of expanded instruction of the Bible in the public schools.

What do these new Bible instruction laws actually seek to achieve? Only in Texas do such laws require that all state public high schools offer every few years an elective course on the Bible for purposes of historical, literary, and cultural study. Under the Texas law, no student is mandated to take the course, and school districts do not have to offer the course if less than 15 students choose to enroll in the course when the school proposes to offer it. In the other states where laws have been passed addressing Bible-centered instruction, the legislation only encourages the offering of such courses or new modules in schools not already making them available to students, or the more frequent offering of such in those districts where they have been taught previously but only episodically. Moreover, only in Texas—due most likely to its requirement to offer these courses—is there any allocation of resources from the state budget to ensure additional teacher training in this instructional area. In three of the other nine states—Georgia, Tennessee, and Oklahoma—the law allows education policy-setting agencies to allocate within existing budgetary outlays resources for course development and teacher training. Interestingly, in South Carolina and Oklahoma, the law encouraging courses on the Bible bars districts from using educational monies to subsidize teacher training or curricular development for biblical courses, in part on the grounds of not draining resources available to other areas of instruction. Also of note, in Florida, the language of the statute is that of merely "permitting" the Bible to be taught in public schools. Since this has always been permitted, the articulation of such an allowance constitutes merely a symbolic endorsement of biblical instruction.[16]

In addition to either mandating or encouraging the offering of these elective courses, each of the ten state legislatures has also addressed the issue of curriculum, that is, the issue of how the Bible is best to be addressed in the courses. Importantly, in each of the ten states where greater attention to the Bible has been expressed in law, there is no attempt to dictate the precise curriculum to be used; each state's law leaves specific decisions about the curriculum to the relevant educational agencies. In this context, it is important to note that in twenty-three states a state-level Board or Department

---

16. As a further outlier, the Florida law reads as follows: "The district school board may install in the public schools in the district a secular program of education including, *but not limited to*, an objective study of the Bible and of religion." Unlike the other states mentioned, Florida's law situates biblical instruction in the context of religion in general and thus comes close to endorsing a multicultural educational perspective. Title XLVIII 1003.45 of the Florida code; emphasis added.

of Education approves or adopts textbooks to be used throughout the state; in the remaining twenty-seven states, the decision on textbook use is made entirely by local school boards. Nevertheless, in each of the ten states with Bible instruction laws, some specific language about curriculum is stated in its legislation.

In Georgia, for example, Democratic sponsors of the legislation favored encouraging the use of the BLP's text, *The Bible and Its Influence*, which drew criticism from Republican lawmakers opposed to the text, an opposition led by State Senator Tommie Williams.[17] Williams, who consulted with NCBCPS's offices in opposing the Democrats' bill, offered an alternative bill that indicated that the Bible be a required textbook for such courses and thus that instruction not depend only on secondary sources.[18] Ultimately, the bill which became law in Georgia mandated the use of the Bible as a primary text, while also indicating that use of secondary sources was appropriate and would be left to the determination of the local school board. This outcome has been replicated in three of the other ten states with Bible instruction laws: South Carolina, Texas, and Oklahoma. Only in Tennessee does the law about Bible coursework not explicitly mandate that the Bible be used as one of the assigned readings.

As the newest participant in the arena of public school instruction on the Bible, the Green Scholars Initiative has not yet fully completed its curriculum, yet it intends to establish detailed curricula to be used in a wide range of schools. The Initiative experienced a short-lived success in the Mustang, Oklahoma Public School District in the form of a proposal to conduct a so-called "beta-test" of its emerging curriculum, yet implementation was held in abeyance, a development we explore in more detail below.

As we have seen, therefore, these new laws surrounding biblical instruction leave considerable discretion to non-legislative educational agencies. First, only in Texas is there a mandate to offer periodic Bible courses should there be student interest in taking them. In the remainder of the states, there is only an encouragement (or permission) that school boards offer these courses. Second, both in those states that have state-level educational agencies and those which rely more heavily on local school boards, each policy-setting body has wide discretion to determine the proper curriculum. This discretion is either plenary, as in Tennessee—that is, it allows the policy-setting body to decide even if the Bible itself will be part of the instruction—or the discretion is only modestly circumscribed, allowing the

---

17. Deckman, "Religious Literacy in Public Schools," 38. See also Gutierrez, "Legislature 2006: Senate Approves Bible Classes in Public Schools."

18. Deckman, "Religious Literacy in Public Schools," 38.

policy-setting body to set specifics of the curriculum while mandating only that the Bible be one text among the materials used. Moreover, in all cases, if the Bible is taught, *how* it is taught—which biblical books are studied, for example—is left to policy-setting bodies, and is left unaddressed by the legislation itself.

Concrete Curricula

How have the institutions of educational governance in states which have passed these new laws chosen to specify the curriculum to be used in Bible courses? As noted, educational policy in the United States reflects the proposition that many, perhaps even most, specific curricular decisions are best decided by local school boards. This longstanding idea is reflected even in those states that have state-level governing agencies—for each state with a state-level education board authorized to set educational policy still leaves a great deal of the specificity of the curricular content of coursework to local authorities. For this reason, the NCBCPS and the BLP, along with the Green Scholars Initiative spend much of their energy working at the local level of government, trying to encourage parents and educators to consider the adoption of elective Bible courses in school districts and encouraging, in turn, that their curriculum be the preferred model for use in the districts.

How have local school boards tended to shape the curriculum in Bible courses in those states that have adopted these laws, or in states such as Alabama, which have had a long tradition of teaching such courses independent of legislative enactment, or in those states that despite the absence of a legislative decree are seeing an increase in Bible courses? More school districts seem to be teaching the NCBCPS curriculum than the BLP curriculum, and the NCBCPS claims that it can project a further increase in the adoption of its curriculum. It states that its curriculum has been adopted in 1,190 school districts, and 2,739 high schools in thirty-nine states.[19] The BLP in turn reports that more than 600 high schools in forty-three states have adopted its curriculum, including the large state of Florida.[20] Some states have recently seen curricular switching from the BLP to the NCBCPS, or curricular supplementation of the former's text with the latter's. Alabama, for example, has a state-level educational policy-setting agency that has a significant influence on curricular formation. Several years ago, the State Board of Education in Alabama approved the BLP's textbook, *The Bible and*

19. National Council on Bible Curriculum in Public Schools. "Alabama Adopts New Textbook for Academic Study of the Bible."

20. See Bible Literacy Project, *The Bible and Its Influence.*

Its Influence, for use in its state's high schools, as part of a larger list of acceptable texts that can be purchased by school districts. However, in 2015, the Alabama Board of Education endorsed the curriculum of the NCBCPS.

Additionally, as noted above, a major new initiative spearheaded by Steve Green is currently in the development phase. Despite an initial setback, the plan is to launch a large number of courses employing a distinctive four-year elective sequence on the Bible. This ambitious proposal therefore would, in principle, allow students to quadruple the curricular attention given to the Bible during the participants' time in high school relative to the usual offering of a single course. The latest curriculum has not yet been finalized, but the rough outlines have been sketched by Jerry Pattengale, director of the Green Scholars Initiative. The idea is to fashion a rigorous, non-devotional curriculum addressing the Hebrew scriptures and the New Testament and their respective influences, spread across four courses, each strictly elective. Despite initial obstacles, Pattengale notes, "The Museum of the Bible remains committed to providing an elective high school Bible curriculum and continues to work on an innovative, high-tech course that will provide students and teachers with a scholarly overview of the Bible's history, narrative and impact."[21] In fact, progress has been made in the public school sector internationally, which could prove of great assistance to the eventual development of public school curricula in the United States. In Israel, for example, six public schools have recently adopted its curricula, and developments in other international public schools look promising.[22]

This curriculum plans to connect with the world-class museum in Washington, D.C, very close to the national mall—the Museum of the Bible. The Museum will be staffed in part by Green Scholars—leading biblical authorities representing a variety of academic perspectives. Green Scholars in conjunction with scholars from around the world are currently developing the detailed curriculum.[23]

In all, therefore, the issue of Bible-centered instruction in public schools is an important one in American public education. The new legislation we have pointed to has taken place within a context, to be sure, which has long permitted instruction on the Bible, even to the point of offering courses exclusively on the Bible's literary, cultural, and historical importance. But now, in addition to this historic connection, biblical courses have been mandated in one state; nine states have recently encouraged greater instruction; several states have seen renewed efforts to pass laws encouraging

21. *Christianity Today*, "Hobby Lobby's Bible Course Cancelled."

22. Museum of the Bible, *2015 Annual Report*.

23. van Biema, "Hobby Lobby's Steve Green Launches Public School Bible Course."

greater instruction; and Bible courses are growing in states where legislative action has not been taken. More Bible courses are being offered now than ever before. The call for greater instruction on the Bible in public education, therefore, merits serious and sustained attention.

Chapter 2 ———————————————

State Religious Education and the Question of Religious Purpose

MANY CRITICS OF ENHANCED biblical instruction, often members of the so-called secular left,[1] believe that there is a predominantly religious motive at work in the recent focus on expanding Bible-centered instruction in public schools. They further argue that for this reason the calls should be rejected as failures of church/state separationism, and this despite any stated secular rationale for expanded biblical course offerings. Critics such as Americans United for Separation of Church and State[2] and religious studies professor Mark Chancey, among a number of others, argue that the call for Bible-focused instruction is intended to promote a religious objective, namely to advance the continued cultural influence of the Bible, the biblical worldview, and biblical values. The criticism is often initially made in the form of two contentions. First, the claim is sometimes made that Bible courses teach the Bible as true. Second, the claim is often made that Bible courses contain what critics consider factual errors—specifically, critics allege that these courses teach what

---

1. Although first used mostly on the far left and far right, the term "secular left" has gained wide usage in public discourse, proving a helpful frame in light of the frequent designation of traditional Christians as members of a "religious right." For its mainstream usage, see for example centrist *New York Times* columnist David Brooks, when he writes that "the real political story of the past decade has been the growing size and cohesion of the secular left, and its growing influence on the Democratic Party." Brooks, "A Matter of Faith."

2. See, for example, Boston, "The Religious Right's New Tactics for Invading Public Schools." Boston is the director of communications of Americans United for Separation of Church and State.

is seen as a falsehood, viz. that the pillars of Western civilization are Judeo-Christian and that the founders of the Constitution were primarily shaped by Christian theology in their work and thus that their design of government bears a pronounced Christian imprint, and that America remains a primarily "Christian Nation."[3]

The Heart of the Criticisms, and a Response

These criticisms represent only the first level of critique. For when it is pointed out that neither the NCBCPS nor the BLP nor the incipient Green Scholars curriculum teaches the Bible as true (beyond what scientific archaeology can prove about sites and dates), and that the claim that the Bible influenced American history and government profoundly is held by a great many reputable historians, the critique moves to a more subterranean level. As Diane Moore of the Harvard Divinity School asserts, the NCBCPS is inappropriate in public schools because it is "devotionally *based*."[4] Hence, a key aspect of her assessment of the NCBCPS is the question of "[W]ho is promoting the curriculum or resource?"[5] And what is their deepest motive? Critic Amanda Colleen Brown resorts to imputations of what she sees as suspect motivations by seeing a possibility that "the NCBCPS [initially] chose not to develop a text in order to give teachers more freedom" to advance their nefarious designs. Indeed, she divines, "even though the NCBCPS has put on a new coat of paint," it is merely a façade to cloak its "deeper agenda."[6] Ian Smith, a staff attorney with Americans United for Separation of Church and State asserts that these laws are constitutionally impermissible because they are based on a pretext—in fact, "the thinnest legal pretext possible"—to cover the malign motive of advancing the Christian faith in public schools.[7] The charge of many critics is not at root that there are historical inaccuracies, or that the Bible is presented as true, or as a text to which one must or should assent;[8] instead, the charge is more foundational: these advocates

3. Deckman, "Religious Literacy in Public Schools," 35. See also, for example, Chancey, "A Textbook Example of the Christian Right: The National Council on Bible Curriculum in Public Schools," 554–81.

4. Moore, "Teaching about the Bible in Public Schools: A Religious Studies Framework," 77.

5. Ibid., 76.

6. Brown, "Losing My Religion: The Controversy over Bible Courses in Public Schools," 193–240.

7. Gryboski, "Arkansas Public School District to Offer Controversial Bible Class Next Fall."

8. One federal district court decades ago agreed with parts of this critique in

cannot be trusted precisely because they advance an objective based on a religious motive, which in itself is seen as constitutionally sinister.[9]

We believe that there is a basic error embedded in the view of the critics of the biblical instruction movement. Specifically, we intend to show in this chapter that the presence of a religious motive cannot be eliminated from policy decision making consistent with the free exercise rights of United States citizens.

As we have seen, the idea that there may be a religious motive informing the work of reform advocates is viewed by some as deeply problematic. However, understanding exactly what is problematic about religious motivation for public policy requires that we attend to a variety of different understandings of the separation of church and state developed by social, political, and legal thinkers. Micah Schwartzman has developed a helpful taxonomy.[10] The most demanding view with support in contemporary thought is the view that law cannot be motivated by a predominantly religious purpose, where purpose is defined as the informing motivation for the policy enactment.[11] This understanding is expressed in the thinking and underlying logic of contemporary constitutional theorist Andras Sajo.

Sajo calls for "a more robust theory of constitutional secularism" than he says currently is upheld in Western countries.[12] The state must become

---

regards to an earlier version of the curriculum supplied by the NCBCPS. A version of its curriculum as it then existed was adopted by the Fort Myers school board in Florida in 1996. The curriculum was challenged on the basis that it impermissibly advanced religion. In the court's judgment, this was due primarily to the way the curriculum was advancing a presentation of the New Testament and the Old Testament as texts to be treated as uniformly historically accurate. Ultimately, in 2000, the state of Florida removed the then-existing NCBCPS course from its approved list. See DelFattore, *The Fourth R: Conflicts over Religion in America's Public Schools*. As we have noted, it has since adopted the BLP curriculum. Moreover, since 1996, the NCBCPS has altered its curriculum in ways that it asserts fully ensure its constitutionality. Yet, the criticisms continue, suggesting that a deeper level of critique is driving the opposition.

9. For example, a blog post by Americans United for Separation of Church and State points to a 2013 speech Green gave to the National Bible Association as evidence of his religious agenda. During the speech, Green said a purpose of the course is to "reintroduce this book to this nation. This nation is in danger because of its ignorance of what God has taught." Highlighting Green's remarks points clearly to a concern not so much about the content but about the underlying motive of reform advocates. Klein, "Hobby Lobby Leaders Hope to Spread Bible Course to Thousands of Schools."

10. Schwartzman, "What if Religion Is Not Special?," 1351–1427.

11. Ibid., 1359. The even stronger view that no religious motive at all enter into the mind of citizens is not, Schwartzman notes, as prominent, nor has it been upheld by any federal court.

12. Sajo, "Preliminaries to a Concept of Constitutional Secularism," 605–29.

"militant" in upholding its core secularist values.[13] This is needed, Sajo alleges, because "the shielding of the political from the religious remains an unfinished project."[14] Why? Because secularism is seen as especially fragile in light of contemporary factors including both its own failure to press its logic forcefully enough in the past, and also what he calls the "reemergence of religion"—or its failure to expire as expected—and specifically the problem of what he calls "strong religion," a definition so broad that it encapsulates all religions whose adherents actually believe themselves bound by divine commands.[15]

What must the secular state do to respond to such "strong" believers? They are entitled to religious freedom, he concedes, and so are entitled to have their religious motives inform their engagement with public decision making.[16] But the secular state must now "take vigorous, prohibitive positions" to protect itself against such strong religionists.[17] Sufficient prohibitory action against religion has not yet been taken, and one area where this has been especially troubling for Sajo is by the state allowing "ostensibly liberal arguments [to be] Trojan horses used to bring religious *concerns* into the citadel of the secular state."[18] How does this occur? One way he is especially exercised about is when "religion seeks to smuggle itself into the public and political sphere using fundamental rights language."[19] What is problematic here for Sajo is that "religious emotion" is driving the deployment of secular rationales for public law.[20] Ominously, religious emotion is operating *within* what he takes to be the boundary limits of secularism: a requirement that agents develop a secular argument for public policy. For these strong religionists, he alleges, are at root developing secular arguments but only as mere Trojan horses for their underlying religious passions, concerns, and motivations. To arrest this, the state must take "preventive measures"

13. See Sajo, ed., *Militant Democracy*.

14. Sajo, "Preliminaries to a Concept of Constitutional Secularism," 622.

15. Ibid., 605–6. Strong religion is defined so broadly that it would include any believer in a religious tenet believed with such intensity that the adherent thinks she should not be compelled to circumvent her religious belief by the state; examples include "a religious community" that "withdraws," believing that though its religious principles cannot be forced on others, "exceptions are to be granted in the sense of being left on their own" (606). In the Judeo-Christian context at least, this would include most who actually believe that there are at least some genuinely divine mandates.

16. Ibid., 607, 628.

17. Ibid., 615.

18. Ibid., 606–7; emphasis added.

19. Ibid., 607.

20. Ibid., 624, 626. See also, Sajo, "What is Militant Democracy? Against What Should We Defend the State?"

against those agents whom he concedes are operating within his preferred rules for the secular state (that pulbic laws have in their support a secular rationale).[21] Although he does not state this explicitly, restraining the poison of religious concerns is so pressing that his newly robust secularism must empower the state to search the substratum of motivational interests informing admittedly rule-following behavior through the state's ensuring that religious motivations (especially motivations informed by "strong religion") are not in fact the driving force behind legislation or policy making.[22] As such, the logic of Sajo's argument is precisely that religious motivations for laws, though permissible, must be subordinate to other less toxic desires.

This understanding is, in our view, much too extreme. Indeed, such a view, or any view similar to it is condemned by a range of thinkers including Paul Weithman,[23] Nicholas Wolterstorff,[24] and Michael Perry.[25] Weithman, Wolterstorff, and Perry have maintained, with good reason, that requiring citizens to observe, in Marion Maddox's words, "a personal wall of separation" is indefensible philosophically, and imposes "a requirement for religiously committed citizens not to argue [robustly] their views on public issues with reference to their theological beliefs that places an unfair burden on [them]; no comparable burden is proposed for the non-religious, whose deepest commitments are presumed safe for public deliberation in ways that religious commitments, on this view, are not."[26] As Perry further notes, "to require a religious citizen to bracket her moral convictions in public discourse would annihilate herself. And doing that would preclude her from engaging in moral discourse with other members of the society."[27] Oxford scholar Roger Trigg agrees: "the problem is that when a significant segment of the population is prevented from voicing their deepest concerns in public, their own commitment to democracy, and their involvement in its processes, can be undermined."[28] Thomas Berg extends this critique with

---

21. Sajo, "From Militant Democracy to the Preventive State?," 2255–94.

22. "Without a strong secularist position . . . a respect for the sacred that [may] motivate [a piece of] legislation . . . may find its way into certain readings of constitutionalism," Sajo, "Preliminaries to a Concept of Constitutional Secularism," 624.

23. Weithman, ed., *Religion and Contemporary Liberalism*.

24. Audi and Wolterstorff, *Religion in the Public Square: The Place of Religious Convictions in Political Debate*.

25. Perry, "Why Religion in Politics Does Not Violate *La Conception Americaine de la Laicite*," 543–60; and Perry, "Herein on/of the Nonestablishment of Religion," 105.

26. Maddox, "Religion, Secularism and the Promise of Public Theology," 82–100.

27. Perry, *Morality, Politics and the Law: A Bicentennial Essay,* 72–3.

28. Trigg, *Religion in Public Life: Must Faith be Privatized?,* 42.

special attention to the real-world political and legal impact of any requirement that lawmaking have so truncated a religious motivation:

> To invalidate laws on secular subjects because of their religious
> motivations . . . discourages religious individuals from stating,
> in public debate, their religious arguments for particular laws.
> Political speech on legislation and public issues "occupies the
> core protection afforded by the First Amendment"; so does
> religious speech. But under any significant secular purpose re-
> striction, such statements can be used as evidence that the law
> was motivated . . . too much by religious beliefs. The result is to
> push people to silence their religious speech as a condition of
> participating in basic democratic processes.[29]

Berg further illustrates the disastrous impact such a requirement
would have had on signal pieces of legislation rightly celebrated as land-
marks in American history.

> The 1964 Civil Rights Act was fueled by a religious protest
> movement in African American churches, and by a campaign
> of mainline clergy and congregants who made thousands of
> phone calls to legislators and held daily protests and worship
> services near the Capitol . . . the pervasive revivalist language
> was necessary . . . in the face of massive resistance and for "many
> participants" the movement was "primarily a religious event,
> whose social and political aspects were, in their minds, second-
> ary or incidental." But under a test of [ ] secular purpose, the
> pervasiveness of religious language could serve as evidence of
> the statute's unconstitutionality . . . [and so adjudging motives
> would lead] a reasonable observer who saw years of rallies in
> churches and speeches soaked in biblical language as Congress
> [sending a] message in the Civil Rights Act of 1964 to say that
> human dignity and equality come from God.[30]

Who would wish away the 1964 Civil Rights Act?

Indeed, opposition to such a strong secular motivation requirement
is supported by a range of additional thinkers, including Robert Kraynack.
Kraynack argues that views such as Sajo's create a "spiritual lobotomy" of religious citizens.[31] Frederick Mark Gedicks makes the same argument, noting

---

29. Berg, "'Secular Purpose,'" Accommodations, and Why Religion is Special
(Enough): A Response to Micah Schwartzmann, 'What if Religion is Not Special?,'" 28.

30. Berg, "Secular Purpose," 31. Internal quotes from Chappell, *A Stone of Hope:
Prophetic Religion and the Death of Jim Crow*, 44, 87.

31. Kraynack, *Christian Faith and Modern Democracy: God and Politics in the Fallen*

how this requirement would cause one to tear oneself apart, as it were, in order to have a right—a right traditionally seen as a constitutionally protected—to make claims in the civic arena on matters of public concern. Gedicks describes the tortured psychological burdens—the "cruel choice"—such understandings of church/state separationism exact on men and women who see their faith as making claims that should be foundational to their existence, yet who are forced to compartmentalize their religious life and their public life, and are required to act as if their deep faith has no impact on the pursuit of public goods.[32] Further, as Trigg points out, the requirement that there be no deep religious motivation can subtly teach a disdain for religion, that it harbors views that have a "deep mismatch" with affirmed public purposes; hence, there is a great risk of "rational discussion be[ing . . .] allowed to degenerate into ad hominem accusations about why someone holds a particular view."[33] Moreover, as Craig Engelhardt remarks, such ad hominem attacks would attach even to those who practice religion only in their familial sphere, since, for example, the act of religious citizens removing their children from public schools would still be subject to the aspersion that "parents who have chosen a religious school are less than good citizens" by abandoning the salutary system of state-defined secular instruction.[34]

For these reasons, we believe that a much more defensible view of the requirements of church/state separation is advanced by scholars such as Brendan Sweetman and Thomas Berg: namely, the requirement only that one aspect of political decision making be the presence of a secular rationale;[35] that is, an articulable argument to the effect that, in the words of Berg, the law in question will "be better for people in this world," or, in other words, a justification or purpose a non-religious person also could understand and, in principle, entertain—no matter the motivations of the law's primary sponsors or principal advocates.

This conclusion respects the rights of non-religious individuals to have policy based on a foundation which is not inaccessible to them, and as such is consistent, we believe, with the non-establishment principle of the First Amendment. In part, this is so because such a requirement does not create the same problems as a requirement that policy not be motivated

World, 270.

32. Gedicks, "Religious Exemptions, Formal Neutrality, and Laicite," 492. See also Gedicks, "Public Life and Hostility to Religion," 671–96; and Gedicks, *The Rhetoric of Church and State: A Critical Analysis of Religious Clause Jurisprudence.*

33. Trigg, *Religion in Public Life*, 40–41.

34. Engelhardt, "The Necessary Role of Religion in Civic Education," 163–86.

35. Sweetman, *Why Politics Needs Religion: The Place of Religious Arguments in the Public Square*, 89–93, 187–92. Berg, "'Secular Purpose.'"

by deeply held religious intentions. The problem with that approach, as we noted, is that it creates an unfair and untoward burden on citizens of deeply religious convictions—that of a muffled political voice, or of a spiritual self-lobotomy. However, a requirement that a secular rationale be supplied, along with whatever motivation(s) a believer may have to pursue a public policy outcome, does not necessarily dampen political activism, or rend the psyche of a believer because believers very often can have deeply religious motives precisely for forming and advancing a secular, that is, a this-worldly goal. As Berg notes, "people who believe that God stands against (or for) certain conduct will also [tend to] believe that the conduct is bad (or good) for human beings in this world."[36] We can think of innumerable examples, such as the Little Sisters of the Poor desiring goals no (sensible) secular-ist would find per se objectionable, such as laws providing health care to those in need, while doing so from a motivation of building the kingdom of God.[37] The secular rationale in this case would be that it is good to serve humans in need in matters of health, while the motivation to do so would be entirely "other-worldly," grounded, for example, in faithfulness to one of nearly an inexhaustible supply of biblical mandates, including "to seek the peace and prosperity of the city to which I have carried you"[38]; or to have the "Religion that God our Father accepts as pure and faultless [ ]: to look after orphans and widows in their distress"[39]; or to be "imitators"[40] of the Savior who "came so that they may have life, and have it to the full."[41]

Moreover, many believers may well wish to advance even more elabo-rate secular rationales for their religiously motivated behavior, such as ar-guments from natural law, or from natural rights, or a state of nature, or even from an original position.[42] Indeed, many religious believers will have

36. Berg, "'Secular Purpose,'" 33.

37. Ironically, the Little Sisters of the Poor expressed no opposition we can find to the initial versions of the Affordable Care and Patient Protection bill, which in part sought to provide health care to those in need and which large numbers of other American nuns supported, only to find the final law exact mandates violative of the very religious conscience that drives the Little Sisters and other religious sisters to help the poor, and that very likely drove the Little Sisters' initial lack of opposition to the bill's earliest versions.

38. Jer 29:7 (NIV). Our work in this volume ranges across centuries, and incorpo-rates thought from a broad array of interpretive traditions. As such, we quote from a variety of versions of the Bible.

39. Jas 1:27 (NIV).

40. 1 Cor 11:1: "Be imitators of me, as I am of Christ" (NRSV).

41. John 10:10 (NIV).

42. We acknowledge that not all Christians will feel comfortable deploying all forms of secular argumentation. Advocates of the Radical Orthodoxy movement associated

a religious motive precisely for engaging the natural reason of their fellow humans. There is often a desire to express this-worldly goods in terms of expanded arguments accessible to those without the eyes of faith, simply as a desire to live out New Testament commands, such as that of Saint Peter to "always be ready to give an explanation to anyone who asks you for a reason for your hope"[43]; or to recognize and affirm the God-given capacity for reason that dwells within one's neighbors; or a desire to witness to the theological claim, derived from Proverbs 20:27, and so well expressed by the so-called Cambridge Platonists, that "reason is the candle of the Lord,"[44] or the theological claim eloquently maintained by Saint Philip Neri, that "a man without prayer is an animal without reason": for Neri's prayer *empowers* reason instead of distracting from it, and a believer may well wish to credit that fact by joining prayer to public rational discourse accessible to the unconverted. Moreover, many other religious traditions besides the Jewish and Christian traditions have similar religious motivations for the giving of fairly developed secular reasoning.

Given this perspective, we can also appreciate the weakness of a softer version of Sajo's thesis: the requirement defended by Robert Audi[45] that citizens of a liberal state hold as a part of their decision making[46] a

with John Milbank and Graham Ward would resist, for example, social science argumentation predicated on what it considers an epistemology of violence inconsistent with Christian discipleship. See Milbank, *Theology and Social Theory: Beyond Secular Reason.* Some very strong forms of fideism would resist secular argument altogether. Christians so strongly fideistic as to see no element of the faith as amenable to rational defense rarely make substantial demands on the state beyond that for religious autonomy, and this demand can be defended on their behalf by fellow believers who do not share the same scruple against secular reason.

43. 1 Pet 3:15 (NAB). One can also bring to mind Isa 1:18: "come now, let us reason together" (KJV).

44. "The spirit of man is the candle of the Lord" (KJV). For a classic study of the Cambridge Platonists, see dePauley, *The Candle of the Lord: Studies in the Cambridge Platonists.* For recent discussions of their continued relevance, see Trigg, *Religion in Public Life,* 75, 80.

45. Audi, *Religious Commitment and Secular Reason;* Audi and Wolterstorff, *Religion in the Public Square.*

46. Audi claims that his position is pertinent mostly to decision making about laws that are coercive, by which he means laws that restrict human conduct. However as Sweetman points out, "all positions that are made the basis of law . . . restrict human conduct. This is true even if an activity is made legal (and not just illegal). If abortion is legalized, it also restricts the conduct of religious believers in the sense that although they want to live in a world where abortion is illegal, they are forced to live in a society where it is legal. Almost everyone who contributes to public debates wants some aspect of their views imposed (usually by law) on those who disagree with them." Sweetman, *Why Politics Need Religion,* 123. On this basis, one cannot exempt from Audi's secular

non-exclusive secular motivation for their actions. On this view, the secular motive need not be the controlling motive—as it appears to be for Sajo—but it must be fairly strong, or what Audi calls "sufficient," meaning that in the absence of any other motives the agent would still act in the manner chosen. In fact, Audi not only does not rule out that other motives may be present, but even allows for the other motives to be stronger in intensity than the sufficient secular motive. Nevertheless, as Sweetman remarks, Audi requires that the agent must to some real extent "deep down be motivated" by a secular motive.[47]

We disagree with a requirement that any secular motive must be conjoined to a secular rationale. This is so, first and foremost, because such a requirement would rule out of bounds the giving of a secular rationale through an exclusively religious motivation. However, as we have just argued, this is a powerful way of approaching the giving of secular reasons, and Audi fails to appreciate how unfair his requirement actually is to many religious believers.

Audi and other defenders of his secular motivation requirement believe that an argument can be made to justify the requirement for a sufficient secular motivation based on the Golden Rule: that one do to others what one would wish done to oneself. This Golden Rule-based justification he believes would satisfy objections to his requirement from religious believers. For he argues that if we do not require that a sufficient secular motive be conjoined to our decision making and public engagement, then religious believers would be opening up the door to atheists advancing public policy with the goal of advancing atheism, and religious believers would not wish for that, he maintains. This Golden Rule argument, however, is empty. This is so simply because Audi's concession that the secular motive (here meaning something like a desire to advance a non-atheism-promoting conception of the good) does not have to be the only motive, and that other objectives might even be motivationally stronger for the agent than the secular motive so defined. What this means is that there is already room for atheists to advance their agendas in the public square, as long as their desiderata are conjoined with motives that do not directly advocate for, or derive their basis from the quest for atheism. So the idea that religious believers have to be careful about what they ask for is, effectively, inert.

A second point is precisely that many religious believers strongly feel (and with good reason)[48] that atheists already are advancing agendas in

---

motivation requirement laws regarding Bible instruction in public schools.

47. Sweetman, *Why Politics Needs Religion*, 122.

48. For several examples of the secularizing force of contemporary law, see

public life even as they advance "secular" arguments and express secular motives for their positions. Hence, an argument that one should allow for others what one allows for oneself becomes an argument that religious believers see as properly directed not at them, but at atheists: since atheists are doing it, religious believers should be able to do so as well. In response, Audi could argue that the fact that atheists are doing something "wrong" does not permit a Christian to do the same. The Golden Rule is, do to others as you would have them do to you, not what they are *already doing* to you; that would replace the Golden Rule with the lex talionis. But this argumentative move presupposes an independent, non-Golden Rule-based argument for why religious motivation is wrong per se in pluralist societies. We fail to see any persuasive force to a per se prohibition on Christians placing their light on a lamp stand, unsheathed from an encasing bushel.[49]

Furthermore, the mandate that there be a secular motive for engaging secular reasoning, even if one is permitted to have other and even stronger motives as well, is close to the state's requiring citizens, in part at least, to assume a Kantian conception of their world—to hold in awe and wonder the mere fact of rationality itself unmoored to any deeper conception of the source or value of human reason. One can think of Kant's holding in rapturous awe the practical law of pure reason he calls the Categorical Imperative. To mandate that a secular motive be present in the absence of a persuasive argument for the demand is very close to the state mandating that we too hold in awe the facticity of pure reason unalloyed by religious considerations. But the state has no business demanding that others hold such a view of their reasoning capacity.[50] To do so is to prejudice religion unjustifiably, and to advance a contestable vision of human agency to the

Garnett, "A Quiet Faith? Taxes, Politics, and the Privatization of Religion," 771–803.

49. "No one after lighting a lamp puts it under the bushel basket, but on the lampstand, and it gives light to all in the house" Matt 5:15 (NRSV). Prudential arguments in light of violent tensions among groupings may be dispositive in some contexts, but Audi seems to need a per se prohibition not a situational counsel of prudence, which no sensible person would reject in the presence of genuine social chaos.

50. Kant goes further than having us view pure practical reason with awe; he argues that the failure to do so is madness. One, of course, can wonder whether there is any necessary connection between Kant's view of groundless human reason and the strident dismissiveness of traditional religion he displays in *Religion Within the Limits of Reason Alone*, where, for example, devotional prayer is considered a sign of mental illness. See Gearon, *On Holy Ground: The Theory and Practice of Religious Education*, 27 for a survey of Kant's "scathing" view of longstanding religious thought and devotional practice. Kant certainly thinks that there is a necessary connection between his conception of unmoored rationality and the rejection of conventional religiosity. Were there in fact any such necessary connection, the state all the more would have no place advancing the Kantian view or views similar to it.

exclusion of alternative accounts of the human person and the source of human rationality.

Moreover, an additional problem exists within Audi's framework. He maintains that a sufficient secular argument means an argument that does not start *or conclude* with anything related to religion.[51] But this too is deeply unfair, as it is in effect a stipulation by the state that one act *als ob* natural reason could never be seen to support the existence of God, or rationally demonstrate any claims with religious content. But why act like this unless one believed it to be true? But to credit this view as true is to give presumptive credence to a claim highly contestable in light of the long tradition and current flourishing of philosophical theology.[52] Once again, this requirement is akin to the state mandating a form of thought functionally similar to Kantianism—that is, a perspective such as that developed in the *Critique of Pure Reason*, which holds that natural reason (or what Kant calls theoretical reason) can never establish the truth of any religious claim. But this, as we have noted, is certainly contestable—and the state has no place taking sides in such a high level metaphysical debate. The state cannot and should not legislate de facto Kantianism, or any similar view that commits the state to the inability of natural reason to establish any claims with religious import, such as the proposition that a God exists.

What this all means is that if a secular argument (one that does not assume as a premise religious commitment) is advanced in public, there should be no prohibition on a non-secular motive also being present.

---

51. Audi holds that an argument is religious and so impermissible "provided that (a) its premises *or* (b) its conclusions . . . cannot be justifiably accepted apart from religious considerations." Audi, *Religious Commitment*, 71; emphasis added. An argument with non-religious premises (such as that matter appears to be divisible) that leads to a religious conclusion (say, that matter has an indivisible and so non-material source, viz., God) is one that cannot be justifiably accepted without a religious consideration, for the conclusion is itself a religious consideration. Audi is even more explicit in his claim that arguments which conclude with God are impermissible in a later work. In 2009, Audi maintains that one way an argument can be religious, and thus impermissible, is if it "evidentially depends on . . . the existence of God." This no matter how the proposition that God exists is arrived at. Audi, "Natural Reason, Natural Rights, and Governmental Neutrality toward Religion," 158. Interestingly, Audi claims not to be a philosophical skeptic about the rationality of religious belief, affirming that there is "no cogent reason to deny the possibility of religious knowledge." Audi, *Epistemology: A Contemporary Introduction to the Theory of Knowledge*, 271.

52. See for example the massive oeuvre of Professor Richard Swinburne of the University of Oxford. As Padgett notes, the "high praise" of Swinburne "from colleagues on both sides of the Atlantic shows the esteem in which Swinburne's thought is held by philosophers of many stripes." Padgett, *Reason and the Christian Religion: Essays in Honour of Richard Swinburne*, vi.

However, an objection to this position could be mounted on the basis of the so-called Lemon Test expounded in *Lemon v. Kurtzman*,[53] a test which, formally at least, has never been overruled.[54] Although Audi would prefer his argument to remain at the normative level, the real world debates over such things as the Bible in public schools requires an appreciation of how the absence of a secular motive might meet with resistance based on legal precedent. The Lemon Test consists of a three pong appraisal, and each prong must be satisfied for legislation to pass Lemon scrutiny: i) the law must have a secular legislative purpose; ii) the principal or primary effect must not be to aid or harm religion; iii) the law must not create excessive entanglement between religion and the state. The first prong, one could argue, is violated when religious motivation undergirds a legislative enactment. However, such an interpretation presupposes that "purpose" is equivalent to motive (or what is sometimes called "input"); however, purpose could instead be construed as simply a rationale or a logical justification,[55] in which case the Lemon Test is perfectly compatible with our argument established above.

However, in the important Supreme Court decision of *Wallace v. Jaffree*,[56] the Supreme Court seemed, at least in parts of its decision, to define purpose as equivalent to an underlying motivation. In the 1970s and 1980s, the legislature of Alabama appeared committed to overturning, or at least scaling back what it perceived to be the excesses of the Warren-era jurisprudence regarding the place of religion in American life, with apparently special focus placed in Alabaman politics on at least mitigating the prayer decisions of *Engle v. Vitale* and *Abington v. Schempp*.[57] In 1978, the Alabama legislature passed a law authorizing school teachers to lead students in public schools in a one minute period of "silent meditation" at the beginning of the school day. In 1981, the legislature added to the law, with the final legislative product reading that teachers were authorized to lead public school students in one minute of "silent meditation or prayer." In 1985, the Supreme Court struck down the 1981 law as unconstitutional by reference to the Lemon Test. The law, the Court maintained, did not have a secular purpose. Why? The Court reasoned that the legislative record established that the *motive* of the law had been to advance prayer, and thus to

53. 403 U.S. 602 (1971).

54. Indiana University, *Prayer at College Events*.

55. See Koppelman, "Secular Purpose"; and Koppelman, *Defending American Religious Neutrality*.

56. 472 U.S. 38 (1985).

57. See Westmoreland, "*Wallace v. Jaffree* (1985)."

advance religion, and therefore that the law failed to pass the secular purpose prong. In other words, purpose was here construed to mean underlying motivation.[58]

This part of the case we object to in principle: motivation is separate
from a rationale, since secular rationales can be advanced, or pursued for
wholly religious motivations. However, the import of the Court's mistake
in *Wallace v. Jaffree* is minimal. First, the Court states clearly that a law's
motivation can be partly religious; it just cannot be entirely religious. This
mitigates the application of its logic to only those cases that are entirely
religiously motivated without a conjunction of other motives, which we
concede is likely to be rare (though not non-existent). Further, later in its
ruling, the Court appears to define motive in reference to secular justifica-
tion/rationale: the majority appears later in its opinion to be saying that an
articulated justification of a secular rationale, or logic is itself proof that
there is a secular motivation. This is what the court later appears to be saying, since the very reason why the Court strikes the statute down is that the
record, on its reading, did not disclose that a secular rationale had been advanced at all. Hence, it appears that *if* a secular rationale had been advanced,
then the case would have survived Lemon review because the Court would
have held, it seems, that that rationale would constitute evidence of a secular
motive. The Court in other words collapses motive and rationale, leaving
the case, in principle at least, innocuous to our position, since we agree that
religious motives should be fortified with a secular rationale.

The error of the Court's reasoning therefore is more abstract than
concrete: it fails to appreciate that secular rationale is not the same thing as
secular motive. For, again, religious agents may indeed have purely religious
motives to secure secular purposes or objectives. Hence, the legal reasoning
of the case as a practical matter does not discomfit our approach. The crux
of the case is simply that the Court's fact finding disclosed to its satisfaction
that there was no secular rationale advanced for the law, and so the law failed

58. The federal courts have occasionally been very heavy-handed about assessing
the presence (to their minds) of an adequate secular motive. In *McCreary County v.
ACLU of Kentucky*, 545 U.S. 844 (2005) a five-to-four majority conducted an inquisition
about secular motivation, as has (by time of publication) Judge Watson, a federal district judge in Hawaii, in his injunction in *State of Hawaii and Ismail Elshilch v. Donald
J. Trump, et al.*, otherwise known as the Travel Ban case. CV. NO. 00050 DKW-KSC.
We follow the view of many jurists and practitioners in anticipating a Supreme Court
reversal of Watson's opinion. Indeed, as of the date of publication, Judge's Watson's
divination of Trump's deepest heart-held secrets and his rejection of Trump's illicitly
religious longings have twice been repudiated by the Supreme Court as the Travel Ban
case has moved throughout the federal judicial system. See Vogue, "Supreme Court
Lets Full Travel Ban Take Effect."

Lemon scrutiny. Assuming its fact finding to be valid (which we question below), we agree with the outcome, since we too agree that religious motive should be conjoined with secular rationale. Thus, the Alabama legislature's failure (or its failure to the mind of the Court) to provide a secular rationale is limp with respect to the theory we developed above.

Despite this, the case has drawn considerable criticism, with numerous scholars finding the *Wallace v. Jaffree* case deeply problematic. Indeed, distinguished educational researcher William Jeynes remarks that "If there was a doubt about an antireligious judicial agenda in the Supreme Court decisions of 1962 and 1963, to Protestants and Catholics in particular such an agenda was apparent now."[59]

One might surmise that a reason for the Court's sloppy reasoning in the *Wallace v. Jaffree* opinion is due to some of the case's interesting context. The petitioner against the 1981 law, secular activist Ishmael Jaffree,[60] first took his case to the federal district court of the Southern District of Alabama. At the district level, the trial judge ruled, based on a detailed historical argument, that the state of Alabama was constitutionally permitted to establish a state religion. Moreover, we should keep in mind that the Alabama legislature had refused to remove from its statute books laws authorizing school prayer (though it recognized the need for new laws as evidenced by the very 1981 statute). Also, the case itself involved allegations that the school teacher was not merely allowing a period of silent prayer, but was leading children in vocalized, explicitly Christian prayers, which the 1981 law never permitted.

The federal circuit court overruled the district court's conclusion of law to the effect that Alabama was constitutionally permitted to have a state religion, as did the Supreme Court, in rather caustic terms.

The excesses of this case might well be attributable to the majority's zeal to swap down the trial judge for striking against the Supreme Court's 1947 decision incorporating the prohibition on an establishment of religion to the states;[61] to swap down the legislature for keeping obsolete laws on its statue books; and to swap down the Mobile school district for having an employee go beyond what the 1981 statute permitted. In fact, it is as if the Supreme Court seemed to view these actors as backwoods 'Bama rubes who would dare revisit the distinguished panel's[62] post-War rulings on church

59. Jeynes, *A Call for Character Education and Prayer in the Schools*, 215.

60. See for plaintiff's background, *Lagniappe Weekly's* "The Legacy of *Wallace v. Jaffree* and the Separation of Church and State."

61. *Everson v. Board of Education of Ewing Township,* 330 U.S. 1 (1947).

62. One might bring to mind Lincoln's ironic use of the phrase "that eminent tribunal" in his First Inaugural Address in March of 1861, a phrase used to express

and state. In this sense the case has a bit of the flavor of *Cooper v. Aaron*.[63] In that case, state leaders had been unwilling to fully uphold *Brown v. Board of Education* (citing such reasons as profound public disapproval, and the need for law and order). The Supreme Court in *Cooper v. Aaron* said in sharp tones that this practice of non-enforcement was intended to up-end a federal court's ruling and so was invalid. The same zeal appears to manifest itself in the *Wallace v. Jaffree* case, and so in an important sense the case was as much about the power of the Supreme Court as about anything concerning religion in public affairs. Its excesses might flow from this emotional and power-charged context. (Note well, we admit we are indulging in speculation, and nothing in our general argument turns on these speculations about the frame of mind of the majority opinion's author, Justice John Paul Stevens.)

In any event, the Lemon Test and its extension in *Wallace v. Jaffree* increasingly have remarkably weak sway in contemporary constitutional law.[64] There is now at least one alternative to it that has been accepted by the Supreme Court; *Lemon* therefore has effectively been overturned *sub silencio* as a uniquely controlling test of church/state separation across the board. A new test is found in the recent Supreme Court case of *Town of Greece v. Galloway*.[65] In this case, the Court established that a religious purpose is permissible if: a) it is non-coercive, and b) the mechanism through which the religious purpose is expressed is open to minority faiths.

Both these elements and the interpretive spirit underling the majority opinion, we believe, should carry important implications for biblical instruction in public schools: the logic of the *Town of Greece v. Galloway* holding should serve to underscore the constitutionality of instructional reform measures. Indeed, opponents of *Wallace v. Jaffree* recognize the *Town*

---

opposition to the Supreme Court's infamous decision in *Dred Scott v. Sandford*, 60 U.S. 393 (1857). .

63. 358 U.S. 1 (1958).

64. Its weakness is manifest. In addition to the points we address most specifically, Philip Hamburger and others (including dissenting Supreme Court justices) argue that the Lemon Test is inconsistent with the original intent of the Constitution. See Hamburger, *Separation of Church and State*, 12–13. Further, the law has never taken the Lemon Test as a stand-alone constitutional litmus test. For certainly one of its central elements is especially dubious, namely, the element that law must nether substantially hinder nor advance religion. This has never been taken as a stand-alone principle. Tax exempt status for churches no doubt very substantially assists religion, as do charitable laws offering tax deductions for donations to churches, but such laws have never been viewed as constitutionally impermissible *simply* on the basis that they have as a primary effect substantial assistance to religion.

65. 572 US__(2014).

of Greece decision's expansive power, beyond the issue there at bar of prayer before governmental meetings. As David L. Barkey, an attorney for the Anti-Defamation League remarks, "while the opinion is facially limited to legislative prayer, there are deep concerns that language from the decision [ ] will be used by lower courts to further degrade constitutionally mandated separation of church and state."[66]

Mr. Barkey is right to see the possibility of *Town of Greece v. Galloway* creating ripples throughout constitutional law. We see it as applicable to debates about Bible instruction in public schools. First, Bible courses—even if their creation is informed by a religious motive—are utterly voluntary and so in no plausible sense coercive.[67] We acknowledge that the Supreme Court has often seen matters pertaining to school children as worthy of more critical censure than those not so directed, but the fact that all the Bible courses we are addressing are offered only as electives and only at the high school level mitigates considerably the scope of this concern. It just seems implausible to equate the social dynamics surrounding football games and commencement exercises with an elective academic course (with its tests, term papers, and homework) offered among a range of other elective options.[68] And this conclusion must follow all the more so given the *non-devotional* nature of the courses in the first place. Talk of coercion, or of psychological harm, therefore, just seems out of place.

Second, the mechanism by which any religious motive underlying these courses might be operationalized—proposals to local school boards—is a process that adherents of all religions, minority or majority, may certainly avail themselves of; local school boards would have to hear on an equal basis any proposal to have minority religions non-devotionally taught in their public schools: Buddhists who would like the historical and cultural legacy of Buddhism taught in public schools are as permitted to argue this claim as are adherents of any other religion, and nothing would stop a school board from adopting a curriculum on the history and influence of Buddhist tradition.

In all, the logic of the *Town of Greece v. Galloway* standard supports the constitutionality of a religious motive if backed by a secular rationale

66. Barkey, "Breaching the Wall: The Real World Impact of *Town of Greece v. Galloway*,"

67. This point is magnified all the more in states such as South Carolina, which explicitly disavow any tax dollar allocation for teacher training and support for such courses.

68. For the Supreme Court's rulings on prayer at football games and commencement exercises respectively, see *Santa Fe Independent School District v. Doe*, 530 U.S. 290 (2000) and *Lee v. Weisman*, 505 U.S. 577 (1992).

or logic. Existing formal precedents therefore are too weak a reed to detain the curricular reform movement. A religious motive for policy making concerning the teaching of the Bible, if annealed with a secular justification, should be seen as perfectly constitutional.

In addition, we need to address a further problem with Audi's argument that policy making always be informed by a sufficient secular motive. This further argument we develop against Audi's view is applicable also to any other argumentation that requires a secular motive, including the strong secularism of Sajo that holds that a secular motive be the predominating motive informing public decision making. Namely, the issue of motive is often unclear. In the argument we deployed so far, we have assumed that the religious motive is clear to all participants. But this is not always the case. A precondition of determining whether either a sufficient secular motive, or a predominating secular motive is present is the determination of what motives are in fact moving policy participants.[69] However, it can be very difficult to determine motives on many occasions. Moreover, this is no run of the mill difficulty—for divining the motive, on Audi's and Sajo's arguments, precondition the enjoyment of what would otherwise be a constitutional value. That is, on the argument of Audi, if a sufficient secular motive does not inform a proposal, then that proposal should not be considered in depth but dismissed *ab initio*; and on Sajo's argument, the absence of a predominating secular motive would be grounds for state nullification of any ensuing law or policy outcome. However, having proposals to one's elected representatives and to one's fellow citizens not dismissed out of hand nor voided inappropriately is a clear constitutional value, a value flowing from our Constitution and the animating principles of the republican form of government. Hence, the determination of whether there is, or is not a motive, or motives of the right kind is a predicate to the enjoyment of a value of great worth—that is, of having one's views open to serious consideration or sustained as public law. We acknowledge that Audi does not propose that the absence of a secular motive be a legal disability—that is, that it be determined by a court of law and that if no such motive be found, then the court invalidate a proposal; instead, he holds it to be a moral, not legal, requirement that one advance only proposals that are informed by a

69. As Berg points out, it is very important not to be confused by the differentiation some scholars maintain between a "subjective" and an "objective" determination of secular motives. An "objective" determination of motivation includes, as Koppelman notes, an assessment of what the law "messages." But as Berg correctly argues, this determination must take into account the totality of the circumstances and thus must "consider all the evidence," including therefore an accurate inquisition of the actual motivations of a law's supporters. Berg, "'Secular Purpose," 30–31. See also Koppelman, "Secular Purpose," 111–12.

sufficient secular motive.[70] Nonetheless, Audi's theory is meant to be taken seriously—it is meant to have teeth. It is meant to impose a *real* requirement, even if the requirement not be seen as concretely justiciable. Think about it this way. If one has a moral obligation to advance views informed by a sufficient secular motivation, then others are morally entitled to dismiss one's views out of hand should one violate this discourse-controlling rule. As such, for Audi as for Sajo, the question of whether there are sufficient secular motives is one of considerable weight.

This adds an additional layer to the argument against defenders of a requirement of secular motivation. The assessment of an actor's motive has to be right; it cannot just be based on a precautionary sense that a motive one disfavors *might* be present. Getting the motive right is of constitutional urgency. Governmental openness to the petitions of citizens may be licitly curtailed on Audi's or Sajo's views if a sufficient secular motive not be detected; but in turn, the constitutional value of governmental openness would be illicitly impacted if a miscalculation of the actual motives occurred.

An additional point is important. There is a significant difference between the predicate determination, that is, the determination of an agent's motive which preconditions the openness of elected officials to debate any proposal, and the determinations made in just such an open debate among elected officials of any particular proposal. This distinction between gate-keeping the enjoyment of the constitutional value, and debating policy in a condition where the enjoyment of this value is certain will be an important point as we proceed in our argument.

Furthermore, although the arguments of Audi are not meant by him to be legally justiciable, which, if they were, would dictate a requirement for publicity pursuant not least to Lon Fuller's magisterial argument about the requirements of the rule of law,[71] a requirement for publicity emerges from his view nonetheless. A driving goal of Audi's argument is to meet others on what both see as *terra communis*. We believe this is satisfied by a secular argument requirement, but Audi does not. However, this means that Audi's

---

70. For Audi, "this restraint is merely a moral duty and it should not be a legal duty." Holzer, *Competing Schemas within the American Liberal Democracy: An Interdisciplinary Analysis of Differing Perceptions of Church and State*, 89. However, Judge Watson, the district judge from Hawaii who enjoined President Trump's travel ban after his inquisitorial review of the administration's secular motivation, purports to know the mind of Donald Trump, much better than Donald Trump. And Judge Watson would hope to impose this clairvoyance by force of law. To be sure, candidate Trump asserted in rambling rallies all sorts of statements. The question requiring clairvoyance is what motive informed this particular decision.

71. Fuller, *The Morality of Law*. Fuller designates publicity as one of the eight elements of the internal morality of law.

argument demands that the motivations of all be determined in a way that itself represents a common terrain for all, and so through a publicly accessible argument: the publicity requirement which would attach were the determination seen by Audi as legally justiciable emerges given his argument's commitment to having public policy questions decided on ground common to all disputants. Hence, one must publicly specify—defending to a watchful yet diverse public eye—the contention that a sufficient secular motive is, or is not present.

But to determine to this level of specificity the motives of another agent when those motives are not explicitly articulated, or conspicuously evident requires that one be informed by what the great Oxford legal scholar H.L.A. Hart called the "internal perspective," or "the internal aspect" of social behavior: observers must see as those whom they are assessing view the world. Observation cannot merely be based on detecting behavior that appears regular and uniform.[72] Hart notes, "the internal aspect . . . is often misrepresented as externally observable behavior." However, the internal viewpoint is only fully disclosed when one sees beyond the observable behavior, and penetrates to the "critical reflective attitude" underlying "certain patterns of behavior" and the "common standard" of evaluation used by the group one is assessing.[73]

But determining motives by assuming the internal perspective is in general a difficult thing to do—again, especially in a context where it preconditions the full enjoyment of constitutional values, and so the determination must meet a very high standard. Quite likely, this standard was not met, for example, in the majority opinion in *Wallace v. Jaffree*. As we argued above, that case is largely innocuous when we see both that it judges rationales and motivations as interchangeable terms, such that the former will *eo ipso* disclose the latter (despite this being a flawed conclusion) and if we further stipulate to its factual predicate, namely, that the record disclosed no presence whatsoever of either a secular rationale, or a secular motive for the law it reviewed. The majority opinion, however, very likely misjudged the motivations of the Alabama legislature, failing to see that the record could rather easily be read to demonstrate that the legislature was informed by at least one incontestably secular motive. As Chief Justice Berger argued with considerable passion in his dissenting opinion, a secular motive was right before the Court's eyes, to which it had become blind: a proper reading of the factual record showed that a moment of silence for either meditation or prayer was motivated by the legislature's desire to clarify that the 1978 law

72. Hart, *The Concept of Law*, 56.

73. Ibid., 57.

did not preclude a student—and note, we are dealing with school children, precisely the young people whom the Court has at times seen as especially impressionable and so in need of protection from all sorts of rather far-fetched forms of "coercion"—that prayer was *not excluded* from the moment of silence. The motivation to clarify constitutional rights, evident upon a proper reading of the factual record, is, Berger notes, abundantly permissible, flowing as it does simply from a desire to fortify civic knowledge.[74] Were it not permissible, should civics courses in public schools that, if worth their salt, will inevitably teach students that they have a legally protected right to worship God now become constitutionally suspect? The Court, instead, appears simply to have misread the record of relevant motivations.

That the majority of the Supreme Court failed to assess motives accurately is perhaps not surprising. As Caleb Lack and Jacques Rousseau and other scholars have shown, many agents are poor judges of other people's motives. Lack and Rousseau demonstrate that many agents suffer from several well-known problems in cognizing social difference, such as confirmation bias and bias based on heuristic accessibility. Specifically, and as many have recognized, a deep tendency exists in human cognition to over-emphasize data points that support one's preexisting views, referred to as confirmation bias. Additionally, bias can result from what psychologists term the availability heuristic: "when making decisions, we tend to be biased by information that is easier to recall; such information could be that which is vivid, well publicized, or recent." The availability of information moves us to make judgments "based on how easily certain points are brought to mind."[75] These deep tendencies in our thinking, however, produce deficient cognition, since availability is distinct from reliability, and confirmatory data must not be over-weighed to ensure an accurate assessment.

These and other well established bias-forming tendencies are likely to inform judgments about the motives of those with whom one disagrees, such as the judgment of the motives of an agent or group of agents defending a policy position one may find troubling. Indeed, the person judging an opposing political group's policy may well be a member of a differing political group, and so have much easier access to argumentation advanced by that group against the group being evaluated. In fact, this would seem to be the case in debates over curricular reform: the debates tend to center around one cluster of advocates, the NCBCPS, the BLP and their allies, against another group of advocates—primarily secular groups such as Americans

74. *Wallace v. Jaffree*, Chief Justice Berger, dissenting opinion, at 88.

75. Lack and Rousseau, *Critical Thinking, Science, and Pseudoscience: Why We Can't Trust Our Brains*, 77.

United for Separation of Church and State, the Secular Alliance, the American Humanists, the Freedom from Religion Foundation, and other allied left-leaning organizations, judges, and professors. Opponents of Bible instruction therefore are likely to have access much more readily to material that casts, or that seeks to cast, curricular reformers in what to their mind is an unfavorable light. When we add this problem to the confirmation bias, it follows that cognition of the motives of those to whom one is opposed can be quite difficult indeed.

In response to these problems, Lack and Rousseau as well as other scholars argue for the central importance of critical thinking skills to empower individuals, officials, and groups to avoid frequent sources of cognitive deficiency. As Lack and Rousseau point out in what appears to be a point of considerable common sense, "the capacity to approach issues in a way that gives us the best chance of making the most justified conclusion is one that needs nurturing and exercise . . . to avoid vulnerability to false beliefs."[76] Such nurturing, they argue, is best achieved by developing and reinforcing firm and supple critical reasoning skills, by which they mean conventional traits such as self-reflection and the capacity to avoid logical fallacies.

However, two issues in this context become especially germane to our discussion of Audi's and Sajo's demand for a secular motivation to public policy making. First, as Lack and Rousseau are at pains to point out, critical reasoning skills are difficult to produce and sustain. This realism as to the current state of public critical reasoning capacities militates against a strong moral position which makes such onerous demands on the public mind (or even on that of such an "eminent tribunal").[77] To be sure, critical reasoning should and must be emphasized, and it may well be more widely distributed than Lack and Rousseau maintain (though such an optimistic assessment should be indulged, we think, only with caution). Nevertheless, a second problem presents itself that adds additional weight to our argument against the secular motivation position.

A new and productive area of research has shown that the problems surrounding the cognition of social difference, including understanding the motives of those with whom one disagrees, are deeper than the difficulty of securing critical reasoning skills as conventionally defined by Lack, Rousseau, and others. Dan Kahan of the Yale Law School and other scholars associated with Yale's Cultural Cognition Project have established that when political disagreement is a central element in situations where one is making publicly relevant determinations of fact, cognitive failure is actually *more*

76. Lack and Rousseau, *Critical Thinking*, 1, 2.
77. See ibid., 47n99.

likely among those who have well developed critical reasoning skills, such as the capacity for self-reflection and avoidance of logical error, especially when issues of political disagreement are at stake.[78] This is so, Kahan's research demonstrates, because those with the traditionally important skills of self-reflection and mental acuity are actually *more likely* to be able to deploy those skills in ways that uphold both their preexisting sense of self and their connections with what to them are socially valuable group allegiances. And both of these aspects are especially accentuated when matters of political disagreement are at issue: deeply contested matters of public law frequently implicate one's preexisting sense of self, and one's connection with groups one sees as socially valuable. In contested policy matters, thoughts such as that "liberals like me don't allow restrictions on abortion" or "my liberal friends wouldn't accept me if I were to endorse restrictions on abortion" are often (but not self-consciously) in participants' minds. Hence, the root of much cognitive failure is not a paucity of skills in the conventional sense (such as logical acuity) but instead is the heretofore unrecognized depth of people's attachments to their sense of self, and their associated group loyalties in matters involving political contestation.

Kahan's thesis is a striking one, and some have argued against it by noting that such a bold claim about our epistemic weaknesses requires in turn especially bold evidence to corroborate it. However, sound data suggests precisely that it is quite likely that secular leaning advocates will misjudge the motives of groups advocating for educational reforms. There does seem to be a very real miscalculation—or at least considerable risk of miscalculation—common among secular groups about the motivations of a range of reformers advancing conservative-leaning policy change, and not just in matters of Bible-centered pedagogy and coursework. This indicates not that these inferences cannot be used in open political debate against conservative positions, but that they are not clearly accurate to the degree that Audi's and Sajo's argument would require in order for them to serve as a precondition for determining the availability of the enjoyment of longstanding constitutionally values—such as the value of having a citizen's policy proposals not be dismissed out of hand. For if one's motives on these views are driven by an insufficient secular motive, then the policy prescription should not be entertained at all, and so the enjoyment of a basic value is preconditioned on a judgment that one's motive is *in fact and demonstrably in fact* x rather than y.

One detects in much of the literature not just about the NCBCPS but about other areas of curriculum reform, a judgment about the motives of

---

78. For detailed overviews, see Kahan et al., "Motivated Numeracy and Enlightened Self-Government."

these groups that assumes them to be proselytizers—one might even say, to be snake-handling proselytizers and backcountry rubes. We can see this misperception of the actions of groups with which they disagree by liberals—and often extremely intelligent liberals—in other areas of educational debate, such as matters of sex education and science education.

To the first issue, the very accomplished liberal educational theorist Marc Rom—a distinguished professor of public policy at Georgetown University, and a man of superb intellectual acuity and professional accomplishment—holds falsely that debates over sex education curricula are debates at root only about revealed religion; that religious views, derived from the Bible, drive a vast percentage of the actors advocating for forms of sex education different than his preferred model ("comprehensive" sex education starting when students are very young), and that these religious motives make the advocates insensitive to secular argumentation. He maintains that "the advocates of Abstinence Only sex education are typically motivated by their religious concerns. But because religion cannot be explicitly used in the classroom, Abstinence Only advocates seek to use secular means to promote their causes. Still, if it were possible, there is little doubt that many Abstinence Only proponents would bring religion into the curriculum."[79]

However, evidence indicates that the Abstinence Only position has sound empirical support, and that reform advocates are motivated (at the very least partly) by this sound data—a possibility vanishingly minimized by the presumed detection by Rom of an unwelcome motivation. At least three lines of argument support this conclusion. First, The American College of Pediatricians, which has come strongly to support Abstinence Education, has recently called attention to a report from the Centers for Disease Control and Prevention that reveals that almost sixty percent of high school students today have never had sex. This represents an increase of twenty-eight percent since 1991.[80] Moreover, a 2011 United States Health and Human Services survey discloses that eighty-four percent of teens view sex as something to be avoided as a teenager.[81] The American College of Pediatricians argues that these reports "demonstrate clearly that Sexual Abstinence Education, is a relevant message for youth and a goal they can achieve."[82] This is all the more so when one appreciates that abstinence programs are

79. Rom, "Below the (Bible) Belt: Religion and Sexuality Education in American Public Schools," 140.

80. Centers for Disease Control and Prevention, "Youth Risk Behavior Survey: 1991–2015."

81. Administration for Children and Families, Report (2011), http://acf.hhs.gov/programs/f 9 ysb/content/docs/20090226_abstinence.pdf.

82. Administration for Children and Families, *Abstinence report*.

holistic in nature, situating sexual issues in a wider assessment of life plans and career goals, and general decision-making skills.[83]

Second, the American College of Pediatricians argues that new CDC data suggests the failure of Comprehensive Sex Education, while new data discloses the positive benefits of Sexual Risk Avoidance (a synonymous term often preferred to Abstinence Only Education, since, as we noted, the instruction does not address only abstinence but situates sexual health in the wider context of career and life success). The American College of Pediatricians notes that "teens who do choose to engage in sexual activity are using less birth control and sexually transmitted infections (STIs) are on the rise, as is adolescent depression, sometimes referred to as the 'emotional STI.'"[84] Given the broad distribution of CSE programs, these nationwide trends suggest the failure of CSE instruction, the College concludes. At the same time, the conclusion of a 2013 National Abstinence Education Association report detailing twenty-three peer-reviewed Sexual Risk Avoidance programs notes that Abstinence Education has "demonstrated significant and positive behavioral change among student participants" in terms of broadly shared metrics such as grades, avoiding risky behavior such as drug use, and teen pregnancy.[85]

Third, the Centers for Disease Control has underscored this conclusion about the importance of sexual abstinence for student success, which suggests that abstinence instruction should be highly prized by educators who, after all, must have the health interests of students foremost in mind. In a first of its kind study, the CDC finds that high school students who have never had sexual intercourse rate substantially higher in almost all health-related behaviors than do sexually active students, with rates of daily smoking, binge drinking, marijuana use, depression, and physical fighting all significantly lower for non-sexually active students relative to their sexually active peers.[86] While the report cannot establish whether sexual activity causes these risky behaviors, or whether students with risky behavior patterns are more likely to seek sex, the conclusions nevertheless are astounding. As Glenn T. Stanton argues, "these findings should be very concerning to all parents and professionals concerned with teens' general health and well-being. The sexual choices and values our young people hold have real-life consequences far beyond

83. Kim, "Family Fact of the Week: The Abstinent Majority," 1.

84 American College of Pediatricians, "Great News for Teen Pregnancy," citing Centers for Disease Control and Prevention, "Youth Risk Behavior Survey."

85. National Abstinence Education Association, "Abstinence Works."

86. Centers for Disease Control and Prevention, "Sexual Identity, Sex of Sexual Contacts, and Health-Related Behaviors Among Students Grades 9–12—United States and Selected Sites."

sexuality itself. Thus, there are indeed compelling reasons to encourage teens to choose not to be sexually active,"[87] especially through programs that situate sexual health in a larger framework of life choices related to a broad spectrum of risky and self-destructive behaviors.

Why shouldn't we assume therefore that the motives of Abstinence Only advocates are to achieve empirically supportable outcomes of sexual health and student well-being? Why impute to advocates a motive informed only, or mostly by a desire for purity grounded only on biblical, or other-worldly values? It seems likely that to some extent, at least, preconceived ideas of what conservative Christians are like has colored the judgment of so distinguished a political and social scientist as Professor Rom—a scholar whose contributions in other areas have been of the first order of excellence and disciplinary significance. This of course is not to have shown that the view he holds on the superiority of CSE has demonstrably been invalidated; rather, it is to show that serious counter-arguments are left unattended due to a likely misperception of the motives of those holding opposing positions.

With respect to debates over science education, the same miscalcula-tion is often in view. Equally insightful and distinguished scholars such as George Bishop and Stephen Mockabee disregard any possibility that support for augmenting the Darwinian view of evolution with a recognition of al-leged points of irreducible complexity could ever be empirically motivated. No, alternatives to the sufficiency of the Darwinian mechanism of evolution are proposed only through the abiding fears of religious people—what they label their "angst."[88] "Gut-level, affective reactions" drive them in their op-position, for they are propelled to act only by an "emotional association" that connects these matters with Godlessness; they have no genuinely reasoned perspective on science issues but, instead, are driven by fear and bemoan contemporary education as the enemy of their city of God.[89] Yet Michael Behe has advanced serious arguments against the sufficiency of Darwinian evolution.[90] Again, this is not to say that his view on evolutionary science is true; it is to indicate a likely miscalculation of the motives supporting contending viewpoints in debates over curricular reform.

These examples, which by no means are unique, suggest confirmation of Kahan's conclusions about the difficulty of cultural cognition, even among highly sophisticated thinkers. This is all the more so because additional data

87. Stanton, "CDC Study Says Teen Virgins Are Healthier."

88. Bishop et al., "American Public Opinion and the 'Culture War' Politics of Teach-ing Human Evolution," 91.

89. Ibid., 107.

90. Professor of Biological Sciences at Lehigh University, Behe is the author of such works as *Darwin's Black Box: The Biochemical Challenge to Evolution.*

disclose that assessments such as Rom's manifest a deeper embedding of an untrue archetype—namely, a deeply rooted yet invidious miscalculation of the conservative mindset. As we have seen the merits of the position to which Rom is opposed are not insignificant, so the imputation of a biblical desire to impose a Puritanic agenda is questionable. But what is more, his and Bishop's and Mockabee's deeper assessment of conservatives' motives—that they are fueled by fearfulness about rising secularity—is at once widely shared but highly suspect.[91] Indeed, reliable evidence indicates that the underlying motives of evangelicals and conservative Christians are less informed by fears of irreligion than many often assume.[92] Such believers frequently have a very strong conception of providence, and of how "the gates of the netherworld shall not prevail against"[93] those to whom God has given the gift of faith. Faith for them is not a delicate fledgling nervously to be brooded, but a gift of God wondrously to be embraced. Indeed, many also have an abiding belief that religious faith will be protected not only by God's providential care for his faithful but by the fact that religion is hard-wired by the creator into the handiwork of his creation. For example, in answer to the question, "why has faith still any chance at all" in light of the growing attacks on God in Western societies, Pope Benedict XVI responded: "I should say it is because faith corresponds to the nature of man . . . only God corresponds to the [nature] of our being."[94] Contemporary philosopher Roger Trigg echoes this sentiment in his work, *Equality, Freedom, and Religion* based on the conclusions of the Oxford Cognition, Religion and Theology Project, which he directed.[95] His research indicates that religious sentiment is hardwired into the nature of humankind and hence that religion will not wither away. "The secularization thesis of the 1960s—I think that was hopeless," Trigg concludes.[96] Secularism may arise and linger briefly, he argues, but it is not likely to remain culturally ascendant. Indeed, many conservative Christians look with unpuzzled nonchalance at the evidence of the predicted decline of secularism that several social scientists demonstrate on the basis of the extremely low birth rates experienced among the non-religious, and the creeping "weariness with life" growing in parts of the Western world.[97]

91. Religious Studies scholar Jason Bivins goes so far as to impute to conservative evangelicals a "religion of fear" plying a "politics of horror." See Bivins, *Religion of Fear: The Politics of Horror in Conservative Evangelicalism*.

92. See Prud'homme, "Conclusion," 185–92.

93. Matt 16:18 (NAB).

94. Ratzinger, *Truth and Tolerance: Christian Belief and World Religions*, 137.

95. Trigg, *Equality, Freedom, and Religion*.

96. Greene, "Religious Belief is Human Nature, Huge New Study Claims."

97. Conservatives look with unsurprised sorrow at developments such as those

As Professor Eric Kaufman of Birbeck College of the University of London points out, due to declining birthrates among seculars, "the future will be more religious and conservative than you think."[98] Such is exactly what a good number of conservative Christians see as rather obvious.[99] Confidence in their faith means many conservative Christians are not dreadfully fearful of growing secularism.[100] Indeed, the highly religious seem to have in turn a relatively lower degree of *overall* anxiety. Data suggests that in general strongly religious people are more trusting of others, and more positively related to their communities than are non-religious individuals. A recent study by the Pew Internet and American Life Project titled "The Civic and Community Engagement of Religiously Active Americans" shows that those who are highly active in religious organizations are more trusting of others, and more positively connected to their communities than those who are not active in church-based organizations.[101] And conservatives and evangelicals, of course, tend toward a very high rate of activity in these kinds of religious associations. Hence, many religious conservatives tend to have not a fretful concern and "ominous"[102] brooding about life, but a positive respect for difference and an openness to the secular world. Indeed, is his extensive survey of American evangelicalism, sociologist Christian Smith

in the Netherlands where "weariness with life" is now counted an incurable disease justifying medical euthanasia, and where a growing movement of "writers, artists and politicians" is advocating for the right of anyone over seventy to be legally euthanized should life lose its charms. See Boomsma and Price, "Western Suttee: Against a Right to Be Killed," 28–30.

98. Kaufmann, "The Future Will Be More Religious and Conservative Than You Think." See also his book length treatment of the same topic, Kaufman, *Shall the Religious Inherit the Earth? Demography and Politics in the 21st Century.* See also Stark, *The Triumph of Faith: Why the World is More Religious than Ever.*

99. Although some of the most conservative of Christians see the world as mired in decline and register this as evidence of the imminent Second Coming, this decline is embedded in what for them is an anxiety-liberating framework of Christian hope. Further, such individuals are accurately described by Peter Lawler as individuals who are inclined toward a longstanding skepticism of public institutions. See Lawler, *Aliens in America: The Strange Truth about Our Souls,* 229.

100. It is perhaps helpful to remember that periods of widespread doubt or institutional deterioration are far from uncommon in the history of Christianity. See Chesterton's "the five deaths of Christianity" outlined in his work *The Everlasting Man.* One such purported death was during the era of the European revolutions. Yet, in the time leading up to this tumult, profound insights on Christian trust were advanced, including in the classic devotional treatise by the eighteenth-century French Catholic priest Jean-Pierre de Caussade, *Abandonment to Divine Providence.*

101. Jensen, "The Civic and Community Engagement of Religiously Active Americans," 30.

102. Bishop et al., "American Public Opinion and the 'Culture War,'" 86.

documents a broad acceptance of social diversity.[103] As John Bartkowski notes in summary of Smith's conclusions, "the vast majority of interviewed evangelicals champion and celebrate America's cultural pluralism."[104] In fact, religious conservatives are, as we have noted, less anxious in general than secularists.[105] Patrick Glynn in his exhaustive work, *God: The Evidence*,

103. Smith, *Christian America? What Evangelicals Really Want*.

104. Bartkowski, Review of *Christian America? What Evangelicals Really Want*, 1204–6.

105. Prud'homme, "Conclusion," 190–91. Our point is certainly not to say that there is no anxiety whatsoever about rising secularity; it is only to say that those concerns are less pronounced than many often assume. Additionally, a very important point to keep in mind is the depth and influence of internal Christian critiques of any anxiety that may arise concerning secularization. One of the leaders in international evangelical theology, the Oxford-trained theologian Thomas Greggs, for example, writes extensively to Christians reminding readers that anxiety about secularism "puts religion above God"—and contradicts core tenets of Christian faith. See, among other works, "Religionless Christianity in a Complexly Religious and Secular World"; and Prud'homme, "Conclusion." Furthermore, some have argued that conservative Christians in the 2016 presidential election were looking for a political savior, a search born of a disposition toward fearfulness. Damon Linker writes, for example, that, "if you're feeling defeated and demoralized, weak and vulnerable, you probably want a president who will serve as your protector." And this is precisely the lot of evangelical and other conservative Christians, Linker asserts. See Linker, "How Donald Trump's Strongman Act Won Over Evangelicals." But the data just does not bear this out. Although conservative Christians did eventually vote resoundingly for Trump, they did so over what appear to have been a great deal of initial skepticism and so not out of a gust of unreflective fearfulness. Further, although the Barna Group's exit reports indicate that Clinton lost the Catholic vote, she did so by approximately one percentage point—not a sign of mass fearfulness by American Catholics. In fact, as of September 2016, Catholic voters were tilting toward Clinton because, as Leah Libresco documented, they harbored extremely negative feelings about Trump. In addition, the LDS Church made a point of explicitly rebuking Trump in December 2015. As to the Protestant vote, for most of the campaign, the real movement toward Trump was among relatively *unchurched* Protestants—people who do not regularly attend church. See Libresco, "Trump is Driving Catholic Voters toward Clinton." It seems to us very unlikely that these unchurched voters were moved by the search for a specifically *religious* protector. Indeed, a great many evangelical Protestant leaders in particular were firm in their opposition to, or caution about Trump's candidacy. In addition, the post-election survey conducted by the Barna Group finds that the "evangelical vote which Trump won is the lowest level of evangelical support for a Republican since 1996" and in turn that "research indicated that perhaps the most significant faith group in relation to the Trump triumph was notional Christians" not born-again believers. See Barna Group, "Notional Christians Big Election Story"; and also Wright, "Nearly 100 Evangelical Leaders Draft a Petition to Denounce Trump." Relevant also is the failure of Roy Moore to win the Alabama Senate seat in December 2017. As Lyman Stone points out, "Roy Moore substantially underperformed among white evangelicals . . . [who] gave Moore the worst showing of any Alabama Republicans Senate candidate in the 21st century." Stone, "Roy Moore Had Lowest White Evangelical Support of Any Alabama Republican in the 21st Century."

summarizes numerous studies that indicate that religious faith "correlates with lower stress, lower depression and greater ability to cope with stress."[106] In all, then, the religiously conservative seem to be quite accepting of the wider world. Based on this understanding, a portrait of conservative reform advocates as frightful souls compelled by self-defensiveness seems strikingly out of place; the idea of hoards of meddling, anxiety-riddled evangelicals or other conservative Christians desperately tinkering with public education, just doesn't stack up.[107]

In all, Kahan's research, which as we have seen is highly germane to educational debates, provides further support to our argument against Audi's or Sajo's requirement of a secular motivation. For in matters of policy, including educational policy, it can be hard to determine accurately what motives those with whom one disagrees actually have, again at the sufficiently high standard of proof their positions require.

What is more, the difficulty for these positions is even deeper when one is called upon to judge the relative weight of the variety of possible motives informing an agent's decision. Audi's argument demands that the secular motive be sufficient, but not that it be the only motive; the secular motive must be strong enough on its own to impel the decision being made, but it need not be the only significant motive harbored by the agent. Judging relative weights of motivational strength is all the more incumbent upon Sajo, since religious motives must be less weighty than secular ones. However, both the work of Lack and Rousseau and that of Kahan and his associates demonstrate just how difficult determining what any of the motives of those with whom one disagrees actually are, much less ranking the range of motives that one might suspect are present based on a lexical ordering of motivational sufficiency or weight.

We therefore have grounds all the more for being very cautious about any approach predicated on accurately divining true motives in contentious debates. For this reason, a secular motivation requirement is doubly suspect. We have two distinct reasons for abandoning it: it is not needed to retain consistency with the First Amendment, and it is quite difficult to operationalize in matters where motives are contested and not transparent.

106. Glynn, *God: The Evidence, The Reconciliation of Faith and Reason in a Post-Secular World*. See also "Faith and Wellbeing."

107. Prud'homme, "Conclusion," 191.

Chapter 3 ─────────────────────────────

In Defense of State Religious Education
A Rationale for State Biblical Instruction

Up to this point, we have argued that religious motives can inform public policy making but only if they are conjoined with a secular rationale, that is, an argument that does not *presuppose* the existence of God or divine revelation. In this chapter, we shall argue that Bible-centered instruction in public schools is supported by just such a secular justification. Our argument is based on five points: i) the constitutional permissibility of courses on the Bible for historical, literary, and cultural purposes; ii) the pedagogical propriety of such courses focusing exclusively or predominantly on the Bible, and not on other sacred texts; iii) an excursus on the cultural and historical significance of the Bible; iv) the acute curricular need for coursework on the Bible given strikingly high levels of contemporary biblical illiteracy; and v) the need to avoid popular cynicism concerning the objectives being served by public schooling.

The Constitutionality of Bible-Focused Reform

To our first point, Supreme Court case law clearly allows the teaching of the Bible for the purpose of affording students a complete education in history, literature, and culture. This principle is stated forcefully in the very Supreme Court case that banned devotional biblical instruction in public schools. In *School District of Abington Township v. Schempp*, the Supreme Court held:

> It might well be said that one's education is not complete without a study of . . . the history of religion and its relationship

to the advancement of civilization. It certainly may be said that
the Bible is worthy of study for its literary and historic qualities.
Nothing we have said here indicates that such study of the Bible
. . . may not be effected consistently with the First Amendment.[1]

Doing just that is the stated rationale of both the laws we have surveyed mandating or encouraging Bible instruction, and of the organizations
promoting these laws. This secular rationale is expressed publicly by both
the legislators and the reform advocates as a secular one; that is, a rationale
held to be accessible to others on the basis of rational argument unaided by
religious inspiration or insight. All state statutes mandating or encouraging
biblical instruction make clear that the courses are to be taught objectively,
and not as devotional religious exercises. Typical is statutory language in the
South Carolina law stating that the course "must be taught in an objective
manner with no attempt to influence the students as to the truth or falsity
of the materials being presented."[2] Each of the pieces of legislation lays out
specific requirements, including that instructors of elective Bible courses be
certified by the state, and that there be no religious litmus tests for course instructors.[3] Additionally, the Texas law expressly calls on the Texas Attorney
General to review all Bible course curricula to ensure that they comply with
the First Amendment to the United States Constitution.

This conspicuous articulation of rational argument, and of reason-
based program design, is reiterated unambiguously by organizations sup-
portive of reform. The NCBCPS makes clear its position that the teaching
of the Bible is constitutional, and that its program is "concerned with education rather than indoctrination of students."[4] Their website states firmly
that they are concerned only with the "foundation and blueprint for our
Constitution, Declaration of Independence, and our educational system,"
which is a proper curricular objective in history courses on the American
polity.[5] The NCBCPS has on numerous occasions revised its curriculum
to underscore that it does not teach as historically true claims key to the
Christian faith, such as the resurrection of Jesus, and that it pays generous
attention to the different translations that exist and so does not promote use
only of one form of the Bible.

1. *Abington Township v. Schempp* (1963).

2. South Carolina State House, "South Carolina A102, R155, S726 [2]: An Act to
Amend Chapter 29, Title 59 Code of Laws of South Carolina, 2007.

3. Deckman, "Religious Literacy in Public Schools," 39.

4. National Council on Bible Curriculum in Public Schools, *The Bible in History
and Literature.*

5. Ibid.

For their part, the BLP states clearly as well that its curriculum is predicated on the basis of secular arguments concerning the need for greater historical, cultural, and literary understanding of the Bible. Typical of its position, the leadership of the BLP noted in a press release that "Our track record of successful implementation and strong community support has given . . . districts confidence that our materials meet the educational needs of their diverse student populations."[6]

Soundly Focusing Curricular Attention on the Bible

In addition to articulating a secular rationale for adding courses on the Bible, it is important to note that reform advocates call for instruction only, or predominantly about the Bible and not on other sacred texts. Yet, this too has a sufficient rational justification independent of argumentation that presupposes the truth or current value of the Bible. The Bible is foundational to American and Western literature and history in a way that no other religious text can possibly be described. On this, experts highly regarded both by liberal and conservative educational theorists agree. For example, Luke Timothy Johnson, a scholar noted for his erudition and moderate views on the role of religion in public life, has defended the proposal for greater attention to the role of the Jewish and Christian scriptures in American and world history courses, a perspective that can be found, for example, in his 2006 piece titled "Textbook Case: A Bible Curriculum for Public Schools,"[7] and which is echoed by a number of other scholars including Craig Engelhardt of Baylor University in his 2009 essay "The Necessary Role of Religion in Civic Education."[8] Indeed, even scholars strongly opposed to Bible courses in public schools such as Kent Greenawalt argue that "no doubt the Bible has affected our literature and broader culture far more than any other religious writing."[9]

Underscoring the Bible's Prominent Place

However, contemporary public education has been greatly influenced by the rising prevalence of multicultural educational pedagogy. This multicultural and multi-confessional orientation is likely a major source of the

---

6. Bible Literacy Project, *The Bible and Its Influence.*
7. Johnson, "Textbook Case: A Bible Curriculum for Public Schools."
8. Engelhardt, "The Necessary Role of Religion in Civic Education."
9. Greenawalt, *Does the Bible Belong in Public Schools*, 137.

controversy surrounding Bible courses. For example, scholars like Diane Moore of Harvard Divinity School who do not believe the Bible should be taught in stand-alone courses very often ask, as she pointedly has, "Why privilege the Bible" in public schooling?[10] Due to the growing influence of such a sentiment, an excursus on the cultural significance of the Bible could only prove helpful. A survey of the Bible's cultural significance will underscore the constitutionality of courses dedicated exclusively on this remarkably important text; its preeminence as a sacred text to Western culture, in turn, highlights the importance of Bible-focused educational reform. Hence, in this section we provide a necessarily adumbral sketch of the prominent position of the Bible in Western civilization, with special focus on the Bible's influence in English and American cultures.[11]

What is more, underscoring the importance of the Bible to England and North America is all the more apposite as the English-speaking world only recently celebrated the quadrennial of the most widely read version of the Christian Bible: the King James Version. This is not to say, of course, that the Bible was unimportant in this context before the King James Version. Indeed, Diarmaid MacCulloch has recently surveyed cogently the importance of the Bible in England before the King James translation.[12] In England throughout the late 1400s, the Vulgate was readily available to even the most minor priest. However, England, in the late fifteenth and early sixteenth centuries, did not have a widely accepted vernacular edition of scripture. This was actually a European anomaly: by this time, the Bible had already been widely translated into high and low German, Italian, Dutch, Spanish, Czech, and Catalan.[13] This anomalous condition was deeply felt by the leading church officials in pre-Reformation England. Indeed, "many leading figures . . . wanted to reform the Church . . . and they were aware of how anomalous it was that England did not have a good Catholic vernacular version of the Bible."[14] Chancellor Thomas More took it upon himself to encourage a vernacular edition, and made considerable efforts to create one.[15]

Despite a reversal that would see Chancellor More repudiate a vernacular translation (due, he said, to the "malignity of the times"), King Henry VIII commanded that there be an English version of the Bible, and

10. Moore, "Teaching about the Bible in Public Schools," 79–80.

11. See also Gearon, "The King James Bible and the Politics of Religious Education: Secular State and Sacred Scripture," 9–27.

12. See MacCulloch, *All Things Made New: Writings on the Reformation*.

13. Ibid., 167.

14. Ibid., 169.

15. Ibid.

one printed in the British Isles to boot.[16] Furthermore, Archbishop of Canterbury Thomas Cromwell in 1536 ordered that there be both Latin and English translations of the Bible in every English church. The most widely distributed English language Bible at this time would soon come to be the 1576 English translation of the so-called Geneva Bible.

But, not for long. The English translation of the Geneva Bible would soon lose its preeminent status. In 1611, the King James Version (KJV) was issued, and soon became the dominant English Bible. The four-hundredth anniversary of the KJV, just recently celebrated, was marked by the publication of a plethora of scholarly as well as popular historical accounts of its origins and subsequent history.[17] Among this wealth of publications is Melvyn Bragg's *The Book of Books*. Bragg's work is one of the most insightful of the histories recently produced. Bragg suggests that "it would be fair to claim that for its first three centuries, the KJV was, in general, the prime educating force in the English-speaking world. Its impact was stronger in the first two centuries. In the nineteenth century, although there was growing competition from popular fiction and literature, it was still the dominant book . . . People learned to read in order to read the Bible and they learned to read by being taught through the Bible itself."[18]

Furthermore, Bragg challenges those who suggest that the Bible was a work that "held back the shaping of the modern world." Instead, he argues vigorously that "the King James Version . . . helped shape it often for the better and was integral in that process." In any case, "few can deny," he notes, "that from 1611 in the English-speaking world, *it was the primary educational work*"—so foundational was the Bible to English-speaking culture.[19] Bragg is surely correct in asserting so strongly the Bible's influence in shaping English and American culture. We shall underscore the Bible's importance by briefly surveying first the role of the Bible in England in the century or so before the American founding and, second, the impact of the Bible on American political and cultural development.

The KJV is the high point of the English Reformation. At a time when Saint Jerome's Latin Vulgate translation of the original Hebrew, Greek, and Aramaic had been Christendom's Bible for over a thousand years, William Tyndale—via Wycliffe—produced the first English translation of the New Testament in 1526. It had been Tyndale's famous hope that the Bible would

16. Ibid., 170.

17. Hamlin and Jones, eds., *The King James Bible After Four Hundred Years: Literary, Linguistic, and Cultural Influences*; Campbell, *Bible: The Story of the King James Version*; Nicolson, *When God Spoke English: The Making of the KJV*; Wilson, *The People's Bible*.

18. Bragg, *The Book of Books*, 261.

19. Ibid.; emphasis added).

be accessible to the "English ploughboy." As noted, for much longer than any European nation, vernacular translations remained illegal in England. Tyndale left England for a life of itinerant scholarship, his translation un-accepted by Henry VIII, but sending an increasingly popular translation "home." At the behest of papal authority and through the betrayal of a fellow Englishman, Henry Phillips, Tyndale was arrested in 1535, imprisoned at Vilvoorde, near Brussels, and executed in 1536. But, after so long being hailed as its defender (Defender of the Faith was a title bestowed to the King in 1521), Henry VIII moved, for well-known reasons, away from Rome. Lutheran and Calvinist theology dramatically increased appetites for English Bibles. Indeed, the KJV, like all English vernacular translations, needs to be seen in the context of a Reformation which emphasized (though Protestants argued about the extent) salvation by faith not works, a faith undergirded by the doctrine of *sola scriptura*. For Christians to read the Bible was, from here on in, essential to their salvation. It was the Bible that provided inerrant knowledge of divine revelation; and since the Bible was God's Word, translation was no light task.

In 1603, James VI of Scotland became James 1 of England. The new king hosted an ecclesiastical conference at Hampton Court in January 1604, in part a response to a Puritan "Millenary Petition" to rid the Church of England of remnants of Catholic practice. Puritans derive their once pejorative title from a desire to purify Christianity and return it, as Calvin had attempted in Geneva, to its primitive origins. Primitive here was accolade not insult.

The Hampton Court Conference was an attempt to heal a divided church. The Episcopal and 'catholic' bishops were led by Richard Bancroft (Bishop of London), the Puritans by John Rainolds (President of Corpus Christi College, Oxford). A simple way to look at the division would be to say that the former thought the Reformation had gone far enough, while the latter thought that it needed to go much further. The idea of a new translation was, in retrospect, a brilliant theological and political move. For the task of translation kept the opposing sides not only busy but working together.

Six "Companies of Translators" were established for the cause of a new authorized version: The First Westminster Company; The First Cambridge Company; The First Oxford Company; The Second Cambridge Company; The Second Oxford Company; and The Second Westminster Company.[20] Fourteen rules, variously adhered to, were in place. Rule 14 determined that the translators attend to the other translations including the Tyndale and

20 For a more detailed treatment, see Campbell, *Bible: The Story of the King James Version*, 276–92.

the Geneva versions. The list of translations referred to is unremarkable except for what it leaves out: no mention is found of the great translation made by the English Catholics in exile at Douai (where the New Testament was translated) and Rheims (where the Old Testament was). The translators ignored this omission.[21] This is an important reminder of the political nature of the biblical translation. There may have been divisions between the Protestant translators, but they were united in antipathy to Rome.

As well as a new national politico-religious identity, the new English Bible began to engender a new national literacy. This was an unforeseen educational consequence of Reformation. Reading would become critical to salvation, even if reading the Bible did not mean you were saved by it. With ever more efficient printing, now well established since the fifteenth century, the new literacy also opened readers, as it has done in the Renaissance, to texts other than the Bible.

Milton's *Paradise Lost* and Bunyan's *Pilgrim's Progress* are two often cited works of seventeenth-century English literary genius that manifestly demonstrate the cultural as well as theological influence of the KJV. But while their literary qualities are undoubted, it was for their authors the Reformed Protestant theology (of Fall, of atonement, of election, of salvation by faith not works, of God's grace) which are important. For Milton and for Bunyan, language is a vehicle for communication of faith not a substitute for it.

Nevertheless, in seventeenth-century England, this new literacy would indeed open wide access to texts far beyond the KJV. Renaissance humanism, bringing to "rebirth" classical Greek and Latin sources had itself, through figures like Erasmus, awakened the European Reformation. The problem of classical or "pagan" learning and Christian education, though, was an old one, far predating the European Reformation. It is reflected in Saint Augustine's *Confessions*, and as a direct problem of Christian pedagogy in *On Christian Teaching*.

In this context, science and political philosophy would exert great influence in seventeenth-century English religious and cultural life. The founding of the Royal Society was a high point. Isaac Newton was its most famous member, and eventual president. Newton was grammar-school educated and the breadth of classical, mathematical, and scientific knowledge he gained at his Grantham grammar school show wide educational currents, even in a land where schooling itself was far from universal. Newton's education was certainly not limited to the Bible, though his knowledge of

21. Nicolson, *When God Spoke English: The Making of the KJV*, 81.

it was extensive, and to his last days his interest in the prophetic books of Daniel and of Revelation never abated.[22]

In political philosophy, the Puritans, as non-conformists, inarguably pushed the case for liberty of conscience—what we would call freedom of religion, though Milton would not have extended this to atheists and idolaters. Given his broadly Reformed (technically Arminian) theology, Milton's surprisingly "liberal" political perspective is evident in his *Areopagitica*. Responding to the Licensing Order of 1643, Milton's 1644 publication was addressed to Parliament. It alludes to Paul's address to the Athenians in Acts 17: 18–34, the setting in around 355 B.C. of Isocrates's *Areopagitic Discourse*. His speech combines scriptural sources from the KJV to justify freedom of publication.

Such liberal politics (based on individual rights and freedoms) as found in Milton would profoundly affect society, with John Locke having an outsized influence. Educated at Westminster School, John Locke towers as the political philosopher of his age. Locke wrote his *Letter Concerning Toleration* in 1693, in the aftermath of the English Bill of Rights (1689). The letter contained his "thoughts about the mutual toleration of Christians in their different professions of religion" in which he esteems "toleration to be the chief characteristic mark of the true Church."[23] It is the KJV he cites. What is striking is that the age's leading political thinker consistently uses the Bible to support his philosophical argument.

Renowned for *Two Treatises Concerning Government*, Locke also wrote *Some Thoughts Concerning Education*, encapsulating liberal political philosophy in pedagogical terms—an approach not without a significant biblical influence. Mindful that education should be responsive to "the child's natural genius and constitution" which "God has stamped," Locke does not set out a precise curriculum. Yet, he gives hints: in paragraph 180 to "arithmetic"; in 181 to "acquaintance with globes"; in 182 he argues that "geography, chronology ought to go hand in hand"; in 183 that it "would be strange if the English gentleman should be ignorant of the law of his country"; in 186 to "rhetoric and logic, being the arts that in the ordinary method follow immediately after grammar"; and in 194 to "physics" and the science curriculum, with deference to "the incomparable Mr. Newton."[24] Although scripture is not central to his educational discourse, it still suffuses all of his political and pedagogical writing.

---

22. Ackroyd, *Newton*, 15–24.

23. Locke, *Some Thoughts Concerning Education*, 179–99. See also Morgan, ed., *Classics of Moral and Political Philosophy*.

24. Locke, *Some Thoughts concerning Education,* 179–99.

Over time, Locke's thought, as with so much in the history we have surveyed, would come to be deeply influential on American history, and political and cultural development. To a brief review of the Bible's influence on America we can now turn.

New World migrations of English Puritans in the first decades of the 1600s spread the KJV to America. As Adam Nicolson remarks, it is likely that "on the Mayflower it was the Geneva Bible they took with them . . . It is perhaps somewhat paradoxical that the KJV, for which one animating purpose had been nation-building in the service of a ceremonial and Episcopal church, would become the guiding text of Puritan America."

Yet, a guiding text it surely became.[25] Its core function in education is one of the most important reasons. As Alexis de Tocqueville, the French Catholic visitor to early 1830s America whose *Democracy in America* reflects on early colonial schooling, suggested quite rightly, it was "by the mandates relating to public education that the original character of American civilization is at once placed in the clearest light." And the Bible was front and center of colonial and early eighteenth and nineteenth-century American education. Tocqueville observed that "the municipal authorities were bound to enforce the sending of children to school by their parents; they were empowered to inflict fines upon all who refused compliance; and in cases of continued resistance, society assumed the place of the parent, took possession of the child, and deprived the father of those natural rights which he used to so bad a purpose." Yet, this education was underpinned by biblical faith for Tocqueville: "in America religion is the road to knowledge." It was also seen by this external observer to be for Americans the road to civil prosperity, for in America, he notes, "observance of the divine laws leads . . . to civil freedom."[26]

Historians suggest, to be sure, a strong drift from formal Christianity in certain parts of colonial America. Yet, the late seventeenth century and early eighteenth century were decades of religious revival. In 1730, Jonathan Edwards obtained a copy of the KJV. Known as his "Blank Bible" because it contained interleaved blank pages, over a period of thirty years Edwards annotated the text, demonstrating the primacy of the KJV to this Great Awakening.[27]

Further, these were decades defined partly by a drive to found new and expanded educational institutions. In New England, where the 1630s

25. For a detailed and masterly account of the profound role of the Bible in American public life, see Noll, *In the Beginning Was the Word: The Bible in American Public Life, 1492–1783.*

26. Tocqueville, *Democracy in America* 19–20.

27. Edwards, *The Works of Jonathan Edwards: Blank Bible.*

would see the founding of Harvard College (principally for clerics), Tocqueville surmises that "education and freedom are the children of morality
and religion."[28] And this conviction led to a condition wherein education
in seventeenth and eighteenth-century America was, in ubiquity if not in
sophistication, well in advance of education in England.

In the post-Revolutionary period, the close connection between the
Bible and civil prosperity would be questioned by some;[29] yet reacting to a
spiritual need but also against Enlightenment intellectualism,[30] early nineteenth-century preachers, inspired by the example if not always the theological substance of the earlier leaders like Jonathan Edwards and George
Whitefield, rekindled the Bible-oriented Christian teaching to an America
where churches were losing hold on state and government (about which we
reflect later in this chapter). Emphasizing personal experience in salvation,
in many ways the so-called Second Great Awakening was a religion of the
wilderness, at least primarily. Since Enlightenment influence on frontiers-
men was limited, such men and women could understand a message that
spoke of this life's precariousness and warned of future judgment. Moreover,
in post-Revolutionary America, the American Bible Society produced its
own editions of sacred writ.[31]

Hence, early nineteenth-century religious life after the Revolution was
forged by the Second Great Awakening, which consolidated the movement
led by Edwards and others in the eighteenth century. And by the end of
the nineteenth century—including through the turmoil of the Civil War,

28. Tocqueville, *Democracy in America*, 191.

29. In fact one revisionist historian, Amanda Porterfield, holds that the influence
of religious skepticism was so considerable in the post-Revolutionary period that the
new nation could be said to be "conceived in doubt." Her account most likely overstates
the role of religious doubt in America in the 1790s, tending, for example, to associate
the high regard for Thomas Paine with an acceptance of his heterodox religiosity, when
the legendary *Common Sense*—which made no unorthodox assertions—was much
more likely in the minds of his admirers. Also, she bases the depth of skepticism in part
on accounts of college students at William and Mary and Yale. But since when have the
exploits of college students been barometers of religious piety in wider society? Porterfield, *Conceived in Doubt: Religion and Politics in the New American Nation*, 17–18.

30. In further contrast to the trend asserted by Porterfield, one might point to the
work of an extensive array of Federalists in the decade following ratification. Alexander
Hamilton, toward the end of his life, expressed the conviction of an indispensable need
for a vibrant Christian faith for the common good of the new nation and entertained
forming a so-called Christian Constitutional Society, a sentiment of Hamilton's (perhaps politically driven, perhaps not) that was widely adhered to at the time, a point
Hartog documents in *Politics and Piety: Federalist Politics and Religious Struggle in the
New American Nation*. Notably, Hamilton and the very devout John Jay spearheaded
the anti-slavery New York Manumission Society.

31. See Campbell, *Bible: The Story of the King James Version*.

in which, as Lincoln remarked, both sides used the same Bible—scripture stood at the center of culture, if at times as the centerpiece of considerable contestation. Indeed, five important debates (only a small number of the areas in which the Bible was influential, and which are here only very briefly surveyed) can serve to underscore just how central the Bible was to American political and cultural life. These debates are sometimes incorrectly seen as only battles between biblically grounded religious movements and secular forces. However, the debates are much more complicated than that, indicating just how central biblical ideas were in all sides of a large number of cultural debates throughout American history.

First, the Bible was at the core of debates surrounding state-level disestablishment. The non-establishment principle in the First Amendment originally applied only to actions of the federal government, yet this changed in the early nineteenth century.[32] A wide range of arguments were made for state-level disestablishment, but as Philip Hamburger has shown, one of the most prominent was advanced in 1800 by Tunis Wortman in a piece entitled *A Solemn Address to Christians and Patriots*. A core component of Wortman's argument was his solicitude for the purity of biblical religion: without disestablishment "Christianity becomes no longer the religion of God—it becomes the religion of temporal craft and expediency and policy." For "when a church becomes directly or indirectly connected with the state, it may still retain its external form and appearance, but Christianity no longer remains, the heavenly virtues become extinct, and the pure spirit of piety disguised by its avarice, ambition and impiety take wings and flies to the heaven."[33]

However, strong biblically based counter-arguments were also maintained, and many were not so easily dismissed. Indeed, the separationist argument so passionately advanced by Wortman was met with the charge that if religion be so delicate that any admixture "direct or indirect" of it with the state ensures its corruption, then this very logic commits one to see true religion as a quite sensitive flower, indeed; and it would then seem sensible that so delicate a plant might need nurturance and support against the corrupting influences to be found in many of the non-governmental forces in society, a protection which the government might just, in the final tally, be the least worst agent to secure. Arguments such as these, fortified by direct references to holy scripture, empowered the thought of the defenders of state establishments, among whom perhaps the most prominent was

---

32. See Adams and Emmerich, "A Heritage of Religious Liberty," 1559–1622. See also Tarr, "Church and State in the States," 73–110.

33. Hamburger, *Separation of Church and State*, 122.

Lyman Beecher of Connecticut, for whom establishment ensured a measure of defense against rising social immorality.[34]

Yet, here Tocqueville observed a disjuncture: "Religion in America takes no direct part in the government of society, but it must be regarded as the first of their political institutions; for if it does not impart a taste for freedom, it facilitates the use of it."[35] This benign element to disestablishment was itself underscored by no less a figure than Lyman Beecher himself, who came to see disestablishment as "the best thing that ever happened to the State of Connecticut," creating in its wake a zealous clergy who "by voluntary efforts, societies, missions, and revivals" could "exert a deeper influence than ever they could [before]."[36] Hence, it "cut the churches loose from dependence on state support [and] threw them wholly on their own resources and on God."[37] Such a view became widely shared, and it had previously been fundamental to the thought of the architect of national disestablishment, James Madison. As the historian Garrett Sheldon demonstrates:

> Madison revealed his Christian approach to human nature and society in his attitude toward religion and politics or church-state relations. Religious freedom for Madison was, perhaps ironically, primarily to serve the cause of Christian evangelism . . . Madison's advocacy of religious freedom before, during, and after his presidency (and then in the whole United States through the Constitution's First Amendment) was primarily to help spread Christianity and spiritually awaken Americans to their sinful natures, and need for repentance and faith, which in turn had the benefit of creating a healthy, honest, conscientious, and morally upright nation. Social virtue was dependent on religious morals, and true religion was best spread through religious freedom and toleration.[38]

As legal scholar and former federal judge Michael McConnell argues:

> It is anachronistic to assume, based on modern patterns, that governmental aid to religion and suppression of heterodoxy were opposed by the more rationalistic and supported by the more intense religious believers of that era. The most intense religious sects opposed establishment on the ground that . . .

---

34. See Beecher, "An Address of the Charitable Society for the Education of Indigent Pious Young Men, for the Ministry of the Gospel."

35. Tocqueville, *Democracy in America*, 120.

36. Encyclopedia.com, s.v. "Beecher, Lyman (1775–1863)."

37. Christianity Today, "Lyman Beecher: Revivalist Who Moved with the Times."

38. Sheldon, "Religion in the Thought of James Madison," 100–101.

guaranteed state support was thought to stifle religious enthusiasm and initiative.[39]

However, it is also important to remember that even after formal
disestablishment took place, American law was still heavily inflected with
religious concepts based on biblical warrant, such as the belief in the religious foundations of moral commitments. As Arlin Adams and Charles
Emmerich note, although the Founders represented a broad spectrum of
views they were "virtually unanimous in the belief that the republic could
not survive without religion's moral influence. Consequently, they did not
envision a secular society, but rather one receptive to voluntary religious
expression."[40] The salutary influence of religion was given some measure
of state assistance after disestablishment, though not by direct tax support
or mandatory church attendance, but instead through the maintenance of
such things as blue and blasphemy laws and religious tests for office holding. Indeed, as Jonathan Zimmerman documents, after disestablishment,
"many states extended or even sharpened their anti-blasphemy laws."[41] As
Adams and Emmerich further note, religious tests for office at the state
level "endured with remarkable tenacity" until the 1960s.[42] The bulk of the
work of seeking moral and religious vigor, however, was now conducted by
newly unleashed voluntary associations, with the law a decidedly secondary
instrument.

Second, the Bible played a critical role in the debates surrounding the
American Civil War. Indeed, the Bible was so central to the Civil War that
Mark Noll calls the war a "Theological Crisis" in his important work of the
same title.[43] Central to the Civil War, of course, was slavery. There were,
no doubt, biblical arguments advanced to support slave holding, mostly
arguments grounded on Leviticus 25:44–46[44] and often conjoined with
Genesis 9:25,[45] which was interpreted (bizarrely) as a reference to Africans
(or at least those Africans living from the sixteenth century on). In addition,
the Epistles were referenced, such as Paul's letter to the Ephesians and to

39. Glenn, "Disestablishing Our Secular Schools," 1.

40. Adams and Emmerich, "Heritage of Religious Liberty," 1595.

41. Zimmerman, "Anti-blasphemy Laws Have a History in America."

42 Adams and Emmerich, "Heritage of Religious Liberty," 1579.

43. Noll, *The Civil War as a Theological Crisis.*

44. Lev 25:44–6, "[T]hey shall be your possession. And ye shall take them as an
inheritance for your children after you, to inherit them for a possession; they shall be
your bondmen for ever" (KJF).

45. Gen 9:25, "And he said, Cursed be Canaan; a servant of servants shall he be
unto his brethren" (KJV).

Philemon,[46] and the first letter of Peter.[47] Indeed, it is true that the words of scripture were often relied on, but it is also true that the words were often interpreted, as Noll has shown, by a very specific form of exegesis that became almost exclusively that of Protestants in the antebellum United States: Protestant Christians elsewhere in the world refused, much more often than not, to concur in Southern Protestants' biblical defense of slavery.[48] "Powerful as the orthodox defense of slavery seemed in the United States," Noll highlights, "it had virtually no influence outside the country, even among those who shared the conservative theology of slavery's defenders." Indeed, for conservative Christians across England, Scotland and Canada, Noll points out, "there was only contempt for efforts to defend Southern slavery on the basis of the Bible."[49] Additionally, Southern Protestants' biblical arguments for slavery always tended to have an air of academic abstraction about them. The arguments were almost always about slavery *in abstracto*, and not as it was presently exercised across the South.[50]

In addition to arguments for the rectitude of slavery adduced directly from biblical proof-texting according to their peculiar form of biblical literalism, some defenders developed more nuanced arguments, some even of a limited persuasive appeal, which in turn formed part of the substantial Southern intellectual mindset that John Genovese has perhaps done the most to remind modern readers of. Shorn of references to race, some Southern defenses of slavery as a set of economic relations constituted a position which, to the minds of Genovese and Fox-Genovese, at least, "remain unanswered"—that is, in comparison to demands for immediate abolition.[51]

46. Eph 6:5: "Servants, be obedient to them that are your masters according to the flesh, with fear and trembling, in singleness of your heart, as unto Christ" (KJV).

47. 1 Pet 2:18: "Servants, be subject to your masters with all fear; not only to the good and gentle, but also to the forward" (KJV).

48. "The foreign Protestants who most clearly resembled American Protestants were, in sum, exercised primarily by the evil of slavery . . . in expressing their opinions they showed little of the hesitation that held back so many of their American contemporaries." Noll, *The Civil War as a Theological Crisis*, 106. For Catholics, Pope Gregory XVI in 1819 condemned the slave trade in terms so vehement that "it could be seen as an attack on the institution of slavery as well." Quinn, "Three Cheers for the Abolitionist Pope," 1; quoted in Noll, *Civil War as Theological Crisis*, 131.

49. Noll, *America's God: From Jonathan Edwards to Abraham Lincoln*, 400.

50. Shanks note that proslavery divines were always "anxious to get the discussion on the plane of the abstract question." Shanks, "The Biblical Anti-Slavery Argument of the Decade 1830–1840," 132–57. As to the question of slavery as then practiced, ministers were quite anxious to decry abuses and call for substantial improvements to the treatment of slaves in the South. See Genovese and Fox-Genovese, *Mind of the Master Class*, esp. 508, 520–21.

51. Genovese and Fox-Genovese, *Mind of the Master Class*, 527.

As the distinguished theologian Guenther Hass has recently argued in echo of several antebellum Southern thinkers, and which the Genoveses find compelling, if an institution so deeply mired in the human condition as slavery were per se evil in every conceivable form; if it could be expressed in no imaginably positive way for even the most evanescent segment of time, then it follows that the created order itself stands in utter contempt. Yet such a complete rejection of the creational order entails "drift[ing] about on a sea of historicism (and implicit relativism)."[52] Additionally, a further argument that moved beyond literalist proof-texting was the rather simple point advanced by Richard Fuller to the effect that since the earliest followers of The Way had admitted slaveholders into the movement, slaveholding did not *eo ipso* condemn one to the position of a Christ-denying Judas.[53] For Fuller, to reject that slaveholders could be welcomed into the communion of faith (i.e., to reject that slave owners did not always have to cease immediately their position as slave owners to move closer to Christ through membership in His church) was tantamount to rejecting all the lessons of primitive Christianity and, as such, to undermine all faith in the Spirit-filled witnesses of the earliest apostles. These points, then, as now, remain arresting.[54]

Nevertheless, it is important to remember that many Northern[55] (and some Southern)[56] intellectuals and divines advanced Bible-based arguments

---

52. Haas, "The Kingdom and Slavery: A Test Case for Social Ethics," 74–89.

53. Holifield, *Theology in America: Christian Thought from the Age of the Puritans to the Civil War*, 498.

54. See Genovese and Fox-Genovese, *Mind of the Master Class*, 527, based on Haas's "The Kingdom and Slavery." In furtherance of the Genoveses' and Haas's point, one can look to men such as Elizur Wright, an Ohio insurance pioneer and immediatist antislavery advocate, whose frustrations drew him from his youthful Calvinism toward radical free thought movements described as exceedingly close to atheism. See Goodheart, *Abolitionist, Actuary, Atheist: Elizur Wright and the Reform Impulse*. A further example can be seen in the trajectory of New England abolitionist Stephen Pearl Andrews, whose immediatism would merge with anarchism and (heretical) spiritualism. See Stern, *Patriarch: A Biography of Stephen Pearl Andrews*.

55. The opposition by Northern divines has deep roots and includes the advocacy in the eighteenth century of ministers such as Samuel Hopkins of Newport Rhode Island (1721–1803), Jacob Green of New Jersey (1724–1790), Levi Hart of Connecticut, author of the vehemently anti-slavery sermon *Liberty Rescinded and Recommended* (1794), and Jonathan Edwards Jr., author of the impassioned sermon *The Injustice and Impolicy of the Slave Trade and the Slavery of the Africans* (1791). Hart and Edwards Jr. would found the anti-slavery organization, The Connecticut Society for the Promotion of Freedom and the Rights of Persons Unlawfully Holden in Bondage in 1790.

56. There always remained a rather unsung minority of ministers in certain slaveholding regions who bitterly resisted the proslavery interpretation of the faith. Indeed, it is not unworthy of note that there were indeed Southern evangelical ministers throughout the two decades before the War who neither owned slaves nor supported

against slavery with great passion, and many were of the first order of intellectual sophistication and persuasive appeal.[57] Indeed, the noted historian Daniel Walker Howe argues that in nineteenth-century America, given its depth of racism and bigotry—malignities, we should add, all too common in the historical record—it was only religion, and specifically "the institutional and emotional resources of Protestant Christianity" that could empower Whites to adopt abolitionism.[58] These points deserve further recognition and so we dilate upon them a bit more fully here.[59] A brief survey of five major forms of biblical argumentation against slavery should suffice.

First, opponents of slavery responded to the text with the text. To every reference in the Old Testament to permissible slaveholding, opponents

---

the institution. For example, Revs. Robert Breckinridge and Robert Livingston Stanton, of Danville Theological Seminary in Kentucky, and Rev. John G. Fee, founder of Berea College, were adamantly opposed to slavery. As Noll says of Rev. Fee, "he argued boldly that slavery . . . was fatally flawed." Noll, *America's God*, 414. Perhaps the best work documenting the labors of the anti-slavery evangelical ministers of the antebellum south is David B. Chesebrough, *Clergy Dissent in the Old South:* 1830–1865. As Chesebrough relates, "A creative minority of ministers spoke and wrote boldly in denouncing slavery as unjust, un-American, and ungodly," *Clergy Dissent in the Old South,* 86. Also prominent in opposing slavery were several influential Episcopal ministers. Episcopal theologian Rev. William Sparrow of the Episcopal Theological Seminary of Alexandria, proved himself an outspoken critic of slaveholding. For this and much throughout this chapter, see Prud'homme, "Evangelical Ministers in the Antebellum South and Guilt over Slavery: The Incoherence of Evangelical Pro-Slavery Thought," 205–58.

57. Among the wealth of antislavery sermons and disquisitions advanced by Northern ministers, see Sunderland, *The Testimony of God against Slavery, or a Collection of Passages from the Bible which Show the Sin of Holding Property in Men* and Barnes, *An Inquiry into Scriptural Views of Slavery.* Of special note is Francis Wayland's correspondence with Richard Fuller in *Domestic Slavery Considered as a Scriptural Institution.* Perhaps the most famous of the Christian anti-slavery pieces (both at the time and subsequently), Rev. Wayland's remonstrance against his fellow Baptist minister (and co-founder of the Southern Baptist Convention) Rev. Fuller spawned numerous commentaries at the time, including William Hague's *Christianity and Slavery: A Review of Doctors Fuller and Wayland, on Domestic Slavery.* It is important to remember that despite Fuller's passionate defense of a biblically based rejection of abolitionism, he came later in the antebellum period to embrace gradual emancipation as a Christian mandate.

58. "In the America of the nineteenth century, it was the institutional and emotional resources of Protestant Christianity that typically empowered humanitarian reform. For example, religion was central to the antislavery position of virtually all white abolitionists. Blacks could formulate an antislavery position without invoking religion, but whites could not." Howe, "The Evangelical Movement and Political Culture in the North during the Second Party System," 1216–39. Although Blacks could and some did advance non-religious arguments against slavery, many more advanced Bible-based arguments against slaveholding, arguments we explore below.

59. See Shanks, "The Biblical Anti-Slavery Argument," 137.

responded with searing passages of their own. As Holifield summarizes, "the problem was that the battle when fought on literalist . . . terrain always seemed to end in stalemate."[60] To every statement about the Patriarchs holding slaves, anti-slavery advocates could point to scriptural statements or segments embarrassing slavers, such as Leviticus 25:10: "proclaim liberty throughout all the land unto all the inhabitants thereof."[61] Indeed, President Lincoln himself adopted the mode of anti-slavery literalism, with a special focus on the Old Testament, a text which "fascinates him. Constantly. Constantly."[62] In 1864, he wrote to a group of Baptists abiding a literalist interpretation by referring to a literal reading of Genesis 3:19. Lincoln asserted that "to read in the Bible, as the word of God himself, that 'In the sweat of your face you shall eat bread,'[63] and to preach therefrom that 'in the sweat of other man's faces shalt thou eat bread' to my mind can scarcely be reconciled with honest sincerity."[64] Indeed, this textual literalist impasse can be seen perhaps most vividly by the work of antebellum African American ministers, all of whom opposed passionately the sin of slaveholding. As Noll recounts, "African American Christians were as likely to be champions of 'the Bible only' and of biblical literalism as their white contemporaries"— repudiating, for example, a lasting Noahic curse on all Africans with the psalmic proof-texting that, instead, "Princes shall come out of Egypt and Ethiopia shall soon stretch out her hands unto God."[65]

So both sides could say of the other the words implied by Christ in the fourth chapter of the Gospel of Matthew, and made explicit in poetic phrasings by the English Bard: even the devil can quote scripture, if only for his own purpose. Due to this impasse, the spirit of the sacred word and the context of scriptural passages were often repaired to. In fact, for many, the repairing to the spirit of sacred writ was propelled by the word itself, literally read. Had not Paul in 2 Corinthians 3:6 demanded, in strokes of boldness, that "the letter killeth, but the spirit giveth life"?[66]

In the move to an exegesis of the spirit of the sacred text, ministers read Paul as saying the spirit confers first and foremost the gift of spiritual

---

60. Holifield, *Theology in America*, 495–504, esp. 496.

61. Lev 25:10 (KJV).

62. Allen Guelzo, interviewed and quoted in Feiler, *America's Prophet: Moses and the American Story*, 163.

63. Gen 3:19: "In the sweat of thy face shalt thou eat bread, till thou return unto the ground" (KJV).

64. Lincoln, "Reply to Delegation of Baptists on May 30, 1864," In Basler, *Collected Works of Abraham Lincoln*, 368.

65. Ps 68:31 (KJV). Noll, *America's God*, 404, 406.

66. 2 Cor 3:6 (KJV).

rebirth—the gift of great price of being "a new creature."[67] However, the spirit was read also as giving life not only to a new individual, but to an entirely new nation: the spirit would make not only a new creation in Christ, but it had already made a new nation under heaven. For the spirit-based reading of scripture had fueled America's War for Independence. As James P. Byrd documents in his recent work, *Sacred Scripture, Sacred War: The Bible and the American Revolution*, non-literal readings of the word of God through a hermeneutic of the spirit was at the center of a great deal of revolutionary sermonizing in defense of the revolutionary cause. One of the most widely referenced theological justifications for the Revolutionary War was the biblical story, found in Judges 5, of the elderly woman Jael fighting righteously for the cause of God.[68] Were the Colonists, then, enfeebled widows? No; what had happened, rather, was that the letter—including the letter of Paul's own strictures about obedience to earthly sovereigns in Romans 13:1[69]— had been read in light of his own letters' indwelling spirit: The spirit of the word burst to the surface.[70]

William Ellery Channing in his 1835 work, *Slavery,* struck against the literalist cause precisely along these lines by reminding the defenders of slavery that Paul's words to Christians to "be subject to the higher powers of the magistrate," because they were "written during the reign of a despotic emperor" served to "create[ ] problems for theologians who insisted on literal readings of scripture yet approved of the American Revolution."[71] Since the American Revolution was the mother's milk of American patriotism for all but the most radical abolitionists, the move toward biblical exegesis based on the spirit of the word was doubly difficult for slave defenders to rebuke.[72]

Nineteenth-century biblical debates about the spirit of the scripture in regard to the slavers bondage of fellow humans came to be predicated on

67. 2 Cor 5:17: "Therefore if any man be in Christ, he is a new creature: old things are passed away; behold, all things are become new" (KJV).

68. Byrd, *Sacred Scripture, Sacred War: The Bible and the American Revolution.*

69. Rom 13:1: "Let every soul be subject unto the higher powers. For there is no power but of God: the powers that be are ordained of God" (KJV).

70. A spiritual hermeneutic looked to the indwelling spirit of the sacred text, often claiming the assistance of the Spirit of the Holy Godhead and third person of the Blessed Trinity; hence, a hermeneutic of the spirit was often doubly spirit-based.

71. Holifield, *Theology in America*, 499.

72. Snay has documented how the southern scriptural defense of secession—and the rebellion against an earthly sovereign the act necessarily entailed—overlooked a literal reading of Saint Paul in favor of sweeping claims that the indwelling logic of the sacred book disclosed the South as the new most-favored nation of God. See Snay, *Gospel of Disunion: Religion and Separatism in the Antebellum South*, 189–96.

readings discerning the underlying spirit of the Old Testament, the writings of the Apostles, and the life and teachings of the Savior Himself. Fought on the terrain of a spirit-based hermeneutic, anti-slavery ministers could assert with deepened confidence that, in the words of Presbyterian minister Albert Barnes's 1857 exhortation, future generations would "look back upon defenses of slavery drawn from the Bible, as among the most remarkable instances of mistaken interpretation and unfounded reasoning furnished by the perversities of the human mind."[73]

So first the spirit of the Old Testament was invoked against Southern slaveholding. The Mosaic law defines man-stealing as a capital crime warranting death.[74] What were slaves if not descendants of those poor souls whose lives had been stolen, in one way or another? And the prophetic witness of Jeremiah and the minor prophets was also intoned. The stern command, "woe unto him that useth his neighbor's service without wages, and giveth him not for his work" made Jeremiah an inexhaustible resource;[75] did this not cast doubt on permission for unpaid slave labor as such? Further, reference was made to the minor prophets' descriptions of the destruction by Yahweh of Tyre—a center of the slave trade—as condemnation of her grave iniquities.[76]

As to the spirit of the Apostles, apostolic exhortations found in Paul, James, and Peter were underscored and their disposing underlying logic referenced. Ministers frequently made reference to the Prince of the Apostles teaching to "honour all men," and to the "brother" of the Lord, James, demanding that "if you have respect to persons, you commit sin"[77]—a point Paul echoes in Galatians: "There is neither Jew nor Greek, there is neither bond nor free, there is neither male nor female: for ye are all one in Christ Jesus."[78] Indeed if such were not enough, James was seen to speak even more directly to the issue of slavery: "Behold, the hire of the labourers who have reaped down your fields, which is of you kept back by fraud, crieth: and the cries of them which have reaped are entered into the ears of the Lord"—all

---

73. Barnes, *An Inquiry into the Scriptural Views of Slavery*, 381; quoted in Holifield, *Theology in America*, 494.

74. Exod 21:16: "And he that stealeth a man, and selleth him, or if he be found in his hand, he shall surely be put to death" (KJV).

75. Jer 22:13 (KJV).

76. See Amos 1:6–9; Joel 3:4; and Shanks, "The Biblical Anti-Slavery Argument," 146.

77. 1 Pet 2:17: "Honour all men. Love the brotherhood. Fear God"; Jas 2:9: "But if ye have respect to persons, ye commit sin, and are convinced of the law as transgressors" (KJV). See also Shanks, "The Biblical Anti-Slavery Argument," 153.

78. Gal 3:28 (KJV).

while "ye have lived in pleasure on the earth."[79] The spirit of Jesus' earliest followers spoke boldly against unjust enrichment and exploitation of all kinds.

Most importantly, the spirit of the Savior was seen as controlling. An exegesis guided by the spirit of the Lord—or an exegesis guided by what Rev. Andrew Thompson called "the whole spirit, and genius, and tendency of Christianity" and by "its inherent and efficacious power"[80]—disclosed to many ministers that Jesus's message at critical points in His ministry was absolutely inconsistent with a slaveholder's bondage. First, clergy pointed to the announcement of Jesus's mission, where He discloses that "The Spirit of the Lord is upon me, because he hath anointed me to preach the gospel to the poor; he hath sent me to heal the brokenhearted, to preach deliverance to the captives, and recovering of sight to the blind, to set at liberty them that are bruised."[81] They also looked to the Great Commandment "to love thy neighbor as thyself"[82]—including "the least of these"—and saw any failure to do so as being as if Christ Himself had been denied.[83] But what were slaves, if not by their degradation by a lash the "least of these"? Lastly, Northern ministers averred that the benign services of the Comforter promised by Jesus following His ascension must be trusted to work mercy, clemency, and selflessness in the hearts of all believers.[84]

Additionally, and in the same cast of mind that moved ministers to seek the spirit of the Bible's message, the anti-slavery argument from scripture anticipated and responded to such tortured arguments as the inheritance of a servile condition by Africans owing to their lineage from the accused son of Ham. It was often expressed that even should one accept that Africans were the descendants of Canaan—which many Northern antislavery divines most certainly did not[85]—all one could say of the slave relationship between Canaan and his brothers was that a curse had been set by God's law,

79. Jas 5:4–5 (KJV).

80 As stated by the influential Scottish minister Andrew Thompson in his treatise, *Slavery Not Sanctioned, But Condemned, by Christianity*, 6–7.

81. Luke 4:18 (KJV).

82. Matt 22:39 (KJV).

83. Matt 25:45. (KJV).

84. Yet, this argument exposed the North to the counterargument that the Spirit should be trusted indeed, and so abolition by force of human arms was hubristic heresy, a position Rev. James Henley Thornwell of South Carolina developed with vigor. See Genovese and Fox-Genovese, *Mind of the Master Class*, 517.

85. Most "elite theologians" in the North saw the curse as attached only to the Canaanites who received their punishment when Joshua established the Hebrew presence in the Promised Land. Noll, *America's God*, 418.

a law-borne curse involving the burden of involuntary service. Yet, had not Paul himself informed us all that "Christ redeemed us from the curse of the law"?[86] The blood of Christ breaks the burden of every curse.

Additionally, in the form of spirit-based exegesis, the slave defenders' contention that Christ did not explicitly reject slavery though the practice was commonplace in the Roman world was met with the answer that so, too, did he never condemn the tyrannical family laws of the *paterfamilias* who could dispose of his children's life at a whim, nor the savage gladiatorial contests that soaked the empire in blood.[87] Yet, informed by the spirit of Christ and his word in holy writ, both came over time to be overthrown by Christian clemency. And, so must slavery.

Next, antislavery biblical argumentation often looked to the environing context of scriptural passages, and thus to the historical and cultural situadedness of biblical provisions, a form of exegesis, like a hermeneutic of the spirit, that would not countenance mere literalist proof-texting. In this endeavor, a radical diremption was often drawn between slavery as practiced in the period of the biblical Patriarchs—where many slaves were liberated on sabbatical or Jubilee years, were protected from abuse, were not to be turned over should they escape, and were at times so close to their masters as to be trusted with arms[88]—and that form of bondage prevailing throughout the South. Additionally, advocates often pointed to the progressive decline in slavery across Hebrew history, and its virtual extinction, along with its condemnation both by Essenes and Pharisees, at the time of Christ.[89]

A further form of argument not often appreciated in contemporary writings on slavery and the Bible was a distinctive form of contextualization, a contextualizing not of biblical passages as such but of the enterprise of pro-slavery Christian thought itself. A number of Christian opponents of slaveholding developed a fascinating form of guilt by association against Christians defending slaving. Charges were often leveled that the very idea of guiltless Christian slaveholding grew only from a poisonously heterodox intellectual climate, with writers noting how before the 1830s, and so before

86. Gal 3:13 (KJV).

87. See Thompson, *Christianity and Emancipation; or, the Teachings and the Influence of the Bible against Slavery*, 17; and Shanks, "The Biblical Anti-Slavery Argument," 154.

88. See for example Deut 23:15: "Thou shalt not deliver unto his master the servant which is escaped from his master unto thee." And Gen 14:14: "And when Abram heard that his brother was taken captive, he armed his trained servants, born in his own house, three hundred and eighteen, and pursued them unto Dan" (KJV).

89. Thompson, *Christianity and Emancipation*, 16

the emergence of that idea that slavery was a positive good captivated the minds of some across Southern society,[90] a high percentage of the writings arguing that Christianity endorsed slavery were advanced by anti-trinitarian, deistic, or skeptical opponents of Christian scripture. Pastor Joseph Thompson of Broadway Tabernacle Church in New York took great pains to document the frequency of claims that Christianity sanctioned slavery by anti-trinitarian radicals, noting that the charges were intended to "attack Christianity in its central principle and vital essence" in order to justify the radical changes ushered in by the revolutionary zeal of French Deism.[91] Further, the charge was leveled that a similarly heterodox climate was descending on the American South, evidenced in part by the rumors—many of them accurate—that some of her leading lights were Unitarians (such as John C. Calhoun, a donor to and frequent attendee of All Souls Unitarian Church in Washington, DC).

Lastly, we must never forget the superb biblical analysis developed by African American ministers themselves. As we noted, African American ministers often deployed a proof-texting exegesis. Yet, they often also deployed arguments that, though not unique to African Americans, were especially powerfully made in the context of African American Christianity. One especially noteworthy African American preacher and minister, James W.C. Pennington, is singled out for special attention by church historian E. Brooks Holifield. Rev. Pennington is a remarkable man whose history deserves a far broader telling. A runaway slave from Maryland, Pennington received a basic education in Pennsylvania but came to be the first Black student at Yale University. He would pastor Presbyterian churches in New York and Connecticut in the late 1830s until his death in 1870. His biblical

90. Before the 1820s and 1830s, the Methodist church, most Baptist churches, and many Presbyterians held to their faith's longstanding opposition to slave owning. John Wesley, for example, abhorred slavery. Indeed, in 1743 he himself wrote the rule against the buying and selling of human beings into the Methodist General Rules. And this denunciation of slavery was also expressed with unmistakable clarity by a great many early bishops of Methodism throughout America. Bishop Thomas Coke and Francis Asbury, for example, sternly rejected slavery, as did the major Methodist conferences in America in the eighteenth century. The general conference of 1784 declared slavery "contrary to the laws of God, man, and nature, and harmful to society; contrary to the dictates of conscience and true religion." As Takaki recounts, "for years after the [early conferences] the Methodist Church threatened to suspend slaveholding preachers and discipline slaveholding church members." Takaki, *A Pro-slavery Crusade: The Agitation to Reopen the African Slave Trade*, 142–43. Hence, Wyatt-Brown remarks pointedly that "churchmen could not entirely forget their denominations' antislavery past." As a result, the later-day followers of the antislavery founder John Wesley seldom "meddled with the issue at all from their pulpits." Wyatt-Brown, "Church, Honor, and Secession," 91.

91. Thompson, *Christianity and Emancipation*, 6, 5.

argument against slavery drew from a deep reflection on Saint Paul's description of the "mystery of iniquity."[92] God's permission of slavery comports no doubt with the providential intention that from evil good must come, but how it does so is masked by the mystery of the disregard for God's moral government which defies finite human understanding.[93]

The Bible therefore was central in debates surrounding secession, slavery, and the Civil War. And thus it behooves us simply to be reminded of the fact that Lincoln memorably stated respecting Northern and Southern warriors alike: "both read the same Bible and pray to the same God, and each invokes His aid against the other."[94] Nevertheless, it also behooves us to take an even longer-term horizon and to remind ourselves further of what Genovese and Fox-Genovese state so arrestingly: "Today we ask: How could Christians or any civilized people have lived with themselves as slaveholders? But the historically appropriate question is: What, after millennia of general acceptance, made Christians—and, subsequently, those of other faiths—judge slavery an enormity not to be endured?"[95]

Now to our third overarching point about scripture's deep influence in American life. The Bible was front and center in debates about the nature and scope of state-supported public education. With the rise of public schooling in the 1830s, the question of character education became central. It was unquestionable to most that state-supported schools had to inculcate dispositions beneficial to state prosperity. For this, biblical religion was deemed indispensable. Advocates of public schooling, therefore, recognized that the Bible had to be taught in the new public schools. Yet, due to the tremendous esteem accorded holy writ, various denominations saw even slight variations in the Bible and its meaning as gravely serious matters; a failure to be extremely cautious about how the Bible was presented was to risk lowering the Bible's importance as a sacred text. In response, the chief architect of the public school movement, Horace Mann of Massachusetts, advocated a compromise: the non-denominational reading of the Bible without state-dictated exegetical or sermonic content. (A similar compromise would develop over time with respect to prayer in public schools, with the emergence of such vague benedictions as the Regent's Prayer).[96] Remarkably, this simple

---

92. 2 Thess 2:7: "For the mystery of iniquity doth already work: only he who now letteth will let, until he be taken out of the way" (KJV).

93. Holifield, *Theology in America*, 315–16.

94 Abraham Lincoln, Second Inaugural Address, Saturday, March 4, 1865.

95. Genovese and Fox-Genovese, *Mind of the Master Class*, 69–70.

96. The so-called Dominion Prayer was so general as to assert merely this: "Almighty God, we acknowledge our dependence on Thee, and we beg Thy blessings upon us, our parents, our teachers and our country."

solution brought together a wide swath of the Christian community—and this despite considerable differences among various Protestant groups.[97]

However, with growing numbers of Catholic immigrants, this compromise came under pressure. Lay Catholics led by several leading members of the hierarchy saw the reading of the Bible—even without comment—as inherently sectarian due to the fact that the Bible then widely used in public schools was the King James Version, which Catholic theology saw both as unreliable and the fruit of schismatic heresy. Some even preferred that there be no Bible reading than to see this schismatic text used in public education. This conviction in turn caused a crisis—at times a violent crisis, as in Kensington, Pennsylvania and Cincinnati, Ohio.[98] A large percentage of the advocates of public schooling saw an essential link between public schools and the virtues of proper citizenship, and the latter required in the minds of the vast majority a linkage with divine scripture. Moreover, the Protestant majority saw its view as being the charitable position, having already prescinded from commentary on the text and thus, in its mind, having already watered down religious instruction in the interests of Christian comity. Why therefore could Catholics not accept the unadorned word of God—even if it be expressed in verbiage authorized by a king, a king whose very progeny American Protestants had themselves violently rejected through revolutionary warfare?

The hierarchy of the Catholic Church would come over time to the very same conclusion: the Vatican in fact censured episodic efforts by American priests to deny the sacraments to American Catholic parents who took their children to public schools, and it held that public schools were perfectly acceptable options as long as religious instruction was supplemented by private and Sunday school teaching—precisely the position which the Protestant view had been firmly committed to in the first place, since the Bible-without-comment compromise was predicated on having the instructional extension of the meaning of the verses that were announced in school provided through private religious instruction.

As Noah Feldman has documented, over time comity would indeed emerge triumphant, as most Catholics would take their children to public

97. McLoughlin notes that despite growing factionalism, Protestantism at this time tended to overcome these tensions and, in turn, came to "pride . . . itself on its interdenominational fraternalism." McLoughlin, *The American Evangelicals, 1800–1900: An Anthology*, 5.

98. See Feldman, *Divided by God: America's Church State Problem—and What We Should Do about It*, 70; Lacorne, *Religion in America: A Political History*, 74–79; Ravitch, *The Great School Wars*; and Lynn, "Studying the Bible in Public Schools: Sounds Good in Theory, But . . ."

schools while a parallel option of private Catholic schools grew as a viable option alongside the public school system.[99]

A fourth overarching influence of the Bible in American life can be seen in how the Bible was central to debates over science and education policy. The crux of this debate concerned the Bible's relationship to the natural sciences. In 1925, in Dayton, Tennessee, John Scopes, a high school teacher of biology was accused and found guilty of infringing state law against the teaching of evolution, revealing an apparent gulf between scientific knowledge and biblical revelation.[100]

It is something of a cliché to characterize Darwin's 1859 publication of the *Origin of Species* as a landmark challenge to biblical revelation. It is a familiar story.[101] It provoked immediate and very public debate. Subsequent accommodation and conflict within science and religion debates frequently center on evolutionary theory and biblical accounts of creation. Darwin is seen here as a neutral scientific figure dispassionately uncovering the laws of nature, leaving others to comment on how such science might affect religious belief. Certainly on publication of *Origin of Species* and the subsequent *Ascent of Man*, Darwin tended to avoid personal contributions to public controversy.

However, in Darwin's later years, his autobiographical writings (from the 1870s) provide more forthright, little cited expressions of his views on religion:

> Whilst on board the Beagle I was quite orthodox, & I remember being heartily laughed at by several of the officers (though themselves orthodox) for quoting the Bible as an unanswerable authority on some point of morality. I suppose it was the novelty of the argument that amused them. But I had gradually come by this time (i.e. 1836 to 1839) to see the Old Testament, from its

99. Feldman, *Divided by God*, 90–92. In the early to mid-twentieth century, the number of Catholics attending parochial school would in fact double to 12 percent of all school children. Ibid., 92.

100. A similar set of debates, of course, occurred in the United Kingdom. However, it is important to note that in 1870, Thomas Huxley—Darwin's legendary bulldog—offered expansive praise for the King James Bible, which as a scientific guide he had so successfully challenged a decade earlier in his famous Oxford debate. Huxley praised the geographical, historical, and literary qualities of the Bible, as well as other of its educational merits. Huxley, "The School Boards," 1–15. This shows that the centrality of the Bible to history is not diminished by its (alleged) tensions with science. Those very alleged tensions display its very centrality to our history. Huxley's argument can also remind even the most secularly minded individuals of the Bible's enduring importance.

101. For a further account of this history, see Gearon, "The King James Bible and the Politics of Religious Education."

manifestly false history of the world, with the Tower of Babel, the rain-bow as a sign &c &c, from its attributing to God the feelings of a vengeful tyrant, was no more to be trusted than the sacred books of the Hindoos, or the beliefs of any barbarian.

His attacks on religion are then directed specifically to Christianity:

> The question then continually arose before my mind & would not be banished . . . By further reflecting that the clearest evidence would be requisite to make any sane man believe in the miracles by which Christianity is supported—that the more we know of the men at that time were ignorant & credulous to a degree almost incomprehensible to us—that the Gospels cannot be proved to have been written simultaneously with the events—that they differ in many important details, far too important as it seemed to me to be admitted as the usual inaccuracies of eye-witnesses—by such reflections as these, which I give not as having the least novelty or value, but as they influence me, I gradually came to disbelieve in Christianity as a divine revelation.

"I found," he writes, "it more and more difficult, with free scope given to my imagination to invent evidence which would suffice to convince me":

> Thus disbelief crept upon me at a very slow rate, but was at last complete. The rate was so slow that I felt no distress, & have never since doubted even for a single second that my conclusion was correct. I can indeed hardly see how anyone ought to wish Christianity to be true; for if so, the plain language of the text seems to show that the men who do not believe, & this would include my Father, Brother & almost all my friends, will be everlastingly punished.[102]

He adds, with undoubtedly intended irony, "And this is a damnable doctrine." The Bible was therefore central in the Darwinian debate—both to the wider culture, no doubt, but also within the mind and heart of Darwin himself.

However, there is an often forgotten aspect of the story of Darwinism and Christianity: the biblical defense of Darwin, a point ably documented by David Livingstone in *Darwin's Forgotten Defenders: The Encounter between Evangelical and Evolutionary Thought*.[103]

102. Darwin, *Evolutionary Writings, Including Autobiographies*, 391–92.

103. Livingston, *Darwin's Forgotten Defenders: The Encounter between Evangelical and Evolutionary Thought*. Noll notes further that frequently the initial responses by evangelical leaders to Darwin's theory were marked by "far less alarm than would later

A fifth point underscoring the importance of the Bible to American life can be seen in the debates concerning the emergence of Marxian Socialism. Indeed, it is well known that Marx deeply admired Darwin—calling Darwin's view of evolution, in December of 1860, "the basis of natural history for our view."[104] Marx excoriated the biblical notions of an afterlife and of divine providence, seeing them as simplistic tools to further the degradation of the working class and as analgesics consumed by the immiserated masses whose humanity was daily raped by the capitalist class. However, as Frances Knight in her work, *The Church in the Nineteenth Century* describes, the biblically based response to Marx was considerable.[105] In the United States, this took many fascinating turns, with one especially powerful form being the Social Gospel movement of men such as Washington Gladden and Walter Rauschenbusch.[106] The Bible fought back.

Many of these five overarching issues that we have examined[107] continued to inform American cultural dynamics across the twentieth century.[108] We can see this, for example, in the rise of effective forms of religiously grounded anti-communism in the Cold War period. A clear example of the role of biblical religion during the Cold War can be seen in the administration of Harry Truman. As Diane Kirby has recently argued, throughout the period of the Cold War and perhaps most especially during Truman's time

---

be the case." Noll, *America's God*, 425.

104. See Friends of Darwin. Moreover, his close colleague and patron Friedrich Engels announced at Marx's funeral on 22 March 1883 that, "just as Darwin discovered the law of development of organic nature, so Marx discovered the law of development of human history," a point he made to a small funeral audience including as an invited guest the Darwinian champion, Professor Edwin Ray Lankester. See Laughland, "European Integration."

105. Knight, *The Church in the Nineteenth Century.*

106. See Wills, *Head and Heart: A History of Christianity in America*, 382–95, for a balanced overview of the Social Gospel movement.

107. Other dynamics include the debates over higher criticism. Inspired by the work of Friedrich Schleiermacher, David Friedrich Strauss, and Ludwig Feuerbach, nineteenth-century-driven Enlightenment rationalism stimulated new biblical criticism. Campbell gives a good example: the KJV depended upon the *Textus Receptus*, used by Erasmus, but an earlier text, *Codex Sinaiticus*, revealed the latter to exclude the last few verses of Mark's Gospel, specifically Mark: 16:9–20. Campbell, *Bible,* 276. Such criticism had a widespread effect upon Roman Catholic and Protestant traditions. However, Christian responses were powerfully made, such as those found in Green, *The Higher Criticism of the Pentateuch.* See also Schweitzer's indictment of higher criticism in *The Quest of the Historical Jesus.*

108. The Intelligent Design movement is a more recent manifestation of this, and the target of Dawkins's 2006 and 2007 polemics *The God Delusion* and *The Greatest Show on Earth.* In England, in 2008, Michael Reiss was forced from his post at the Royal Society for suggesting ID could be taught in science classes.

in office, "the defense of Western civilization and the defense of Christianity became linked in the minds of people in general, and also in the minds of their leaders." Such was not without cause, given the massive persecution of Christians under the Soviet regime.[109] Hence, Truman could say in no uncertain terms that "I believe honestly that Almighty God intends us to assume the leadership which he intended us to assume in 1920, and which we refused"—leadership against the spread of the menacing ideology of world-wide communism.[110]

We also see the continuation of earlier themes with the role of biblical religion in the Civil Rights movement. As George Marsden points out, in the Civil Rights campaigns, "religion worked against the political consensus," owing in large part to the tireless advocacy of African American ministers who were "community spokespersons in the pattern of Puritan New England, [leaders who] could still challenge the collective conscience of the nation."[111] Important in this context are the significant works of David Chappell and James Findlay Jr., who detail the tremendous indebtedness of the Civil Rights Movement to the strength of America's religious vitality.[112]

In sum, it is incontrovertible that the Bible in America has been (and still remains) a potent force in American politics, and in wider cultural life. Indeed, in 2011, in its 400th anniversary, the Bible's KJV made an appearance in American constitutional politics in a way that underscores both its cultural and political prowess. A Resolution of the House and Senate was passed recognizing how "the KJV's relevance and contributions continue to formatively influence the United States," and honoring the fact that "the KJV has played a significant role in the education of countless individuals, families, and societies."[113]

In all, it seems simply obvious to us—indeed, incontestable—that an elective course focused exclusively on the Bible could never be considered inappropriate on the basis of its subject matter. Students can reasonably be thought to need to know that text, which was, and to varying extents, still

---

109. See for example Froese, *The Plot to Kill God: Findings from the Soviet Experiment in Secularization.* For a classic text documenting the horrific persecution of Christians by the Soviet Union, see Scheffbuch, *Christians under the Hammer and Sickle.*

110. Thomas, Review of *Religion and the Cold War,* by Diane Kirby." Truman, quoted in Kirby, *Religion and the Cold War,* 86.

111. Marsden, "Religion, Politics, and the Search for an American Consensus," 465.

112. Chappell, *A Stone of Hope;* and Findlay Jr., *Church People in the Struggle:.*

113. Congress further decreed its "gratitude for the influence the King James Version has bestowed upon the United States." See King James Bible Online. "Congress Further Decreed Its Gratitude for the Influence the King James Version Has Bestowed Upon the United States."

remains so central to English and American history, politics and culture. As Daniel Dreisbach remarks about the American founding period, "for insights into the founders' political thought and culture, read the Bible."[114] The same rightly can be said of later generations, and of vast areas of the American literary and cultural experience.

The Pressing Problem of Biblical Illiteracy

Our fourth point to support Bible-centered instruction highlights how a focus on the Bible is all the more justifiable because it meets a rising curricular need, that of responding to sharp increases in biblical illiteracy, which is a striking need indeed given precisely the Bible's deep roots in American, Western, and world culture. According to Boston University religious studies professor Stephen Prothero, America has become a nation that is deeply religiously illiterate.[115] Prothero's best-selling book, *Religious Literacy,* documents the lack of basic knowledge that the majority of Americans have about not only minority religions in the United States, but also about Christianity.[116] Among Prothero's findings: only about half of Americans can name any one of the four gospels, and a majority are unable even to name the first book of the Bible.[117] In fact, America is a nation where only thirty-seven percent of adults can name all four of the gospels, and only forty-two percent can name at least five of the Ten Commandments.[118] This conclusion is underscored by the exhaustive *Bible Literacy Report* of 2005. This thoroughly researched investigation documents a nation of "Bible Illiterates." It finds that twenty percent of a representative sample of American high school students do not know what Easter commemorates; twenty-eight percent do not know that Moses led the Exodus; sixty-five percent could not identify a sentence from the Sermon on the Mount; and a vast majority know next to nothing about King David.[119] Such illiteracy is also evidenced by an estimate by a sample of English teachers of their students' biblical understanding: a representative cross section of American teachers disclosed that American educators think that less than a quarter of their high school

---

114. Dreisbach, *Reading the Bible with the Founding Fathers*, 234.

115. Prothero, *Religious Literacy*.

116. See also Deckman, "Religious Literacy in Public Schools," 31.

117. Deckman, "Religious Literacy in Public Schools," 31.

118. Vlach, "Americans and the Bible: Ownership, Reading, Study and Knowledge in the United States." See also Moore, *Overcoming Religious Illiteracy*.

119. Wachlin, "What Do High School Teachers Think Students Need to Know about the Bible?," 6.

students can be counted as even minimally biblically literate.[120] In turn, the American Academy of Religion (AAR), based on its own detailed report has concluded that "religious traditions are often represented inaccurately by those outside of and within religious traditions and communities."[121] The AAR further notes the deleterious effect on religious literacy of the often overdrawn and sensationalizing reports about religious communities so frequently found in the popular media.[122]

Avoiding Cynicism

Hence, a sufficient secular argument has been advanced for increased education on the Bible in public school courses for the purpose of enhancing students' knowledge of history, culture, and literature. Moreover, this is not the only argument available to support increased biblical instruction. Our last argument underscoring the secular rationale for Bible courses is that of avoiding popular cynicism over the purposes served by public education. Given the preeminence of the Bible in Western thought and history, the failure to treat the Bible as preeminent in these areas is likely to produce cynicism and distrust, which we have ample reasons to avoid; thus, once again, we have a secular justification for Bible-centered instructional reform. Indeed, it is helpful in this context to reflect briefly on just how bizarre any argument against teaching the Bible for purposes of understanding Western culture and history actually is. Let us take for example the thought of Kent Greenawalt. As previously noted, Greenawalt writes that "no doubt the Bible has affected our literature and broader culture far more than any other religious writing." But he then proceeds to assert that "a Bible course [in public schools] reinforces the notion that Christianity is by far the most important religion" in terms of American historical and cultural development, and, thus, such courses are to be rejected.[123] It is important to

120. Ibid., 5, 14.

121. AAR Guidelines, quoted in Moore, "Teaching about the Bible in Public Schools," 65.

122. Ibid., 73–74. One could easily bring to mind the Westboro Baptist Church. A congregation of less than fifty people (most of whom are relatives of its founding pastor), this minute and utterly marginal community has received inordinate media attention.

123. Greenawalt, *Does the Bible Belong in Public Schools*, 137. Greenawalt might respond that his fear is that the Bible being showcased in history courses would communicate the idea that the Bible is the most important book in terms of having greater actual value relative to all other religious texts. But surely it need not have this impact. Hegel famously noted—accurately—that history is (mostly) one "blood-soaked

appreciate just how bizarre this argument is, and how likely it is to engender cynicism. The Bible is acknowledged as by far the most influential religious work in Western culture, but courses on Western culture that feature prominently the Bible should not be taught, for that will cause students to think that the Bible is in fact the most prominent religious text in Western culture—or, in other words, they might just be taught the truth. To have teachers so conspicuously avoid teaching what is clearly true can only breed an unhealthy cynicism about the educational process, which we have ample secular reasons to resist.

---

slaughter bench." Does the fact of history's showcasing such bloodshed make bloodshed of greater actual value relative to periods of peace? The facts of history need not incline one to any particular value judgment.

Chapter 4 ————————————————————

State Religious Education and the Defense of Religious Vitality

The Constitutional Motivation for National Biblical Culture

IN THE EARLIER CHAPTERS, we presented arguments that we believe establish the constitutionality of policy advocates being informed by a religious motive in shaping policy outcomes. We conceded that with respect to the issue of Bible-centered education, there *might be*—in addition to the articulation of a justifiable secular rationale—a motive on the part of some reformers to promote among students in public schools an admiration for and an openness—even a possible conversion—to the Hebrew and Christian scriptures. Note well, we are *not* asserting that this is the case. We are only stating that it might be so, at least, among some.[1] Such a motivation we argue is constitutionally permitted. In this chapter we argue, in turn, that it is equally permissible for policy decision-making to be informed—and even explicitly so—by the motive of *protecting* religion from losing its cultural influence, as long as that religious motive is supported by non-religious argumentation as well.

We believe that biblical instruction in public school over time will erode the Bible's influence, and so we reject the expansion of Bible-centered

—————————

1. Dr. Alex McFarland, founder of the religious revivalist organization, Project 2026, seeks to "preserve America and restore the country to the Christian principles it was founded on." He is a supporter of non-devotional biblical instruction in public schools. We have not however confirmed his precise position on Bible courses. Smith, "Project 2026 Launched to Restore Christian Values."

courses in the public education system based on this admittedly religious motivation.[2] To be constitutionally justifiable, on the position we have developed above, it is incumbent that we advance a non-religious rationale for not extending biblical instruction, which can be added to our religious motivation of preserving religious culture. We believe that a non-religious rationale can cogently be defended.

The Centrality of STEM and the Limitation of Resources

A strong non-religious argument involves the important need for improving STEM (Science, Technology, Engineering, and Mathematics) education in American public schools, a need all the more acute given existing shortages of resources, and the fact that American educational standards and outcomes far lag behind other countries in the STEM areas. The United States STEM Foundation coordinates and subsidizes activities that promote greater curricular attention to STEM education in American schools. The STEM Foundation and other organizations have advanced persuasive arguments that the U.S. system of education inadequately attends to science and math education. The U.S. STEM Foundation warns that due to poor STEM instruction, "60 percent of employers are having a hard time finding qualified workers,[3] and that of 65 education systems worldwide, American students rank only 27th in math and 20th in science." Hence it argues forcefully—and persuasively—that STEM education "must be elevated as a national priority." Our nation's future economic prosperity, they contend, depends on this.[4]

2. Our position is analogous to the question of whether a veto of a religion-advancing bill can be made on religious grounds, as was seen for example in 2016 when the governor of Tennessee, Bill Haslam, vetoed a bill adopting the Bible as the state book, which he asserted was done from his religious motivation of avoiding the trivialization of biblical truth. It is noteworthy that little constitutional objection was raised over his religious motivation, a fact owing almost certainly to the pragmatic fact that secularists saw the veto as a victory, even if the logic that supported that victory does not itself uphold the strict separationist position. We acknowledge that even if a secularist reader were unpersuaded by our argument that a religious motive can inform the decision to include Bible courses, she might allow a religious motive to guide its exclusion, simply for pragmatic reasons, however imprudent the concession would be to her long-term defense of strict secularism.

3. In 2012, the manufacturing sector could not find employees with the skills to fill 600,000 high-tech manufacturing positions. See Engler, "STEM Education Is Key to U.S.'s Economic Future,"

4. Metaxas, "Man Does Not Live by Math Alone: Education Is More than STEM." In fact, as the U.S. News/Raytheon STEM Index reports, "if America's performance in math and science simply matched the average for 33 other developed nations, GDP

Substantial amounts of data reinforce this troubling conclusion. Rodney C. Adkins, senior vice president of IBM's Systems and Technology group points out that "America desperately needs more STEM students," in part because STEM workers "are responsible for more than 50% of our sustained economic expansion." However, he further notes that twenty-five years ago forty percent of the world's scientists resided in the United States and now it is only fifteen percent, leading to a striking decline in America's global competitiveness. This lackluster output, he argues, is in part due to the fact that forty percent of incoming college students who plan to pursue a major in a STEM degree end up switching their concentration, a fact due in no small part to the poor initial training received in their secondary and primary schooling.[5] Indeed, well over a quarter of students self-identify as having been ill-prepared for STEM courses at the college level by their primary and secondary schools, and so avoided even considering a position in STEM upon high school graduation.[6] A recent report from the Committee for Economic Development notes that students, if anything, are under-reporting their level of inadequate primary and secondary science training. The Committee finds that sixty-nine percent of high school graduates are not prepared for college-level math or science.[7] In all, therefore, STEM poses a pressing—and financially draining—need for American schools, which argues for avoiding the diversion of resources to other areas, such as elective courses on the Bible.

What is more, the fear of draining resources is a very real one due to systemic underfunding in public schools across the country. There just may not be the resource base to pursue both the necessary investments in STEM and additional elective courses of high quality. American public education is underfunded and under stress. As the Center for Budget Priorities and Policy documented in January 2016, "most states provide less support per student for elementary and secondary schools—in some cases, much less—than before the Great Recession. Worse, some states are *still* cutting eight years after the recession took hold."[8] The Center established the following troubling conclusions:

---

would increase by an additional 1.7 percent each year by 2050."

5. Adkins, "America Desperately Needs More STEM Students. Here's How to Get Them."

6. Engler, "STEM Education is Key to the U.S. Economic Future."

7. Oberoi, "The Economic Impact of Early Exposure to STEM Education."

8. Leachman et al., "Most States Have Cut School Funding, and Some Continue Cutting."

At least 31 states provided less state funding per student in the 2014 school year (that is, the school year ending in 2014) than in the 2008 school year, before the recession took hold. In at least 15 states, the cuts exceeded 10 percent.

In at least 18 states, *local* government funding per student fell over the same period. In at least 27 states, local funding rose, but those increases rarely made up for cuts in state support. Total local funding nationally—for the states where comparable data exist—*declined* between 2008 and 2014, adding to the damage from state funding cuts.

While data on total school funding in the *current* school year (2016) is not yet available, at least 25 states are still providing less "general" or "formula" funding—the primary form of state funding for schools—per student than in 2008. In seven states, the cuts exceed 10 percent.

Most states raised "general" funding per student slightly this year, but 12 states imposed new cuts, even as the national economy continues to improve. Some of these states, including Oklahoma, Arizona, and Wisconsin, already were among the deepest-cutting states since the recession hit.[9]

These cuts have all taken place within a distressing context. Federal funds represent only nine percent of total educational funding, and that percentage has remained mostly stable despite these dramatic state-level cuts. Moreover, the overall educational needs in the United States have grown, as the number of students has risen since 2008 by 804,000 while the number of public K–12 teachers and other school workers has fallen by 297,000.[10]

For these reasons, there is ample secular justification for not adding elective Bible courses. Hence, to add to this argument a further motivational element—that it would harm American biblical culture—is constitutionally unproblematic; the motivational concern for the religious health of the nation is justifiable in this context.

9. Ibid.
10. Ibid.

Chapter 5

State Religious Education and Religious Vitality

When Biblical Instruction Harms

BASED ON OUR ARGUMENTS so far, it does seem that we are entitled to hold a motivational concern that can inform our democratic decision making under the First Amendment that increased teaching of the Bible in public schools would prove harmful to American biblical culture and to the health of religious faith in the nation, and, therefore, should be avoided. The question now becomes, why believe this proposition true?

Before we develop our argument, it is important to avoid an initial confusion. On first glance one might accuse us of indulging in something of a contradiction. In chapter two, we argued that conservatives are not unduly fearful in debates involving educational policy. However, here we shall argue that biblical instruction is something to be concerned with by those who wish to see the Bible retain and expand its cultural importance. Is this contradictory? It is not. This is so because a profound difference exists between well-grounded suspicion and irrational fearfulness; and there is an unhappy tendency for many activists to impute the latter to social and educational conservatives. They are described so often as what we might call "the frightened evangelical," or the "over-anxious Catholic"—individuals emotionally spurred to social action, meddling with public institutions in furtherance of their narrow and passion-fraught agendas. Such descriptions are simply unfair. There are, as we shall see, very well grounded reasons for our concern; we are not engaging in that unthinking hysteria so often imputed to conservative thinkers.

We shall develop our claim about the religiously destructive potential of Bible courses in the public schools through a five-staged argument. We shall: i) address what we call the museumification of a living faith, the legal environment in contemporary public education, the rising irreligiosity among younger members of the teaching corps, and follow with an examination of the ensuing educational double-bind; ii) the rise of a questionable new methodology based on a specific kind of "religious studies" pedagogy; iii) the problem of growing hostility to traditional Christianity among educational elites; iv) the lack of adequate training in biblical studies among most of the teachers likely to lead these courses; and v) empirical examples of the ongoing problem of religious material being improperly addressed in courses not exclusively dedicated to the study of the Bible, leading to the simple conclusion that problems should not be multiplied beyond necessity.

A Museum-piece Curio or a Living Faith? An Educational Double-Bind

To our first point, what does biblical instruction in the public schools today look like? Due to the requirements of constitutional law—which prohibit anything that can be construed as proselytizing in the classroom, including, as the federal court stated in *Gibson v. Lee County*,[1] any treatment that might imply that the biblical text refers (beyond bare archaeological references) to anything which is true—biblical instruction is often simply about rote memorization of phrases and events stored in an ancient almanac. Well, one might ask, what could be wrong with that? Don't students have to memorize long-ago factoids in history and social science subjects all the time? However, when the Bible is taught only as a set of propositions framed in the form of assertions adhered to by a social group in the past, or a demographic subgroup in contemporary society, such an approach is likely to "museumify" a living faith.[2] Indeed, Al Mohler, the president of the Southern Baptist Theological Seminary and a leader in the Southern Baptist Convention, has argued that leaders in contemporary culture have an unwelcome tendency to treat religion in a disparaging way through the manner in which religious conviction is framed in modern life. "I call this the National Geographic syndrome," Mohler states. "It's like the cultural elites all of a sudden discover this tiny little exotic tribe"[3] of faithful people, whom they treat as curios—or

1. 1 F.Supp.2d 1426 (1998).

2. See Prud'homme, "Conclusion," 177–207.

3. Mohler, "Moral Argument in Modern Times: A Conversation with Robert P. George." Indeed, the problem of museumification is widespread in English religious

vestiges of a long-gone era. To reduce the teaching of the Bible to the teaching of a history textbook is to reduce religion to a gallery show piece; it is to make the Bible appear a dead letter and not a living testament and source of strength for millions. Precisely on the basis of conservative Christianity, therefore, we argue that it is best not to teach the Bible if it is to be taught in just this manner.[4]

The concerns we have voiced here actually have precedent in American debates over the educational role of the Bible. As Daniel Dreisbach has documented, the noted educator, lexicographer, and patriotic statesman Noah Webster (1758–1843), early in his career "censure[d . . .] the use of the Bible as a school book."[5] If the Bible is reduced to a common classroom reader, or if it becomes the subject of "frequent thoughtless repetition," then, Webster warned, there is a tendency to trivialize or "lessen the reverence which mankind ought to have for the Supreme Being" and for the "sacred word."[6] Webster later repeated this critique with even greater vehemence, as Dreisbach points out:

> it has often been observed by men of piety, that such a common use of the Bible, is a kind of prostitution of divine truth to secular purposes—that children are insensibly led, by a habit of familiarity, to consider that sacred work, or at lest to treat it as a book of no more importance than any human performance; and that, being accustomed in early life to repeat it often, and many times with the utmost reluctance, they imbibe a disgust for it, which their subsequent conviction of its importance, is seldom able to conquer.[7]

Webster professed, Dreisbach notes, that his concern was born of a genuine zeal for the Word of God, and a desire neither to trivialize its invaluable content nor foster contempt for it through, what Dreisbach aptly calls "coerced familiarity."[8] This historic concern is pressing and cogent—indeed, we believe, all the more so today.

---

education, a point we underscore in chapter 7. The important Ofsted Report of 2010 notes that "many of the resources [fall] short in conveying a real sense of the deeper significance and power of religions in the lives of the believers." Ofsted, *Transforming Religious Education*, 6.

4. Prud'homme, "Conclusion."

5. Webster Jr., *A Collection of Essays and Fugitive Writings: On Moral, Historical, Political and Literary Subjects*, 8. See Dreisbach, "A Handbook for Republican Citizenship?: The Founders Debate the Bible's Use in Schools," 7–29.

6. Webster Jr., *A Grammatical Institute of the English Language, In Three Parts*, 12.

7. Ibid., 3–4, quoted in Dreisbach, "A Handbook for Republican Citizenship?," 17.

8. Dreisbach does note the possibility of an ulterior political motive, or a motive

However, if a treatment that views the Bible in a way that communicates its meaning to so many as a vital living faith were undertaken, schools would likely confront significant legal challenges. To see this, we have to address what a treatment of the Bible as a living document might look like. To attempt to capture the Bible's importance for those who adhere to it is not to proselytize; it is simply to teach the text in a way that treats it on its own terms; it is to convey the Bible's meaning to those who see it as a living wellspring, and not an ancient rune or primitive codebook. To be sure, the Bible can indeed be viewed in some limited sense as a series of propositional claims and assertions that can be memorized like dictionary entries. But the Bible is so much more than that.[9] One major way theorists of religious education have attempted to convey religious content without trivializing it has been through the methodology known as educational phenomenology, an approach growing out of the work championed by the renowned scholar of comparative religion, Ninian Smart.

Ninian Smart (fl. 1952–2001) was highly influential in the academic study of religion, serving as the founding chair of the first university Religious Studies (as opposed to Theology) department in the United Kingdom. As Gearon has noted in depth in previous work, Smart's influence ran much deeper than simply in higher education, as he recognized the importance of taking developments in the academic study of religion into school religious education and succeeded at establishing his preferred method as one of the dominant paradigms in pre-collegiate religious instruction for secular schools across the world.[10]

The phenomenology of religion is a method of sympathetic engagement with religion from the perspective of the religious believer, an effort to understand what religion means to its adherents. Scholars of religion in this school of thought employ practices first described and labeled by Edmund Husserl, centrally the *epoche,* or suspension of belief and preconceptions, coupled with an empathic encounter with the claims and practices one is studying.[11] In a highly influential article in the journal then called *Learning*

---

informed by religious doubt. Interestingly, Dreisbach recounts that "later in life, following a spiritual conversion, Webster reversed his opinion and championed the Bible's place in schools, even writing a lengthy essay on the value of the Bible for families and schools." Dreisbach, *Reading the Bible with the Founding Fathers,* 40. See our concluding chapter for our own resolution of the tensions in these two views advanced by Webster.

9. Prud'homme, "Conclusion," 183.

10. See Gearon, *On Holy Ground,* 100–110.

11. In the academic practice of phenomenology, the method has often sought a later so-called eidetic intuition into the essence of what one has studied. This additional component, however, has played no significant role in its application to secondary or primary education. Moreover, it is increasingly rejected even in academic circles. See

for Living, Smart in 1972 argued for the application of the phenomenological method to state religious education.[12] Since then, as Ben Smidt Hanssen has put it, phenomenology has been a bridge between the scholarly study of religion and religious education, and in many direct and indirect ways it continues to exercise an enormous influence on the pedagogy of state religious instruction.[13] The reason for this outsized influence in large measure has precisely been that the phenomenological method allows for a non-devotional understanding but simultaneously avoids the problem of trivialization described above.

Adopting this method, we must understand that the Bible viewed on its own terms is a record of purported experiences with transcendence and the capturing of intimacy with the divine, and of the urgent call for acceptance of divine love, all stated in beautiful expressions bespeaking the very beauty of transcendent reality. In other words, to convey the Bible on its own terms—not to proselytize but only so that students understand its message—is to convey a work of intimacy, urgency, and beauty. In the United States, however, given its hair trigger legal environment, such an approach would raise innumerable red flags and would likely deter prudent administrators from supporting such courses, rightly weary of legal expenses that would improvidently deplete pressing attention in other curricular areas.

Let us explore what a phenomenological curriculum would look like in more detail. As to the core aspect of intimacy, it has long been noted that the central idea of the Bible is that of at-one-ment with God in a way that retains individual dignity. "The basal conception for the Bible doctrine of atonement is the assumption that God and man are ideally one in life and interests, so far as man's true life and interest may be conceived as corresponding with those of God. Hence, it is everywhere assumed that God and man should be in all respects in harmonious relations, 'at-one.' Such is the ideal picture of Adam and Eve in Eden. Such is the assumption in the parable of the Prodigal Son; man ought to be at home with God, at peace in the Father's house (Luke 15)."[14] The call of the Bible is not abstract, but deeply intimate.

---

the works of Cox, *An Introduction to the Phenomenology of Religion*; and Cox, *A Guide to the Phenomenology of Religion: Key Figures, Formative Influences and Subsequent Debates*.

12. Smart, "Guest Editorial," 5. The journal is now known as the *British Journal of Religious Education*.

13. Hanson, "Phenomenology of Religion: A Bridge between the Scholarly Study of Religion and Religious Education," 14–19. See also Gearon, *On Holy Ground*, 109.

14. *Baker's Evangelical Dictionary of Biblical Theology*, s.v. "atonement."

This call is also urgent—and profoundly so. We agree with Kierkegaard that biblical religion is flattened when basic questions of existence raised in the biblical canon acquire speculative importance and not, instead, urgent, passionate concern.

Thirdly, the Bible is in a very real sense a portrait of beauty—a work on the beauty of the creator, the beauty of the created world, and the beauty of the narrative of human history defined by sin, suffering, salvation, and redemption. But how does one teach the Bible's aspiration to convey beauty? The answer is not entirely mysterious or opaque. To take one example, good art teachers convey the passionate meaning and quest for beauty that informs and infuses great works of art—and they know that to fail to do this is to fail to be true to the artwork itself. How do art teachers convey the full meaning of art to students? Here, we can draw insight from a large body of research in arts education theory. Much of contemporary aesthetic and educational theory is based, directly or indirectly, on Hans-Georg Gadamer's theory of spectatorship as developed in *Truth and Method* and amplified by popular estheticians and educators such as Monica Prendergast.[15] On this approach, the art student "gives himself [sic] entirely to the play of art."[16] Hence, as Janis Carpenter notes, "for Gadamer a work of art is more than an object of study for historical and biographical [purposes] . . . he views a work of art and its study as a dynamic movement that sweeps an observer . . . into an interactive experience" of self-loosening.[17] To understand the claims of art, on this account, is to become immersed in it in some deeply fundamental way. Anything less is not to develop a full understanding of what the art is, or what it attempts to convey.[18]

As a text meant in part to communicate an awe-inspiring beauty, the Bible would have to be treated therefore as in some sense a work of art. Yet it is no doubt a complex and variegated artwork. To do it justice, the art of the overall work, as well as the beauty of the lives of action, service and devotion described in its pages must be brought to vivid account. Indeed, a core of biblical instruction must involve hagiography, or the understanding of the lives of holy people inspired by the intimacy and urgency of the biblical mandate, and must endeavor to understand the beauty of their lives of holy aspiration.[19]

15. Prendergast, "'Playing Attention': Contemporary Aesthetics and Performing Arts Audience," 36–51.

16. Gadamer, *Truth and Method*, 332.

17. Carpenter, "Calderon's Painter, Gadamer's Spectator: Extending the Realm of Play."

18. Prud'homme, "Conclusion," 184. See Prendergast, "Playing Attention."

19. In *On Holy Ground,* a number of examples are provided, including the lives of

The careful religious studies educator would, to be sure, also take care not to inculcate aesthetics as a surrogate expression of religious belief—something Immanuel Kant, and others after him, became complicit. Indeed for Kant, "art is the culmination of the critical philosophy."[20] For in removing religion and, notably, God, from rational judgment, he ultimately came to the *Critique of Judgment*, where we see "almost a yearning for the aesthetic to fill the void that Kant himself had done so much to create."[21] The space vacated by the sacred is taken by the sublimely beautiful. In fact, the *Critique of Judgment*, with all its talk of the sublime, reads almost as if Kant were nostalgic for that which he had labelled "pernicious and disgraceful"—traditional religious conviction.[22] He writes with a passion for the sublime, which has every bit as much fervor as a priest of old writing of the beatific vision awaiting the prayerful soul. Hence, Kant's *Critique of Judgment* provided more than an aesthetic in the limited sense (a way to understand and appreciate art); it provided the means for seeing how art could serve as an emotionally powerful surrogate for the lost consolation of religion.[23] Nevertheless, with an eye to this possible distortion, artistic modes of thought can play a valuable role in biblical instruction.

To be able to teach the Bible so as to capture its calls of intimacy, urgency, and beauty in a public school setting is possible to conceive in principle but tremendously difficult to exercise in point of fact. Education at this level—education, that is, that could convey to students how the Bible can elicit an overwhelming and passionate devotion by millions, who, seeing its truth, are also enraptured by its beauty, are inspired by its urgency, and are committed to its claims of intimacy—is not very easily undertaken in contemporary schools for at least two reasons.[24]

First, we must acknowledge concerns over lawsuits in the contemporary legal environment. That environment would dissuade curricular changes; changes that could be characterized (fairly or not) as overly sympathetic to religion: a rendering of the passionate intensity of belief recorded in biblical narratives, and an effort to capture something of the Bible's awe-inspiring beauty to those whose lives have been changed by it, in the past, as in the

---

Saint Alpnsus Ligouri, Saint Therese of Lisieux, and John Bunyan.

20. Gearon, *On Holy Ground*, 135.

21. Ibid.

22. Ibid., 138.

23. Ibid.

24. Based on the reasoning we develop here, it is perhaps no surprise that, in the words of Kent Richter, "beauty is the most . . . overlooked part of religion in many Introduction to Religion studies." Richter, *Religion: A Study in Beauty, Truth and Goodness*, 149.

present, is a form of legal Russian roulette. Although, as we have noted, the Supreme Court's majority decision in the *Abingdon v. Schempp* case states that literary, historical, or "objective" study of the Bible in public schools satisfies the strictures of the Establishment clause. Daniel Dreisbach, Barry Lynn, and many others have pointed out that the legal environment that pervades public education! is fraught with a litigiousness that can motivate administrators to err on the side of legal caution.[25] This hair-trigger legal environment—where issues of religion are litigated with considerable zeal—is found not only in liberal-leaning havens, but also in fully "red" states. The ACLU after all has chapters in each state, and a growing dues-paying membership nationwide.[26] The ACLU and organizations similar to it are, as one (to be sure unsympathetic) observer puts in, "a bottomless pit in supporting litigation," which they pursue all across the country.[27] Indeed, in areas that some might suspect are especially prone to support biblical instruction in schools, such as in rural school districts, the mere threat of litigation often causes school boards quickly to fold on a variety of issues for fear of the financial consequences of lawsuits.[28] As one commentator remarks, "small districts have to sacrifice books, maintenance, and salaries to defend themselves in court."[29] In fact, GOP governor "Butch" Otter vetoed the Idaho Bible instruction bill, despite overwhelming legislative support, largely out of just such a fear of swelling litigation costs.[30]

We can take the state of Oklahoma as another example of this litigational self-defensiveness. As we have seen, in 2014 the Mustang, Oklahoma school district initially approved—by an overwhelming vote of its elected

25. Also evidenced by Diane Moore of the American Academy of Religion, whose position as an expert can serve the litigation efforts of opponents. She states starkly that a phenomenological pedagogy is "inappropriate as a lens to represent religion in the public schools." Moore, "Teaching about the Bible in Public Schools," 82n6.

26. Membership in the ACLU has increased notably across the country, including in states such as Wyoming and Texas. See ACLU.org.

27. See report of the American Civil Rights Union entitled "ACLU Supports Smutty Photos of Teenagers as 'Free Speech.'" As the ACLU website states, "our extraordinary growth has allowed the ACLU to expand its nationwide litigation." See ACLU, Anthony D. Romero, Executive Director. Other organizations increasing national litigation in areas involving religion include the Freedom from Religion Foundation, which has recently initiated a nationwide campaign of legal challenges against perceived violations of the Establishment Clause.

28. The Freedom from Religion Foundation's 2011 annual report notes the number of legal victors for its side secured through the mere threat of litigation, and thus "without having to go to court!" See "2011 Year in Review."

29. Prud'homme, "Conclusion," 183–84. See also report of the American Civil Rights Union entitled "ACLU Supports Smutty Photos of Teenagers as 'Free Speech.'"

30. Corbin, "Otter Vetoes Bible-in-Schools Bill."

school board (there was only one abstention)—the adoption of the Green Scholars Bible curriculum. Yet, due to protests by the avowedly antireligious Freedom from Religion Foundation[31] and other secularist organizations, the school board was forced indefinitely to table the adoption of the Bible curriculum.[32] The school board stated explicitly its fear of costly lawsuits and sought as a condition of its adopting, simply on a trial basis, the new curriculum that it be guaranteed by Mr. Green that any litigation costs would be covered without expense to the school district, a point to which Mr. Green saw himself unable to commit (being burdened with funding a world class museum in its early stages of construction).[33] No doubt he and the small district were afraid of teams of well-funded lawyers,[34] aflame with passion for their cause, draining resources from an already financially strapped public school system.[35] The mere threat of litigation, therefore, drove the school district to overturn its overwhelming support for adoption of this entirely optional elective Bible sequence. In the face of such well-funded opposition, financial prudence alone demanded the outcome. Not content with their victory, moreover, Americans United for Separation of Church and State and other secularist pressure groups sought to marginalize further the instruction of the Bible in Oklahoma public schools by their opposition in 2015 to a symbolic bill offered in the Oklahoma state legislature declaring only that the teaching of the Bible is legally permitted in public schools—in other words, they opposed a bill that effectively did

31. The Freedom from Religion Foundation (FFRF) proudly espouses and energetically promotes atheism and non-theism, and encourages and celebrates criticism of religion by publicly prominent individuals, e.g. through its annual The Emperor Has No Clothes award for the year's public repudiation of religion the FFRF judges to be best. For reasons such as these, Hansen in *Religion and Reaction* numbers the organization not as a civil rights organization but as an atheist/agnostic one; it is of the same sort as organizations like Kids without God, an atheist advocacy program directed at children. See Kids without God. See also Hansen, *Religion and Reaction: The Secular Political Challenge to the Religious Right*.

32. Christian Today, "Hobby Lobby's Bible Course Cancelled by Oklahoma School District."

33. Banks, "Hobby Lobby President's Bible Curriculum Shelved by Oklahoma School District."

34. As secularist Susan Hansen reminds her readers, "secular organizations . . . have billionaire donors, such as George Soros." Hansen, *Religion and Reaction*, 152.

35. Oklahoma faced in FY 2016 a $1.3 billion shortfall in the state budget. As a result, public schools alone faced a $110 million shortfall in FY 2016. Oklahoma City Public Schools, for example, must fill a $30 million budget hole. "No part of the organization will go untouched," Superintendent Robb Neu has said. He notes that the district is cutting 208 teaching positions. "We have no choice," Neu said. Querry and Fultonberg, "208 Oklahoma City Teaching Positions Will Be Cut because of 'Catastrophic Budget Crisis.'"

nothing but re-articulate the holding of the United States Supreme Court in *Abingdon v. Schempp* as well as the legislature's own 2010 law encouraging greater instruction of the Bible in state public schools. The bill in question would not have immunized the state from lawsuits over curricular content in Bible courses, but instead would only have reaffirmed the right of the state to adopt Bible courses without being subject to legal challenges concerning the exercise of their right to have non-religious Bible courses in the first place. As a result of well-funded advocacy against curricular reform, even this very small measure was defeated in the state senate—all, let us not forget, in Oklahoma and not in Oregon, Vermont, or Washington state. Given the dire consequences of litigation in many cases, and the desire of many organizations to pursue litigation aggressively, we should not be too unsurprised if pedagogies for biblical instruction beyond the mere memorization of long-ago tales of distant tribes were viewed by frugal administrators as simply too risky. Yet, such is precisely what we believe should not take place for fear of marginalization and exoticization that could undermine the witness of the living faith.

Second, Kahan's research in light of the religious demographics of younger teachers is important to the issue of phenomenological religious studies education. For even if we assume that a legal environment were to exist where teachers and administrators felt comfortable adopting a phenomenological pedagogy, the question arises as to whether teachers—and especially younger teachers—are well suited to engage phenomenology effectively. We need to remember the difficulty of entering into someone else's perspective, especially when that perspective is foreign to one, and when one is intellectually bright. Teachers are no doubt frequently some of our brightest citizens. Yet, there is an increasing alienation from religious knowledge and religious viewpoints by the teaching corps in the United States, especially among younger teachers. Derek Anderson has documented just such a trend, which to a large extent is a function of the striking trendline in religiously unaffiliated millennials. The Pew Research Center puts the number of religiously unaffiliated millennials in 2015 at thirty-six percent.[36] This dramatic increase in religious alienation by younger Americans is having its inevitable impact on the teaching profession. As Anderson notes, in 2011, thirty-one percent of teachers were over fifty years old, with twenty-two percent of teachers younger than 30 years old.[37] Hence, Anderson notes that "given the overall national trend regarding religion, it is safe to assume that

36. Pew Research Center: Religion and Public Life, "America's Changing Religious Landscape."

37. Feistritzer et al., *Profile of Teachers in the US, 2011*. Quoted in Anderson, "Characteristics of Atheist Pre-Service Elementary Teachers."

younger teachers are more likely to be non-religious than older teachers . . . with a rapid increase in the number of nonreligious teachers entering the profession as Baby Boomers retire."[38] To be sure, we readily concede that these trends toward secularism are reversible (and likely are already reversing in important areas),[39] but the near term prospects appear to align well with the demographic accounts of American young people advanced by scholars such as Susan Hansen in her hortatory account of secularism in the United States, *Religion and Reaction: The Secular Political Challenge to the Religious Right*.[40]

We should accept therefore an increasing lack of biblical knowledge among teachers in a (perhaps temporarily) secularizing world. The present condition is one in which many young teachers are unlikely to know biblical religion thoroughly, yet our teachers are so often very bright young men and women. They are, therefore, according to the underlying logic of the research of Dan Kahan, likely to prove poor communicators of religious claims when those claims are advanced through the empathic process that defines the phenomenological method.

What emerges from this discussion is an educational double bind: either religion is museumified and drained of vital witness, or it is taught phenomenologically, in which case the schools become litigation targets, and phenomenological teaching is poor in quality.

Questioning the New "Religious Studies" Alternative

An interesting pedagogical alternative has recently been advanced by the American Academy of Religion and its Taskforce on the Teaching of Religion in Public Schools chaired by Diane Moore of the Harvard Divinity School (who also teaches at Philips Andover Academy). This approach seeks to avoid an account of religious propositions based on memorizing claims

---

38. Anderson, "Characteristics of Atheist Pre-Service Elementary Teachers."

39. As Hansen points out, Hispanics are much more religious than Anglo Americans, including those under thirty: twice as many Hispanics under thirty view the Bible as the literal word of God compared to Whites, and three quarters of Hispanics under thirty view religion as important to their daily lives compared to six out of ten Whites under thirty. The Hispanic population has increased profoundly since 1965, and will only increase for the foreseeable future and so we should anticipate increased religiosity in the longer term. Hansen, *Religion and Reaction*, 147. Data points also to a *potential* reversal in the United Kingdom, where for the last six years three Pentecostal churches have opened for every one Anglican church that has closed. Burgess, "Migrants Put their Faith in Britain"; and NatCen, "The British Social Attitudes Survey."

40. Cited above.

embedded in believers' religious tradition, where faith lives are treated as almanac pieces, while simultaneously rejecting the phenomenological method. In the AAR's *Guidelines for Teaching About Religion in K-12 Public Schools in the United States*, it calls for what it terms a "religious studies" pedagogy in public schools.[41] This approach is founded on a base of three interwoven methodological assumptions. We shall first itemize these assumptions while underscoring areas where each is problematic. We shall then highlight some internal contradictions within the AAR's curricular agenda.

The first assumption of the AAR's form of "religious studies" pedagogy is the premise that "religions are not internally homogenous but diverse."[42] This assumption may be true of some (perhaps even many) religions, but it is unsafe to generalize it to all religions. Jains, for example, are remarkably consistent in their adherence to a common metaphysical system. Moreover, even if some (or indeed many) religions do express significant internal diversity, they most often express that diversity as something over and against an underlying set of common principles and beliefs recognized by all, or almost all as theologically basic. It just is not right to say that Buddhism has such internal diversity that Buddhists can meaningfully be described as espousing bodily hedonism: diversity has real limits. The serious concern we have with this premise is its intellectual imposition upon the data of religious life. That is, it seems to have the *goal* of privileging the existence of, or the search for diversity, at the expense of the commonality that is so often a profound aspect of religious communities. It seems, we suspect— though we admit that it can be hard to determine motives—that there is an agenda working under the guise of academic method: the agenda to decenter religion as a force that could convey an absolute truth-claim as truth is traditionally understood, since truth is historically seen as one and not the Nietzschean flux of contending diversity.

The second premise is related to the first, namely, that "religions are dynamic . . . and constantly evolving."[43] This may be true of certain aspects of religion and of some religions. Yet, again, it seems tendentious to say it should constitute the core of the study of religion. "From [our] perspective, there is no such thing as a 'single meaning' of a given tradition, practice or belief system," the AAR's Guidelines remark.[44] To be sure, it is interest-

41. American Academy of Religion, *Guidelines for Teaching About Religion in K-12 Public Schools in the United States*.

42. Moore, "Teaching about the Bible in Public Schools," 74.

43. Ibid., 75, 67.

44. Ibid., 75.

ing and meaningful to note, in the Christian context, that there may not be those "traditions" and teachings which Paul says he "received" from the earliest followers of Jesus, and which is said to have formed an early creed passed down from the beginning of the Jesus movement, and which is held to form a deposit of faith vouchsafed throughout the ages.[45] But, then again, there may well be. Why should the high school pedagogy of religion assume that there is not? Again, an agenda seems at play: to decenter religions as a force that could speak a univocal truth.

The third premise echoes the earlier two. The AAR's instructional methodology asks teachers to see all religions as always "embedded in culture and *influenced by* culture."[46] Again, what concerns us is the impositional character of this pedagogy. Certainly, aspects of religions to varying degrees may be socially conditioned. But it is just not clear, for example, that the Qur'an was in fact influenced by itinerant Christian heretics, diasporaic Judaism, or the indigenous religiosity of Arabia.[47] This view may be an imposition on religious data. Why should such a controversial view be privileged, if not to advance the agenda that religion must be seen as a social effluence, and never a conduit of absolute truth?

A further problem at the heart of the AAR's Guidelines is the presence of troubling internal contradictions. The AAR defines the desideratum of reducing religious tensions as a justification for its pedagogical interventions. The AAR seeks to arrest "prejudice and antagonism [which] hinder efforts aimed at promoting respect for diversity, peaceful coexistence, and cooperative endeavors in local, national and global arenas."[48] Yet, the highlighting of diversity in religious life would necessarily call for highlighting, for example, Muslim adherents of a literal reading of the Verses of the Sword and certain hadiths, and Qur'anic and hadithic interpretations supporting Jihad[49]—however out of the mainstream these Muslim voices may now

45. See 1 Cor 11: 1–2: "I praise you for remembering me in everything and for holding to the traditions just as I passed them on to you"; and 1 Cor 15:3: "For what I received I passed on to you as of first importance" (NIV). As the Catechism of the Catholic Church maintains, "The apostles entrusted the 'Sacred deposit' of the faith (the *depositum fidei*), contained in Sacred Scripture and Tradition, to the whole of the Church" (45) and, therefore, "God graciously arranged that the things he had once revealed for the salvation of all peoples should remain in their entirety, throughout the ages, and be transmitted to all generations" (31), Vatican Archives, "Catechism of the Catholic Church."

46. Moore, "Teaching about the Bible in Public Schools," 76; emphasis in original.

47. See for example Andrae, *Muhammed: The Man and His Faith*.

48. Moore, "Teaching about the Bible in Public Schools," 64.

49. Qu'ran 9:5: "When the sacred months are over kill the idolaters wherever you find them. Arrest them, besiege them, and lie in ambush everywhere for them."

be—since, after all, on the AAR's Hericlitean view of religious flux, there scarcely seems to be any mainstream one can speak of. In order to respect its methodology that privileges the margins as much as the mainstream, these Qur'anic and Hadithic verses would have to be credited and explored in depth as fully Islamic statements—as statements neither to be discarded as marginalia nor dismissed as error. How could this sensibly be seen to promote interreligious solidarity? It would instead likely alienate young moderate Muslims, and deepen suspicions of Islam among young non-Muslims. (Let us not forget, it is young teenagers this curriculum is meant to speak to). Additionally, although the AAR is not to be criticized for pointing to genuine instances of change, social influence, and internal diversity in religious life, clear examples of these categories are often quite recharche. Agreed, there are small groups of Muslims in Berber tribes and in Northern Nigeria who see themselves as bound to pray fewer than five times a day, and there are statistically very marginal Muslim groups who reject hadiths altogether (such as followers of the Ahle Qu'ran movement and the Submitters in the United States).[50] Yet, one of the core premises of the AAR's

The Koran with Parallel Arabic Text (trans. Dawood). See also Surahs 2:193 and 9:29. Mushsin Khan, the translator of the noted Islamic thinker and compiler of hadith Muhammad al-Bukhari, states, for example, that the later surahs, which contain several so-called verses of the sword, were revealed to command Muslims to fight all pagans and People of the Book. See Muhammad al-Bukhari, *Sahih al-Bukhari*, xxiv–xxv. Each of the four main schools of Sunni jurisprudence has elements that have supported offensive religious warfare. Abi Zayd al-Qayrawani, a tenth-century jurist of the Malakite school stated that "we maintain that it is preferable not to begin hostilities with the enemy before having invited them to embrace the religion of Allah except where the enemy attacks first. They have the alternative of either converting to Islam or paying the poll tax, short of which war will be declared against them." Ibn Abi Zayd al-Qayrawani, *The Epistle*, 165. Eleventh-century Shafite scholar Abu'l Hasan al-Mawardi argued that it is forbidden to attack an infidel without invitation to join the faith of the Prophet, but "if they refuse to accept after this, war is waged against them." Abu'l Hasan al-Mawardi, *al-Ahkam as-Sultaniyyah*, 60. In the famous twelfth-century *Al-Hidayah* of the Hanifite scholar Burhan Uddin al-Farghani al-Marghinani, it is written that "if the infidels, upon receiving the call, neither consent to it nor agree to pay capitation tax, it is then incumbent on the Muslims to call upon God for assistance, and to make war upon them," 40. The fourteenth-century Hanbalite scholar Ibn Tamiyya spoke as follows: "[S]ince lawful warfare is essentially jihad and since its aim is that the religion is God's entirely and God's word is uppermost, therefore according to all Muslims, those who stand in the way of this aim must be fought," Peters, *Jihad in Classical and Modern Islam*, 49. Based on such a consensus among the madhabs, the great North African fourteenth-century Muslim thinker and chronicler Ibn Khaldun describes Islam as uniquely committed to warfare to advance the faith: "[T]he other religious groups did not have a universal mission, and the holy war was not a religious duty to them, save only for purposes of defense." Khaldun, *The Muqaddimah [Prolegomenon]: An Introduction to History*, 183.

50. See for example Uskel, *Manifesto for Islamic Reform*.

instructional intervention is the widespread ignorance of Americans about religion: a "fundamental premise[ ] is first [that] there exists a widespread illiteracy about religion in the United States."[51] But the AAR seems to wish students to race from religious ignoramuses to advanced students of the remotest forms of religious difference. Doesn't the premise of widespread religious ignorance mean that students should be taught first and foremost the basics of the Five Pillars, and the practice of five-daily prayer? The goal of streaking to the extremes risks seriously under-instructing students in the core of religious belief, allowing in turn that religious ignorance the AAR rightly bemoans to calcify and fester.

Growing Hostility in Educational and other Elite Circles

We suspect that the AAR's agenda is part of a larger trend. Our third argument that biblical instruction in public schools would harm biblical culture derives from the fact that the public education environment seems to be informed precisely by a rising hostility to traditional religion, and thus that the Bible risks being not merely museumified but taught in a way that reflects active hostility. This increasing hostility to traditional Judeo-Christian religion in public education can be found in several forms. First, it can take the shape of a desire to decenter, as we have seen. Second, it can take the form of a desire to critique the Bible for contributions to injustice. Third, it can take the form of what might be called a willful, that is, advocatory relativism of religious belief and unbelief. Fourth, religious hostility can be seen in the standardized tests newly adopted by educational elites. Fifth, we can see hostility stated at times quite explicitly in the theoretical work and public advocacy of a rising number of educational leaders. Sixth, vocal hostility to traditional religion has become commonplace in certain parts of the country, and has as a result entered explicitly into the local school board debates and decision making.

To be sure, as we have argued above, determining the motives of those in a policy environment with whom one disagrees can often be difficult. However, all our argument needs to establish, to counsel caution concerning biblical courses, is the real possibility of such views being maintained, and not the much higher standard which Audi's or Sajo's views concerning religious motives necessitate, since we are not arguing that the claims of the AAR be dismissed out of hand due to their violation of a discourse-controlling rule, such as Audi's rule that policy claims have a sufficient secular motivation. We are instead debating the AAR's contentions in a policy context,

---

51. Moore, "Teaching about the Bible in Public Schools," 64.

in which a large number of arguments can safely be advanced, including arguments about motives.

First, we see a cause for concern based on religious hostility in the AAR's Guidelines, since as we have noted, it privileges certain questions that have the effect of decentering traditional religiosity.

Second, the AAR's hostility to traditional religion becomes even more explicit in certain parts of its Guidelines. A major push of Diane Moore's curricular agenda for the public schools is her wish for courses "to engage the ways the Bible has been and *continues to be used* to promote and justify acts of cruelty and injustice such as slavery, colonization, and the oppression of marginalized communities in a variety of cultural, historical, and *contemporary* contexts."[52] So, a supposition of this prominent educational theorist at the heights of higher education is that the Bible is a force for contemporary injustice. She does not provide specifics, but perhaps one might suppose she means such things as Bible-based oppositions to the LGBTQIA agenda. Yet, to call opposition to this agenda unjust is to presuppose answers to highly contested questions in political and moral debate. It is, in other words, to assume that the Bible (in certain interpretive expressions) is wrong, and the text there to be buried. In the same spirit, educational theorist Carolyn Evans argues that religion should be addressed in public schools in a manner that highlights "the ways religions have undermined human rights, betrayed their own values or caused human suffering in both historical *and modern contexts*."[53] Evans demands that "the views of those who are critical of religion" be included in public school curricula.[54] Indeed, this idea of critiquing religious commitments as a part of public schooling is developed energetically by a growing chorus of educational theorists, including Paul Clarke, who argues strongly that critical assessments of religion—what he calls "religiously controversial" materials—need to be included in contemporary education.[55] For these reasons, opponents of biblical instruction have grounds for caution concerning the likely ways the Bible would be treated by scholars who harbor such hostile views of the Bible and its legacy.

Third, educational theory in the United States has seen a growth in what we call the willful, by which we mean advocatory, relativism of belief and the absence of belief. We can see this relativism of belief and unbelief

52. Moore, "Teaching about the Bible in Public Schools," 78; emphasis added.

53. Evans, "Religious Education in Public Schools: An International Human Rights Perspective," 471; emphasis added.

54. Ibid.

55. Clarke, "Religion, Public Education and the Charter: Where Do We Go Now?," 351–81. Similar trends are present in England as we demonstrate in chapter 7.

clearly in the work of the noted University of Wisconsin educational theorist Harry Brighouse, who argues that "autonomy facilitating" education should be provided in broad curricular areas within public schools. Brighouse suggests that this requirement should involve students in the study of a range of religious, non-religious, and anti-religious viewpoints, all seen on an equal footing. Students in elementary and secondary public schools should "be exposed to . . . the kinds of reasoning deployed within atheist views . . . and how [atheists] see the attitudes of [religious] proponents toward non-believers, heretics, and the secular world . . . and the diverse ways, including non-reason-based ways, in which . . . religious thinkers have dealt with moral conflict and religious disagreements, and with tensions in their own views."[56]

Views such as these are often advanced in the form of proposals for enhanced character education in schools. To instill in students the appropriate character for citizenship in a contemporary democracy, scholars such as Tianlong Yu and James Giarelli, for example, argue that "today we need to teach *about* religions, and teach about them *critically*."[57] Prominent educational theorist and activist Nell Noddings, currently the Lee Jacks Professor Emerita of Education at Stanford University and the John W. Porter Chair in Urban Education at Eastern Michigan University, develops this point in detail through a proposal she calls "educating for intelligent belief or unbelief." She asserts that educators need "to make religious belief [and unbelief] a subject on inquiry" as a means to enhance the character traits needed in a pluralist society.[58] On her model, "public education requires us to both appreciate and critique religion's role in defining morality, and to use religion as a reference, not an ultimate and dominant source; to engage students in moral reflection; and to encourage students to inquire and explore the ultimate, the sacred, and the existential meanings and purposes of life," including religious, non-religious, and anti-religious viewpoints seen on an equal basis.[59] Indeed, many now speak of affirming a decidedly non-religious sentiment under the label "spirituality." M. Clinton and G. Rossiter, for one, argue that the state must affirm the new "secular spirituality of the youth."[60]

---

56. Brighouse, *On Education*, 24.

57. Giarelli, foreword to *In the Name of Morality: Character Education and Political Control*; emphasis in the original.

58. Noddings, *Educating for Intelligent Belief or Unbelief*, ix.

59. Yu, *In the Name of Morality: Character Education and Political Control*, 125. See also Halford, "Longing for the Sacred in Schools: A Conversation with Nell Noddings," 28–32.

60. See Crawford and Rossiter, "The Secular Spirituality of Youth: Implications for Religious Education," 133–43.

Eamonn Callan—professor of Education at Stanford University—has long echoed this sentiment and has argued for it passionately. For Callan, the concern for autonomy over religious conviction is so pressing that he recommends *even in primary school* a pedagogy he concedes "casts a rather dark shadow" over traditional religious practices that have long formed an indispensable part of the religious life of parents, and thus are "prominent in the religious socialization of many children."[61] Specifically, he argues that the state must impose on such a perennial constituent of the religious life as the transmission of religious values to one's offspring practices that compel children "to participate in social settings where the 'correct' religious affiliation is not taken as settled," a setting that allows the child "some psychological distance between the self, qua centre of evaluation and choice, and any prior religious loyalties. For instance, the study of other religions might be encouraged, and not just as a means to greater tolerance and understanding. The purpose would rather be *to foster in the [young student] receptiveness to religious traditions other than those of his or her parents*, traditions that might well turn out to be more spiritually fulfilling than the latter. Similarly, atheism might be examined as a stance towards religion, which is commended by powerful philosophical arguments and which many people have taken without any sense that the choice made their lives less meaningful."[62] Educational theorist John Goodlad agrees, and implores schools to "liberate students from the ways of thinking imposed by religions and other traditions of thought."[63] The elites are reveling in the purported persuasive appeal of religious unbelief.

Fourth, further inferences to the effect that there is quite widespread hostility to religion among educational elites can be established by reference to the new AP European History exam the educational establishment has recently imposed. As the Bible itself holds, in Matthew 7:16: "you will know them by their fruits" (NASB). The new AP World History exam, as has been reported by a number of educational oversight organizations, embeds deep hostility to religion. The National Association of Scholars notes that "the test weds the exaggeration of modernization to a secularized definition of modernity. It does this by distorting and minimizing the role of religion throughout European history." These distortions include "the reduction of religion to an instrument of power and the elimination of religion's role to foster and shape economic modernity . . . These distortions redefine modernity around secularism by reducing the explanatory power of religion—and

61. Callan, "Justice and Denominational Schooling," 373.

62. Ibid., 374–75; emphasis added.

63. Goodlad, "Education and Community," 92.

even religion's mere presence."[64] Its treatments of religion represent in fact the test's "worst distortions."[65] These distortions, the Report argues, can only be ascribed to a willful secularism hostile to the historic contributions of religion to European culture and progress. Such is the stuff of the multi-cultural ethos that elite educators see as needful in modern public schools.

We readily concede that our arguments so far are based on inference, and some measure of conjecture as to the way curricula could be transformed over time. As we noted above, in policy debates this can be unavoidable, whereas it is highly problematic in preconditioning determinations related to the enjoyment of a constitutionally cherished value, viz. the value of political leaders and fellow citizens not dismissing one's policy positions *tout court*.

Fifth, in addition to inferences and predictions of religious hostility, we should note that several prominent educational theorists have clearly stated how *positively* hostile they are to traditional religious faith.[66] Their influence—again especially in schools of education—is not insignificant. Historically, John Dewey, "the father of progressive education," whose work *Democracy and Education* remains a staple in schools of education, was a strong secularist whose shadow remains prodigious. As Gearon notes, "philosophies adversarial to religion have become integral to teaching about it."[67] As a result, the work of those promoting "the secular life," such as Sociology professor Phil Zuckerman[68] and, even more forcefully, Peter Boghossian—former Research Fellow of the National Center for Teaching and Learning, philosopher of Education at Portland State University, and

---

64. Randall, "The Disappearing Continent: A Critique of the Revised Advanced Placement European History Examination," 13.

65. Ibid., 37.

66. Although advocating for conciliation between religious scholars and those advancing secularism, Noddings herself states that she "believes religion has outlived its usefulness and does more harm than good" and her essay "Understanding Unbelief as Part of Religious Education" is mostly a brief for atheism and "intellectual objections to religion" and "moral objections to religion." Nodding, "Understanding Unbelief as Part of Religious Education," 19–33. See also Nodding, "Public Schooling, Democracy, and Religious Dissent." See also Jeynes, "Are America's Public Educational Institutions Anti-Religious?," 172–75.

67. Gearon, *On Holy Ground*, 41.

68. A serious sociologist whose research is not to be dismissed, Zuckerman's work from time to time does bleed into atheist advocacy. See Zuckerman's *Living the Secular Life*, which far from simply chronicling secularists in the United States ends by avowing his intent to "ameliorate" their position in contemporary public life.

author of the work *A Manual for Creating Atheists*[69]—continue to acquire further influence on American public schools.

Indeed, educational secularity is taking place within a wider context of rising hostility to religion in the broader professoriate and policy advocacy worlds and across academic areas.[70] As Trigg recently notes, the trend in contemporary social, legal, political, and educational thought sees contemporary thinkers now coming to reject the neutrality that liberalism at least purported to represent in the 1970s through the 1990s. This trend goes against older ideas of liberalism—such as that of John Rawls—that held liberal theory not as a substantive doctrine but as a procedural one. Instead, many thinkers now see religion as intrinsically intolerant and opposed to the ideas of a liberal society and, thus, as a view meriting rejection and disavowal as a substantive vision of the human good.[71] This growing movement has and will continue (in the near future) to have a significant influence on social institutions, including public schools.

Such stridently secular social theorists include David A.J. Richard of NYU Law School, whose works include the clamorous polemic *Fundamentalism in American Religion and Law: Obama's Challenge to Patriarchy's Threat to Democracy*.[72] The recent work of Jason Bivins echoes Richard's charge. In his work, *The Religion of Fear: The Politics of Horror in Conservative Evangelicalism*, he rallies like a secular Saint Bernard of Clairvaux a social crusade against conservative evangelicals: "If academics and citizens alike will not name and criticize this demonology [traditional or conservative evangelicalism] with the clarity that is our moral and political responsibility, then we have failed to respond not only to fear's challenge but to the crisis of legitimation in American political life."[73] Equally acerbic is the work of University of Chicago Law Professor (and part-time Nietzsche devotee) Brian Leiter.[74] In his work, *Why Tolerate Religion?*, Leiter finds that "there is no apparent moral reason why states should carve out special protections

69. Boghossian, *A Manual for Creating Atheists.*

70. For the broadening culture of religious hostility, see Garry, "The Cultural Hostility to Religion," 121–31.

71. Lecture to the Institute for Religion, Politics and Politics, June 27, 2016 at Oriel College. On file with the authors. For an assessment of the hostility in contemporary political thought to religion, see also the important work of Legutko, *The Demon in Democracy: Totalitarian Temptations in Free Societies*, 145–75.

72. Richard, *Fundamentalism in American Religion and Law: Obama's Challenge to Patriarchy's Threat to Democracy.*

73. Bivins, *Religion of Fear*, 234.

74. Leiter indulges his interests in "Thinking Out Loud about Nietzsche's Philosophy," and exploring Nietzsche as a moral guide for modern life.

that encourage individuals to structure their lives around categorical demands that are insulated from the standards of evidence and reasoning we
everywhere else expect to constitute constraints on judgment and action,"[75]
by which, of course, he means religion. Leiter finds religion "a phenomenon
characterized by insulation from common sense and the sciences."[76] Michael McConnell rightly finds these expressions "disquieting."[77] However,
a fairly considerable range of contemporary legal scholarship does not,
including the writings of Suzanna Sherry, which describe religion as "su-
perstitious, primitive, anti-rational beliefs that no enlightened, reasoning
person today would accept,"[78] as well as that of Micah Schwartzman, which,
though less acerbically than Leiter or Sherry, still marginalizes religion by
advancing straightforwardly analogies between religious adherence and
mental insanity.[79] Lastly, this trend has found perhaps its most provocative
crescendo in the recent work of law professor Yossi Netushtan in a remarkable new book titled *Intolerant Religion in a Tolerant Liberal Democracy*. In
this work, professor Netushatan argues that "there are meaningful, unique
links between religion and intolerance, and between holding religious beliefs and holding intolerant views (and ultimately acting upon these views)."
As such, "religion, on the whole, should not be tolerated in a tolerant-liberal
democracy."[80] This from the director of a major university's program in
"Human Rights, Globalization and Justice"![81]

75. Leiter, *Why Tolerate Religion?*, 63.

76. McConnell, Review of *Why Tolerate Religion?*, 81.

77. Ibid.

78. Paulson, "God is Great, Garvey is Good: Making Sense of Religious Freedom,"
1597–1626, summarizing Sherry's position in her works such as "The Sleep of Reason,"
453–84, and "Enlightening the Religion Clauses." Importantly, Professor Sherry simultaneously seeks to influence education debates to advance "republican citizenship,"
which underscores our concern about how state religious education could take shape
given the expressly anti-religious views of many educational advocates. See Sherry, "Responsible Republicanism: Educating for Citizenship," 131–208.

79. Schwartzmann, "What if Religion is Not Special?," 1383. Michael Garvey—president of the Catholic University of America—famously developed the analogy between
insanity and religion but his purpose was not to credit it as a plausible account of religion but simply to use it as a model guiding discourse. Schwartzman, however, enter-
tains the analogy on substantive grounds, which Garvey never intended. See Garvey,
"Free Exercise and the Values of Religious Liberty," 779–802. To be sure, Schwartzman
points out that the crediting of religion as insane would be an odd way to defend religious protections, but that does not change his willingness to embrace the substantive
analogy, which religious believers are right to find troubling.

80. Netushtan, *Intolerant Religion in a Tolerant Liberal Democracy*.

81. Nehushtan's argument is easily dismissed, and we present it only to indicate
the growing depth of hostility to religion by members of the liberal intellectual class.

A further aspect of explicitly stated hostility to religion has received less notice than it merits, and that is the rise of what we call a "reinvigorated secularization thesis." What we detect across the literature on religion and society is a view held by a growing number of intellectual elites that religion's demise, although still (putatively) inevitable, has taken longer than anticipated, and that religion must be contained and "managed" between now and its inexorable though delayed demise. Sajo's fears of "strong religion" seem to fit this bill. We suspect this conception will continue to influence educational and policy elites in the decades ahead.

Our point is that educational elites such as those named above exert real influence on educational policy—especially as formulated in schools of education—and that their proposals concerning the need for a critical assessment of religion in public education, or their explicit repudiation of religion as such, give grounds for worry about how their influence would shape the development of curricula on biblical instruction, especially should Bible courses come to be taught on a broad scale.

Lastly, in addition to the arguments developed above, we should point out that hostility can be voiced not merely by educational elites but through the local-level decision making that predominantly defines the process of educational policy setting. Given the power of local school boards, it is critical to note that American religious adherence is sharply divided geographically, a point ably documented by Mark Silk and Andrew Walsh in their work *One Nation, Divisible*.[82] A recent example of how regional differences in levels of religiosity can play out in the context of public schooling can be seen in the Pacific Northwest. One well-documented case took place just

The author bases his contention that religion should not be tolerated on a scattering of tissue-thin empirical research indicating that religious individuals do not energetically support "civil rights" as much as non-religious individuals, and thus that the religious are systematically more prejudiced than the non-religious. For Nehushtan, civil rights mean such things as abortion on demand for females of all ages, absolute rights to marriage for homosexuals, and state-funded surgeries for transgenders, which confers on his contention a conspicuous circularity. Were civil rights defined to include support for religious freedom, his work would draw a far different conclusion. Moreover, bits of evidence can be showcased to suggest all sorts of prejudices for all sorts of reasons. Lesbians, for example exhibit, one study indicates, greater prejudice against attractive women than do heterosexual women; by his logic, therefore, lesbians should not be tolerated to exercise any public function of trust that might put them in contact with the general public, a non-negligible percentage of whom will likely be attractive women. This is ridiculous, of course. But to Dr. Nehushtan we might say: welcome to your principles. See Buunk and Dijkstra, "Evidence from a Homosexual Sample for a Sex-Specific Rival-Oriented Mechanism: Jealousy as a Function of a Rival's Physical Attractiveness and Dominance."

82. Silk and Walsh, *One Nation, Divisible: How Regional Religious Differences Shape American Politics*.

north of Seattle in British Columbia, with many parents agitating to see instructional materials incorporated in a public school's curriculum with the goal of creating "dissonance" in the minds of children so to foment a critical distance from religion. As the leaders of this popular groundswell maintained: "dissonance is neither avoidable nor noxious," but something "that is part of living in a diverse society," and so should be affirmed both for religious and non-religious students alike.[83] How would notoriously irreligious western Oregonians, for example, treat the Bible in *their* public schools should conservatives in Eastern Oregon succeed in adopting statewide reforms? Such actual or anticipated articulations of bias against religion would also likely occur in regions less uniformly liberal than the Pacific Northwest or the Northeastern Seaboard.

Lack of Teacher Training

Even when there is no overt hostility being voiced against traditional religion, there is an instructional lacuna in most teacher preparation programs and in teachers' career developments, which leads to our next argument. The Bible is likely to be taught poorly simply due to the lack of any training in religion, even at the most basic level, in most teacher training programs. The AAR notes this striking lack of teacher training in religious matters. Based on its research in this area, the AAR asserts without qualification that "most educators lack the training . . . to provide the appropriate information about religion relevant to the texts that are studied."[84] Indeed, the data supporting this conclusion is partly drawn from teachers' own self-assessments. A 2005 survey of teachers conducted by the Harvard Divinity School found that "teachers report that they lack the knowledge base . . . to address the historical complexities of religion adequately."[85] Further survey data discloses that it is "not uncommon for educators to hold erroneous beliefs about the legality of using the Bible and Bible literature in public schools," assuming falsely that the Bible is strictly off limits—a conclusion unthinkable were the Bible taught with any regularity in teacher preparation programs.[86] In this con-

83. Collins, "Culture, Religion, and Curriculum: Lessons from the 'Three Books' Controversy in Surrey, BC," 353. In England, the great foe of organized religion, Richard Dawkins, has recently advocated for greater exposure to the Bible in state schools as a means of discrediting it in the eyes of schoolchildren. See Schapiro, "Atheist Richard Dawkins Supports Bibles in Schools."

84. Moore, "Teaching about the Bible in Public Schools," 72.

85. Ibid., 71. See also Harvard Divinity School Study, "About Religion in the Schools" and "Religious Literacy Project."

86. Wachlin, "What Do High School Teachers Think Students Need to Know

text it is important to note that only the Texas statute specifically earmarks funds for teacher training in Bible courses. And although states like Georgia and Tennessee allow school districts to allocate educational resources to curricular development and teacher preparation for Bible courses, they do not mandate the allocation of funds for such training, and pressing needs in other areas make it unlikely (and imprudent) that these courses would get sustained financial investments. In fact, one state, South Carolina, positively prohibits use of state educational dollars to fund curricular development and teacher training in Bible courses, in part to ensure that no resources are drained from other areas of the curriculum deemed to be much more in need of fiscal and programmatic attention. These funding shortfalls mean that teacher preparation and monitoring of Bible courses are likely to be questionable.

This clear lacuna in teacher preparation is we suspect itself expressive—in part at least—of a subtle anti-religious hostility. That departments of education do not teach traditional religion very much at all is a fact due in part to the influence of the secularizing educational elites referenced above. Further, an anti-religious bias can be sensed to some degree in the "liberatory" pedagogy that has become normalized in educational theory and teacher career development. This pedagogy of liberation betrays a tendency toward sustained critique of traditional religiosity, and also constitutes a kind of a replacement for traditional spirituality, a point documented by Susan Hansen in her survey of "the secular political challenge" to America's traditional religious life.[87] In any case, the pedagogy of liberation, even if not construed as religiously hostile, does have the effect of crowding out studies of religious traditions in teacher formation programs. Indeed, a pedagogy of liberation and of vaguely defined "democratic praxis" consumes much of the intellectual oxygen for issues outside the basic forms of instructional aptitudes in graduate and undergraduate education programs. As Alison Dover points out in her work "Teaching for Social Justice and the Common Core: Justice-Oriented Curriculum for Language Arts and Literacy," many public school teachers now face an "imperative to apply justice-oriented approaches."[88] This is so in part because the National Council of Teachers of English (NCTE) recently adopted new standards for the initial preparation of secondary English teachers that "prioritize candidates' social

---

about the Bible?," 16.

87. Hansen, *Religion and Reaction*, 96–109.

88. Dover, "Teaching for Social Justice and the Common Core: Justice-Oriented Curriculum for Language Arts and Literacy," 517–27.

justice orientations and skill sets."[89] Standard VI, for example, requires candidates to "demonstrate knowledge of how theories and research about social justice, diversity, equity, student identities, and schools as institutions can enhance students' opportunities to learn in Language Arts."[90] As the NCTE report states, "in addition to this knowledge, candidates are expected to plan and implement English language arts and literacy instruction that promotes social justice and critical engagement with complex issues related to maintaining a diverse, inclusive, equitable society."[91] Mastering religious traditions risks in turn falling by the wayside.

It is important that we appreciate how these arguments conjoin to form serious causes for concern. This worrisome conjunction can be stated as follows: increasing numbers of younger teachers have little knowledge or interest in religion, and face an ambient culture of increasing hostility to traditional religiosity; the lack of disciplinary training means that the ambient forces have a greater possibility of infecting their pedagogy. In all, teachers are coming into the profession with less biblical knowledge, due to rising secularity among the teaching corps, and to some real extent are exposed to positive hostility during their formative career instruction.

Current Problems and Ockham's Razor

We lastly draw attention to an aphorism famously ascribed to medieval theologian William of Ockham: *Non sunt multiplicanda entia sine necessitate*—entities should not be multiplied beyond necessity. All responsible courses in literature and world history will necessarily have to address, at least to some extent, the Bible. This is a component of any respectable American and world history course, and of intellectually honest courses in a range of English and literary fields. But herein lies a real potential for problems: namely, biased readings of the Bible in these "ordinary" courses given all the issues we have itemized above. In the inevitable references to religion in ordinary classes, for the reasons stated we should not be surprised that empirical cases can be pointed to suggesting reasons for concern in the "regular" curriculum. These concerns would only be amplified all the more in courses with sustained attention to the Bible. We shall explore

89. Miller, "Cultivating a Disposition for Sociospatial Justice in English Teacher Preparation," 44–74.

90. National Council of Teachers of English, "Beliefs about Social Justice in English Education."

91. Ibid. See also Education for Liberation Network's EdLib Lab database.

briefly several problematic cases in the United States[92] addressing religion, and we shall then ask, in turn, why problems, like entities, should ever be multiplied beyond necessity.

First, in La Plata Maryland, sworn testimony indicates that a public high school teacher reiterated to her class as a fact the dubious contention stated in the school textbook that "[m]ost Muslims' faith is stronger than the average Christian."[93] This was part of a section on World History where, again according to sworn affidavits, the class spent two weeks on Islam and only one day studying Christianity.[94] Secondly, a list of problematic curricula in the public schools has been documented by the Institute for Jewish and Community Research. In its report, published with Rowman and Littlefield titled *Trouble with the Textbooks: Distorting History and Religion,* the Institute finds classrooms across the country mischaracterizing Christian and Jewish religion, for example by claiming that "Christianity was founded by a young Palestinian named Jesus," a point likely to cause confusion among schoolchildren since Palestine was not a term widely in use during the life of Jesus.[95] A further set of examples comes from Florida where public monitoring of religious instruction has been extensively conducted. Caution must be exercised in assessing claims of bias, as private watchdog organizations can often have biases of their own, a point made by scholars such as David Brockman of the Brite Divinity School at Texas Christian University.[96] Nevertheless, errors, ambiguities, mischaracterizations, and distortions such as the statements from textbooks and lesson plans detailed below have been documented in the Florida public schools. And we know that lesson plans and texts have an outsized influence on in-class instruction, as Tobin and Ybarra document: "School teachers and school administrators . . . count[ ] on—and, more significantly, trust" the texts and supplementary lesson plans textbook publishers provide. This is especially so "in sensitive and complex subjects."[97] Hence, problems with religion in textbooks have significant

---

92. For examples in the United Kingdom, see chapters 7 and 8, and especially our discussion of the work of Barnes, "The Misrepresentation of Religion in Modern British (Religious) Education, 395–411.

93. Complaint at ¶ 6, *Wood v Charles County School District,* (USDC D. Md., No 8:16-cv-00239-GJH) (Filed 27 January, 2016). See also the important earlier work of Vitz, *Censorship.*

94. Complaint at ¶ 6, *Wood v Charles County School District,* (USDC D. Md., No 8:16-cv-00239-GJH) (Filed 27 January, 2016).

95. Tobin and Ybarra, *Trouble with Textbooks: Distorting History and Religion.*

96. See Brockman, "Expert Details Importance of Teaching Religion in Public Schools."

97. Tobin and Ybarra, *Trouble with Textbooks,* 21–22.

impact. Note well, our argument here does not automatically presume the truth of the Bible nor presuppose its falsity. Rather, our point is that these statements are either inaccurate records of what the overwhelming number of Christians or Jews have and continue to believe, or are heavily and unfairly biased in a direction opposed to orthodox faith. Examples include the following :

- "During the era of Roman control, a Jewish man named Jesus . . . taught that faith and love were more important than Judaism's many laws."[98] This is highly questionable given Matthew 5:20: "For I tell you that unless your righteousness surpasses that of the Pharisees and the teachers of the law, you will certainly not enter the kingdom of heaven" (NIV).

- "[Jesus] was essentially a rabbi, or teacher, and offended . . . by the perfunctory nature of mainstream Jewish religious practices in his time, he prescribed a return to the personal faith and spirituality of an earlier age."[99] This too is highly questionable, not least in reference to John 10:30: "I and the Father are one" (NIV), a statement foreign to rabbinical thought and for which no documented example of rabbinical usage has been detected, nor any usage in the "earlier age" of Moses, the Judges, or the Prophets.

- "Judaism is a story of exile."[100] This statement is so ambiguous as to merely sow seeds of confusion.

- "Many scholars today doubt that the early books of the Hebrew Bible reflect the true history of the early Israelites. They argue that the early books of the Bible, written centuries after the events described, preserve only what the Israelites came to believe about themselves and that recent archaeological evidence often contradicts the details of the biblical accounts."[101] This is an unbalanced statement that neglects archaeological evidence for the Torah discovered through professional studies of the relevant areas.[102]

98. Korach and Saxton, "Corrections to Islam-biased Content in Florida's K-12 Textbooks."

99. Ibid., 28.

100. Ibid., 34.

101. Ibid., 63.

102. See for example the work of Kenneth Kitchen, emeritus professor at the University of Liverpool, including *On the Reliability of the Old Testament*, and Keith N. Schoville, Professor Emeritus at the University of Wisconsin-Madison, including *Biblical Archaeology in Focus*.

- "A few loyal followers of Jesus spread the story that Jesus had overcome death . . . and then ascended into heaven . . . "[103] This leaves undefined what is meant by "a few" and seems as a result to contradict Corinthians 15:6 that notes over 500 witnesses to the resurrection.

- "According to Jewish conception, there is but one God, called Yahweh, who is the creator of the world and everything in it. The Jewish God ruled the world; he was subject to nothing. All people were his servants, whether they knew it or not."[104] The use of the preterit ("ruled" and "was") vividly evidences what we call "museumification"; moreover the passage neglects such biblical declarations of the nature of God as Psalm 11:7: "For the Lord is righteous, he loves justice" (NIV), and replaces them with a divine capriciousness (being "subject to nothing") foreign to the Jewish tradition.

These problems flow from textbooks, textbook-provided lesson plans, and sworn affidavits about classroom instruction. As to the first two, no doubt the hope of curricular reform advocates is that textbooks in Bible courses would not exhibit so many mistakes or ambiguities. Yet, the existence of numerous mistakes and miscommunications in standard history textbooks today fails to bode particularly well for the long-term future of Bible courses. As Tobin and Ybarra document, textbook publishers rarely start out with an intention to offend purchasers (that is, democratically accountable school districts); instead, the process of revising and adapting new editions allows for intrusions of bias and ill-framed communications over the long haul of the production cycle. Hence, problems such as these would likely corrupt the courses on the Bible in the public school system. Why, then, would we multiply the problems? Indeed, true to Ockham's aphorism, problems, like entities, should not be multiplied beyond necessity.

103. Korach and Saxton, "Corrections to Islam-based Content," 66.
104. Ibid., 65.

Chapter 6 ————————————————————

Securitizing American Public Education in the Age of Multiculturalism

AN ADDITIONAL SET OF problems confronting the proposal to mandate greater attention to the Bible in public schools arises in relation to what Gearon has labelled the process of educational securitization. Gearon's work has made substantial strides in this area of research.[1] A major issue in this regard relates to the extremist expression of Islamic faith, and the response by governments in the form of their attempting to define as "genuine" one (widely embraced) expression of Islam—the view that Islam is intrinsically irenic—while branding any other version of the Islamic faith fallacious, all for the purpose of religious instruction serving state security interests. Our fear is that this securitizing tendency is deeply rooted, and will over time shade into state efforts to define whatever version of Christianity it might prefer as "genuine," and all others, false.

Over the last decade, a core element of the response of many political leaders in the West to Islamic radicalism has been what the former senior state department official, former dean of the Woodrow Wilson School of Public Policy at Princeton University, and current president of the New America Foundation, Anne-Marie Slaughter, has called the "the moderate Islam project."[2] As described by Slaughter and also by Cheryl Benard, director of the RAND Initiative for Middle Eastern Youth, "over the past de-

---

1. See Gearon, "The Counter Terrorist Classroom: Religion, Education, and Security," 129–47; and Gearon, "The Counter Terrorist Classroom: Countering Extremism through (Religious) Education?,"

2. See Benard, "'Moderate Islam' Isn't Working."

cade, the prevailing thinking has been that radical Islam is most effectively countered by moderate Islam. The goal was to find religious leaders and scholars and community 'influencers'—to use the lingo of the counter-radicalization specialists—who could explain to their followers and to any misguided young people that Islam is a religion of peace, that the term jihad refers mainly to the individual's personal struggle against temptation and for moral betterment, and that tolerance and interfaith cooperation should prevail."[3] Indeed, this was to be done by moderate Muslims themselves: "The task . . . was to help moderate Muslims spread the word."[4] Yet the stakes are so high—and the failure of the Moderate Islam project up to this point so conspicuous, she asserts—that the project must no longer be left to the Islamic community itself to raise up a corps of moderate Muslim influence makers. Hence, Bernard advocates the astounding proposal that in the United States, government must:

> establish a vetting and a certification process for Muslim clerics as a requirement before someone can head a mosque, run a religious education or a youth program, officiate at religious ceremonies, or term himself an imam. This will raise the quality of religious information and instruction being offered to the community, and bring greater transparency. There are precedents for this. In Austria, for example, after many disturbing experiences with Islamic religion teachers and complaints from parents, the government decided to set up its own theological certification program. In Bosnia and many other Muslim-majority countries, training of imams is overseen by the government, and in many places, Friday sermons are either vetted or centrally provided to all mosques to guarantee correct substance.[5]

Note the state's control of religious leaders to "guarantee correct substance." Ms. Benard—an influential analyst in a senior position at an influential research organization—advocates prior restraint of religious speech of American faith leaders by the government. This indicates the depth of the securitizing tendency of American leaders regarding Islam in the United States. Such a perspective is not unique to RAND; in varying degrees, it permeates American thinking. Elizabeth Shakman Hurd has done exceptional work documenting the control of religion by state officials in her book *Beyond Religious Freedom: The New Global Politics of Religion.*[6] She documents

3. Ibid.

4. Ibid.

5. Ibid.

6. Hurd, *Beyond Religious Freedom: The New Global Politics of Religion.* See also

the strongly interventionist strategy of state officials regarding religious leaders: "Policymakers seek out representatives of moderate religion to create peaceable partnerships, while co-opting or sidelining their rivals."[7] Noting how this has been especially (but not exclusively) true regarding Islam, she records how "good" forms of Islam are "celebrated as sources of morality, community and discipline, while 'bad' ones are criticized as the root of all global instability and insecurity . . . [and thus] Islam is seen as an agent that . . . needs careful management."[8] If Muslim leaders in America—despite First Amendment protections—can be inspected by a state inquisition, how much more can America's teachers, who generally enjoy far fewer First Amendment protections than do private religious leaders?

Yet, it might still be argued that this Austrian model of ministerial vetting by government bureaucrats remains unlikely in the United States. Perhaps this is so. Yet as noted, teachers in public schools are afforded much less explicit protections under American constitutional law than are religious leaders[9]; so what might not develop with respect to faith leaders might well develop with respect to educators in public institutions. Further, the very profundity of the failure of the Moderate Islam project, which not only Benard but also Anne Marie Slaughter and many others point to, creates its own gravitational effect in this direction. As Benard argues, "with a track record of well over a decade, it does not seem as though this is working."[10] The project of *encouraging* Muslim leaders in the United States to articulate a moderate message has not been an outstanding success, they bemoan. "Even granted that an undertaking of this magnitude . . . takes time, it's unfortunately more than just a matter of progress being slow. Incontrovertibly, things are getting worse. We now have ISIS, a magnification of Al Qaeda. We have vicious branches springing up in nearly every part of the world. We have thousands of radical recruits streaming into Syria from Europe and the United States. We have Paris. We have San Bernardino."[11] Hence, much bolder methods are necessary. In light of the depth of the problem of Muslim extremism, the measures Benard advocates—to inquisitorially monitor and to vet religious speech—will likely only become more persuasive to many over time. And indeed, the election to the presidency

Ali, "A Problem From Heaven: Why the United States Should Back Islam's Reformation."

7. Hurd, "How International Relations Got Religion, and Got It Wrong."

8. Ibid.

9 See *Garcetti v. Ceballos*, 547 U.S. 410 (2006) for a recent case defining the limitations that can properly be placed on public school teachers and other public employees.

10. Benard, "'Moderate Islam' Isn't Working."

11. Ibid. See also Adamson, "Islam in Europe: The Challenge of Institutionalization."

of Donald Trump, whose campaign underscored suspicions about some Islamic leaders, might make this approach even more of a possibility.

Indeed, the confluence of the American left and right on this issue will make such calls potentially harder to resist. Benard and Slaughter represent the political left, however the political right has many elements within it likely to find this course attractive, threatening in turn a bipartisan coalition for more state religious inspection. The right has a conjunction of two forces that, when pulled together, would likely add additional support to the project of actively intervening in the life of the Islamic faith in the United States. Namely, many on the right in American public life see Islam as what we might call congenitally suspect to extremist movements. They assert that a susceptibility to violent extremism is inherent in Islam's founding documents, the Qur'an and the hadith. Hence, the prominent conservative Catholic writer, professor and priest James V. Schall, S.J. argues in his widely circulated essay "Realism and Islam" that:

> [when] we recall [ ] recent events from '9/11', the bombings in Spain, England, Mumbai, Bali, Fort Hood, San Bernardino, twice in Paris, Lahore, and Brussels, not to mention the persecutions and beheadings in Pakistan, Iraq, Yemen, Nigeria, Libya, Somalia, Chad, Syria, and the Sunni/Shiite inner-Muslim battles, what is the most plausible way to judge such continuing violence and its origins? To make this assessment, we have to acknowledge that Islam, in principle, is actually and potentially violent . . . [because] the designated and determined goal of the conquest of the world for Allah has been reinvigorated again and again in world history from the time of Mohammed in the seventh century. These revivals and expansions, which have only been temporarily halted by superior counterforce, have roots in the Qur'an itself . . ."[12]

As further proof of this deeply rooted conviction among many conservatives, the prominent columnist Andrew McCarthy—writing in the influential conservative publication *The National Review*—asserts that the problem with Islamic extremism resides in Islam's "aggressive scripture." "Islam . . . is not a religion of peace. It is a religion of conquest that was spread by the sword. Moreover, it is not only untrue that jihad refers 'mainly' to the individual's internal struggle to live morally; it is also untrue that the Islamic ideal of the moral life is indistinguishable from the Western conception." These problems flow from the text of Islamic sacred books themselves. "Alas, the[se] are direct consequences of Islamic scripture and sharia, the

12. Schall, "Realism and Islam."

law derived from scripture." Many "want[ ] Islam to be moderate, but its scriptures won't cooperate."[13] Further, a Trump administration's selection for National Security advisor, Lieutenant General (Ret.) Michael Flynn, has said such statements as that Islam itself is a "political ideology" pretending to be a religion.[14]

Moreover, many influential conservatives endorse the possibility of successful advocacy for a moderate Islamic viewpoint—they just see the enterprise of ensuring that moderate voices become more authoritative as a much more difficult task than even Benard and others suppose. McCarthy argues that "Islam could conceivably become peaceful. Nor is it to say that jihad could not be reinterpreted such that a decisive majority of Muslims would accept that its actual primary meaning—namely, holy war to establish Islam's dominance—has been superseded by the quest for personal betterment." Yet, his point and that of many other conservatives is that "to pull th[is] off . . . will require a huge fight." Indeed, they argue, it will require a redoubling of the systematic intervention in the life of a world religion which Benard and Slaughter advocate.[15]

Due to this confluence of conservative and liberal advocacy, a broad coalition supporting the active regulation in the United States of one of the world's major religions appears potentially in the offing.

What makes this development so troubling for the proposal to teach the Jewish and Christian Bible in public schools is that a drive of this nature will not, given human nature and real world political pressures, remain constrained to the interventionist inspection of Islamic instruction. First, habits can develop and calcify, and institutional inertia take over. Once the government, in order to serve its own interests, has started to intervene to define aspects of one religion, it is hard to stop that practice, as practices over time can ossify. Moreover, not only inertia but an active will to control should never be underestimated. Did not the famed Publius assert, wisely, "power is of an encroaching nature"?[16]

Additionally, contemporary political dynamics give little cause to conclude that state regulation of religion will stop at the inspection of Islamic teachings. For one thing, many in the liberal side of the interventional collation will demand parity—or at least rough parity—between Islam and Christianity. Indeed, the national leadership of the Democratic Party and

13. McCarthy, "The Problem with Islam Is Aggressive Scripture, Not Aggressive 'Traditionalism.'"

14. Ibid.

15. Ibid.

16. See Madison's *Federalist* no. 48.

the leadership among many cultural elites more generally has made it clear
that it will not tolerate any *singling out* of Islam. This leveling requires both
that Islam be seen as at least as peaceful as Christianity, and that Christianity be seen as at least as equally prone to violence as Islam. As Hurd, whom
we referenced earlier, states: "Islam is seen as an agent that—*like other religions*, only more so—needs careful management."[17] Note the telling phrase:
"like other religions."

    Evidence of this equalizing tendency is actually commonplace.[18] Pro-
fessor Schall himself has long pointed it out. He has maintained firstly that
"unless we understand the content and history of religions—their truth
claims and aberrations—we will be unable to see the actual forces that swirl
through the political world. An education that lacks a proper and accurate
study of the theology and theologies peculiar to each different religion is
not really an education. It could not prepare anyone to deal with a world in
which religions, in their differences, are a reality." Secondly he documents
just how little this has been the case given the overarching trend among
Western elites to "lump . . . all religions together." As a result, Schall notes,
"in America in the last half century or longer, this sanitized education is
what decades of students have been given"—a sanitized, state-directed education in which religious difference is "everywhere forbidden and excluded
from any consideration."[19] The result, Schall argues, is that in contemporary
society *all* religions are now "defanged and wholly subject to state power."[20]

    17. Hurd, "How International Relations Got Religion"; emphasis added.

    18. One mechanism to equalize is to deemphasize Islam and heighten attention to
actual or perceived problems in Christian thought and history. To this end, Tobin and
Ybarra argue that "Islam enjoys a privileged position . . . it is not criticized or qualified,
whereas Judaism and Christianity are." Tobin and Ybarra, *The Trouble with Textbooks*,
78. Take this example from a Florida textbook: "'Beginning in the 1000s, western European armies fought the Crusades—a series of brutal religious wars—to win Palestine,
the birthplace of Christianity, from Muslim rule,' in a textbook without a single negative
adjective describing any period of Islamic expansion." Korach and Saxton, "Corrections
to Islam-based Content," addendum, 3, and 57.

    19. This trend has long been detected in English religious education. Barnes notes,
"By challenging notions of religious uniqueness and an exclusive attitude to religious
truth, religious educators in Britain believe themselves to be challenging the roots
of religious intolerance and prejudice, and contributing positively to the social aims
of education. Pursuit of the thesis of the essential unity of the religions has been a
defining characteristic of British education over the last four decades, and a string of
methodologies and approaches have been employed by religious educators in its service." Barnes, "Michael Hand, 'Is Religious Education Possible?,'" 69. See also Gearon,
"Counter-Terrorist Classroom."

    20. Schall, "Realism and Islam." An example from Florida textbooks illustrate this
point: "Another duty is jihad, or struggle in God's service. Jihad is usually a personal
duty for Muslims, who focus on overcoming immorality within themselves. At other

Moreover, such a trend has only become more acute in the last two decades. For example, President Obama's administration famously banned State Department officials from even referring to Islamic extremism, requiring the locution "violent extremism" instead.[21] It also made significant investments in preventing domestic (by which it means non-Islamic) terrorism through surveillance and prosecution at the same time that it has maintained heightened attention to the Islamist threat.[22] President Obama's rhetoric underscored the intentionality of this effort to create parity between Islam and the other religions of the world. In this regard, one should further note how at the National Prayer Breakfast on February 5, 2016, President Obama famously counseled what Raymond Ibrahim characterized as "non-judgmental relativism."[23] The president scolded Christians, and admonished them to "get off their high horse" and see how often Christianity has been used to support oppression—clearly betraying a desire to avoid singling Islam out.

To be sure, the Trump administration might appear to be a brake on this development. Indeed, former National Security Advisor Michael Flynn, whom we quoted above, has stated that he believes that not all cultures are "morally equivalent," by which he means to isolate Islam as particularly problematic.[24] Yet, no one can or will operate in a political vacuum. In fact, the forces of the political left have already begun to redouble their efforts in light of their 2016 defeat.[25] This view therefore will meet opposition from many and be watered down, filtered, or appropriated in all sorts of unpredictable ways.

---

times, jihad may be interpreted as holy war to defend Islam and the Muslim community, much like the Crusades to defend Christianity." Korach and Saxton, "Corrections to Islam-Based Content," 58. This statement lacks historical nuance, and can create confusion concerning the study of Islamic expansion.

21. President Obama's administration insisted that in all its work it "does not advocate on behalf of any particular set of religious beliefs, or express a preference for one faith over another—or even for religious belief over non-belief," a point forcefully made by Secretary of State John Kerry, who went on to say "religion is part of what drives some to initiate war, others to pursue peace; some to organize for change, others to cling desperately to old ways and resist modernity; some to reach eagerly across the borders of nation and creed, and others to build higher and higher walls separating one group from the next." Kerry, "Address to Rice University."

22. See Harte et al., "U.S. Eyes Ways to Toughen Fight against Domestic Extremists."

23. Ibrahim, "Obama: Get Off Your 'High Horse' and Stop Criticizing Islamic Terror."

24. Khan, "Donald Trump's National Security Adviser Mike Flynn Has Called Islam a 'Cancer.'"

25. See, for example, *Hill News*, "Hillary Clinton's Attack Dog David Brock Forming Koch Like Donor Network with George Soros and Others."

In all, as the drive to internally control Islam continues, the project will most likely shade into—perhaps gradually, perhaps not—a similar effort regarding Christianity. That project will come to color the way public school instructors are told to educate children about the Christian faith. This in turn can do three things: it can foment a drive toward syncretistic amalgamation of world religions resulting in serious distortion. In addition, it can become an approach that will all too often exaggerate[26] the genuinely negative elements of Christian history.[27] Lastly, it can become an approach that misinterprets the religion of Christianity in areas where it may on the surface appear to be problematic, but where a deeper understanding of the faith has always (or almost always) held otherwise; in other words, this trend could not just exaggerate the scope of actual harm but see harm where none is actually present. Take for example the passage where Jesus says "I have come to bring not peace but the sword."[28] Or, when He says, "I have come to cast fire upon the earth; and how I wish it were already kindled!"[29] A superficial reading might see trouble in these passages, but deep thinking internal to the Christian tradition almost never has. Yet, if Christianity is colored as problematic, this will serve the objective of legitimizing the penetration into modern American Muslim life of the surveillance state, while also allowing left-leaning state officials to promote their own negative views of Christian thought. The Jewish and Christian Bible, therefore, *will almost certainly be securitized*, to the detriment of instruction in genuine biblical religion. This cannot bode well for the health of Christianity in the country.

26. Identifying this as already a considerable problem of imbalance in English religious education, Gearon provides a corrective in part by highlighting reminders that the post-Enlightenment, increasingly secularized centuries were scarred by dangerous political extremism, particularly in the form of totalitarian ideologies and regimes. Gearon, "The Counter-Terrorist Classroom."

27. In the United States, examples collected in Florida include such statements in textbooks and lesson plans as the following: "The Roman Catholic Church grew strong during the Middle Ages . . . Church leaders became rich and powerful. Sometimes kings and queens did not agree with church leaders. However, because of its power, rulers often decided to obey the church." Note how rulers are driven not by piety or sincere conviction but only by acquiescence to the political power of popes. Or another example: "[W]hile Islam sometimes followed the path of Arab warriors, they rarely imposed their religion by force on the local population. In some instances, as with the Mongols, the conquerors made no effort to convert others to their own religion. By contrast, Christian monks, motivated by missionary fervor, converted many of the peoples of central and eastern Europe." This lesson implies that seeking conversion to Christianity is a vice, and (more subtly) that conversion to the faith involved force of arms. Korach and Saxton, "Correction to Islam-based Content," 79–80.

28. Matt 10:34 (NAB).

29. Luke 12:49 (NAS).

Chapter 7

State Religious Education, Further Reasons for Concern

The English Example

THE CALL FOR BIBLE courses in public education in the United States bears remarkable parallels to the practice which has long been seen in English schools. State religious education has been conducted in England for a considerable period of time. England has a state-sanctioned national religion, the Church of England. Hence, debates about the Bible in state-supported schools have a somewhat different character than they do in the United States. The debates have been on the basis of policy and not constitutional stricture. However, as we shall survey in this chapter, political pressure transformed devotional Bible reading into "objective" religious studies education, and thence into threadbare attention to the Christian faith and even curricular celebration of atheism. Hence, we believe that the English example provides very useful guidance for an assessment of recent calls for biblical instruction in American public schools. The importance of English-American cross analysis is shared by some scholars. Indeed, Suzanne Rosenblith and Beatrice Bailey argue that the current system of religious education in England should serve as the paradigmatic role model for developing state biblical instruction in the United States.[1]

We draw precisely the opposite conclusion. We do so because we argue in this chapter that state religious education in England has not aided religious vitality but rather in part has contributed to persistent religious

1. Rosenblith and Bailey, "Cultivating a Religiously Literate Society."

decline. The English example is, for the United States, a curricular tocsin. We first survey the history of religious education in English schools[2] and then address its role in the decline in—or what sociologist Callum Brown calls the very death of—Christian Britain.[3]

A Brief History of State Religious Education in England

In 1870, parliament passed the Elementary Education Act, drafted by Liberal MP William Forster, which mandated attendance in and provided free public access to elementary education up through the age of 13 for all English children. Although all were now required to attend school, parents could still opt to take their children to religious schools, most of which were affiliated with the national church.

Religious schools at this time all offered religious instruction as a compulsory subject. Pursuant to the 1870 law, religious instruction was likewise made a compulsory subject in each of the new state schools. As Gearon has documented, the context is important to keep in mind: at this time, religion was under attack by a range of scientific and sociological arguments. The law was a response intended to fortify the faith of the English nation. However, with the intent mostly of accommodating the children of dissenting Protestant families, Section 7 of the law allowed parents to withdraw children in state schools from classes in religious instruction, hence religious education was never rendered strictly obligatory. Moreover, again with the goal of accommodating the diversity of Christian perspectives present in the country, in the new state schools, Section 14 of the law—commonly called the "Cowper-Temple clause," after Liberal MP William Cowper-Temple—prohibited any "religious catechism or religious formulary which is distinctive of any particular denomination."[4] Determining the propriety of school curricula on religious matters was left—as with all disciplinary and curricular issues—to determination by local school boards, and thus control over the religious educational curricula was vested at the local level, with county-level boards implementing curricula through "local agreed syllabi."

2. See also Gearon, "The King James Bible and the Politics of Religious Education," from which we draw throughout this chapter.

3. Brown, *The Death of Christian Britain: Understanding Secularisation, 1800–2000.*

4. Quoted in Gillard, *Education in England: The History of Our Schools.* See also Copley, *Teaching Religion.*

Parents under the 1870 Act could still enroll their children in church schools if they wished, and this resulted in the emergence of what educational historians call the dual track system. Indeed, more parents did just this after the 1870 Act: the Act did not diminish but accelerated Christian churches' provisions for schools in England. In fact, in the two decades following the Act, the number of children attending church schools doubled to two million.[5] With improved ecumenical relations between the churches in the years immediately following World War I, dissenting and national church schools began to work together in setting the curricular standards for religious education in state as well as church schools.[6]

The next important milestone in religious education came in 1938 with the publication of the *Spens Report on Secondary Education*. The *Spens Report* reflected optimism in the current state of, and future potential for, religious instruction. The *Report's* writers note how they "believe that there is a wide and genuine recognition of the value and importance of religious instruction and the teaching of Scripture in schools . . . and so the present temper of public opinion" supports it. However, the *Spens Report* is anxious to underscore that the value of the religious instruction on the Bible is not grounded on sociological factors in terms of levels of current religious belief, nor is the value of biblical instruction to be based on the purely literary, cultural, and historical importance of the Bible. No, the *Report* states, "the principal justification for giving a place in the curriculum to the study of the Scriptures is that the Bible is the classic book of Christianity, and forms the basis of the structure of Christian faith and worship. The content of the Bible has, therefore, inevitably its own dignity and associations. It can neither be treated merely as a part of English literature, nor can it be merged in the general study of history."[7]

This understanding of the intrinsic value of religious education focusing on the Bible began to be questioned as a result of a further milestone in English educational policy, the Education Act of 1944. The work of R.A. Butler, the 1944 Act mandated attendance at and provided free public access to secondary education across England. The Act further mandated that all state-supported secondary schools have religious instruction as a classroom subject, and that they provide frequent collective acts of worship,

5. Gillard, *Education in England*.

6. Bates, "Christianity, Culture and Other Religions (Part 1): The Origins of the Study of World Religions in English Education," 6–7.

7. *The Spens Report on Secondary Education*, 206–17. Cf. Hamlin and Jones, eds. *The King James Bible after Four Hundred Years: Literary, Linguistic, and Cultural Influences*.

all of which had to follow the Cowper-Temple clause and, therefore, be non-denominational.

What is invariably forgotten is that the framework for religious education now became not simply non-denominational, as it had long been, but *secular.* The latter word appears repeatedly in the Act. Albeit the section headed "secular instruction" is seemingly in contrast to "religious instruction," the former effectively frames the latter.

In the decades that followed the 1944 Act, especially in the 1960s and 1970s, the secular tendency of the 1944 Act became more visible. English religious education demonstrated a concern with sociological and psychological theory—theories which in fact had often been deployed as reductionist frameworks seeking not simply to account for but to explain away religion per se. Harold Loukes in 1961 and 1963, Ronald Goldman in 1964 and 1965, and Edwin Cox in 1971 followed this line of work in their analysis of the role of the Bible in religious education.[8] Their collective argument was that, bearing in mind the psychological development and sociological condition of children, children in England lacked, to use the Loukes/Goldman term, "readiness for religion."[9] Using a seemingly benign child-centered methodology and outlook, these religious education researchers particularly targeted the Bible as inappropriate for children.[10] Instead, a so-called child-centered education was deemed to meet the children's needs in preparing for adult life, and such an educational approach increasingly took the curricular center stage. Religious education in English schools in turn increasingly became aligned to Personal and Social Education, and became less focused on the Bible. On the basis of these influential researchers, therefore, Bible teaching declined. In fact, readiness for religion research provided a ready-made excuse for educators already ill-equipped to teach the Bible to jettison it from their curricula.

By the middle of the 1960s, charges arose, however, that the new "child-centered" approach to teaching religion ill-prepared children for life in an increasingly diverse society. Religious plurality and the teaching of world religions in schools would now come to dominate the raison d'être

---

8. Loukes, *Teenage Religion*; Loukes, *Readiness for Religion*; Goldman, *Religious Thinking from Childhood to Adolescence*; Goldman, *Readiness for Religion: A Developmental Basis for Religious Education*; Cox, "Changes in Attitudes towards Religious Education and the Bible among Sixth Form Boys and Girls," 328–41.

9. See especially Goldman, *Readiness for Religion.*

10. For a discussion of this thesis and the works that espoused it, and their lasting importance, see Hyde, *Religion in Childhood and Adolescence: A Comprehensive Review of the Research.*

of religious education—as it continues to do so to the present.[11] Indeed, the real defining moment for the secularization of religious education came with an approach to the study of religion in schools expressed in a 1969 edition of the noted journal, *Religious Education*. In his article, "The Comparative Study of Religions and the Schools," distinguished scholar and professor Ninian Smart stated: "I am deeply committed to the secular principle in state education. That is, I am sceptical as to whether the present pattern of religious education in England, which assumes that for those who do not contract out on grounds of conscience, etc., the content of religious education shall be Christian, is right or viable."[12] Based in large measure on Smart's advocacy, the Schools' Council Working Paper No. 36 in 1971 soon began to shape religious education into the teaching of world religions.[13]

Religious plurality and the teaching of world religions in schools would now come to dominate the raison d'être of religious education. Thus, in 1985, an official British Enquiry into the Education of Children from Ethnic Minority Groups, chaired by Lord Swann, published *Education for All*.[14] The so-called Swann Report included a substantial section on the role of religion in schools and came down, in the words of L. Philip Barnes, "decisively in favour of a nondogmatic, nondenominational, phenomenological approach to religious education."[15]

The Swann Report, along with the Schools' Council Working Paper in 1971 and Smart's approach to the study of religion, shaped the 1988 Education Reform Act. This was the most significant education act since 1944. Its implication for religious education was substantive. Part 8 (l) Section 3 reads: "Any agreed syllabus which after this section comes into force is adopted or deemed to be adopted . . . shall reflect the fact that the religious traditions in Great Britain are in the main Christian whilst taking account of the teaching and practices of the other principal religions represented in Great Britain."[16] This law was seized upon to further advance a multi-cultural educational

11. See Jackson, *Rethinking Religious Education and Plurality: Issues in Diversity and Pedagogy*; Jackson and O'Grady, "Religious Education in England: Social Plurality, Civil Religion and Religious Education Pedagogy," 181–202. See also Grimmitt, ed., *Pedagogies of Religious Education*.

12. Smart, "The Comparative Study of Religions and the Schools," 26.

13. Schools Council. *Working Paper 36: Religious Education in Secondary Schools*.

14. Committee of Enquiry into the Education of Children from Ethnic Minority Groups, *Education for All*.

15. Barnes, "What is Wrong with the Phenomenological Approach to Religious Education?," 445.

16. Quoted in Gillard, *Education in England*.

perspective. The teaching of the Bible was on its way truly to becoming only a minor part in a complex panorama of world religions.

Due to this developing transformation, in 1994, for the first time, the Schools' Curriculum and Assessment Authority met with leaders of a wide array of faith communities to draw up a model curriculum, which would accurately reflect the leaders' religious traditions.[17] This trend was amplified in 2004 when *The National Non-Statutory Framework for Religious Education* was produced; its broad aims reiterated in *Religious Education Guidance in English Schools.*[18] In this new trajectory, school materials for teaching world religions—primarily Buddhism, Christianity, Hinduism, Islam, Judaism, and Sikhism—make marginal references to the Bible.[19] So, in 2010, the Bible as an element in religious education had all but disappeared; where it still exists, it does so as snippets of text to illustrate moral or ethical points. Indeed, ethics is a fast-growing aspect of religious education, where biblical study is in fast decline.

This de-centering of the Bible occurred despite counter-movements being tried; these defenses of the Bible's traditional place proved fruitless. Terence Copley and Sarah Lane engaged in a rearguard action, including Copley's Biblos project,[20] as well as their wider attempts at "inspiring faith in schools."[21] Indeed, Copley bemoaned what he saw as "indoctrination" into liberal secular values by state-maintained religious education—a position which many experts on religious education also detected.[22] Indeed, L. Philip Barnes says "Many modern British religious educators seem to want to minimise the acquaintance of pupils with religious beliefs because they fear that coming to understand the beliefs will lead to pupils' acceptance of them!"[23] Copley's Biblos initiative showed a profound, personal, and professional commitment to the teaching of the Bible. Movements such as this, however, have borne very little fruit.

While ultimately feckless defenses of the traditional position of the Bible were advanced, two new developments took hold across the field of

17. Schools Curriculum and Assessment Authority, *Model Syllabuses for Religious Education.*

18. See The Qualifications and Curriculum Authority, *Religious Education in English Schools.*

19. Jackson et al., *Materials Used to Teach about World Religions in Schools in England.*

20. See Copley, *Teaching Religion*; Copley et al., *On the Side of the Angels: The Third Report of the Biblos Project.*

21. Felderhof et al., eds., *Inspiring Faith in Schools.*

22. Copley, *Indoctrination, Education and God.*

23. Barnes, "Michael Hand, 'Is Religious Education Possible?'," 69.

religious education that have moved the discipline perhaps as far from its traditional roots as one could possibly imagine: critical religious studies, and the embrace of atheism as a form of belief deserving sympathetic treatment in religious education curricula. As Gearon has documented, state religious education in England now means "the inclusion of religiously skeptical philosophical stances, which, historically and in contemporary context, remain hostile to religion . . . philosophies adversarial to religion have become integral to teaching about it."[24] Indeed, in 2015, a high-profile Commission—the Commission on Religion and Belief in Public Life sponsored by the Woolf Institute, and chaired by former High Court Judge Baroness Butler-Sloss—chided English school administrators for not adopting even more aggressive religious education policies that would deter even more strongly all schools from "omit[ting] the role of religions in reinforcing stereotypes and prejudice around issues such as gender, sexuality, ethnicity and race."[25] In fact, one influential set of education professors argues that the future of religious education must be found in a subject "set free from religious concerns," in which educators philosophically dissect, criticize, and historicize the baseless claims of religion.[26] Another leading figure in religious education in England argues that the discipline can only find its justification if traditionally core elements of religious life—such as religious intuitions, grace-inspired conversions, a sense of divine mystery, and that very fear of the Lord which is held to be the beginning of all wisdom[27]—are explicitly stated to have no basis in truth; indeed, only if core aspects of religion are analogized to literary fiction can religion have any toehold in the secular state.[28]

What is more, many educational theorists and policy advocates now demand that the lacuna created by dismantling traditional religious education be filled by the cultural celebration of atheism. One prominent theorist, Professor J.M. Hull, director of The Centre for Spirituality and Religion in

24. Gearon, *On Holy Ground*, 41.

25. Butler-Sloss, *Living with Difference: Report of the Commission on Religion and Belief in British Public Life*, 35. Despite a grave and government-sounding name, the commission was not initially convened by, or at the request of any governmental body.

26. Charter and Erricker, *Does Religious Education Have a Future?*. See also Gearon, *On Holy Ground*, 42.

27. Psalm 111:10: "[T]he fear of the Lord is the beginning of wisdom" (NIV).

28. Hand, *Is Religious Education Possible? A Philosophical Investigation*. Hand, "A Response to Philip Barnes," 71–75. Jim Mackenzie states this point as follows: "Hand has expended a great deal of labour . . . [to tell us] that understanding statements about gods in religious texts has something in common with understanding statements about fictional characters in novels." Mackenzie, Review of *Is Religious Education Possible? A Philosophical Investigation*, 790.

Education at the University of East Anglia, argues that religious education must "illustrate atheism's spiritual and moral potential."[29] This from the director of a major research center on religious education!

It is worthwhile to ruminate briefly on how astounding has been the career of religious education in England. Mandated as an area of instruction for all in 1870 at a time when religion was under attack by a range of atheist thinkers, it was intended to provide "nurture" to Christian faith in troubled times.[30] Now, it nurtures the precise viewpoints its founders sought to shield from the youth of England: the foxes of religious critique now guard the henhouse of the English faithful.

In conclusion, the Bible as a part of religious education has all but disappeared in England. Resultantly, the one tradition with which school inspectors in England recently found serious weaknesses in teaching, was Christianity.[31] In religious education, its role has become much diminished, almost, at least in formal schooling, to the point of extinction. In England, a country with a long history of state religious education, the Bible today has barely any educational influence at all.

The Decimated State of Religious Life in Contemporary England and the Inference of Causal Connections

We now wish to examine the consequences of the history of state religious education in England. This involves no doubt some speculation around the statistics about the state of religious life in England. Our speculation centers on a little examined potential casual factor in English secularization: the role of religious education itself. We are deeply concerned that state religious education has enervated the state of religious life in England.

Let us begin then with the numbers concerning the state of English religious vitality. Many sample sources of data could be used to present a picture of the state of religious life in England. Here, we have chosen to look mostly at one significant source: the British Social Attitudes Survey. The British Social Attitudes Survey is a useful measure not only because of its longevity (established over several decades) but because of the consistency of its comparative methods. It statistically measures British attitudes to a

---

29. Watson, "Can Children and Young People Learn from Atheism for Spiritual Development? A Response to the National Framework for Religious Education," 49–58, quoted in Gearon, *On Holy Ground*, 41. See also Watson, "Including Secular Philosophies such as Humanism in Locally Agreed Syllabuses for Religious Education," 5–18.

30. See Hull, "From Christian Nurture to Religious Education," 124–43.

31. Ofsted Report, *Transforming Religious Education*.

range of ethical and moral, social and political, and other values over time. It also draws upon and compares its findings with the UK Census, which has a good amount of data and is extremely valuable for a range of statistical information, but its data only recently, in 2001, included references to religious beliefs and values.

Statistics rarely speak for themselves. Yet, those statistics, which present some determinate and shifting picture of the state of religious life in England, seem to speak with a loud voice. The 2012 British Social Attitudes Survey included a chapter on religious life, including both the more easily identified and measured religious practices (how often might people visit a place of worship, for example) and the less easily charted religious attitudes, beliefs and creeds. Its chapter on religion provides the following narrative summary, the thread of which is encapsulated in its interrogative and provocative title: "Losing Faith?"[32] In posing this question, it asks: "How religious is the British public and how has this changed over time?" Conceding that obtaining "an accurate picture of the importance of religion in people's lives matters is difficult," the study nevertheless brings to light some startling figures. The chapter examined "levels of religious affiliation, whether someone was brought up in a religion, and whether they regularly attend religious services." It concluded with these headline figures:

> Half (50%) do not regard themselves as belonging to a particular religion, while the largest proportion (20%) of religious affiliates belong to the Church of England. Nearly two thirds (64%) of those aged 18–24 do not belong to a religion, and 28% of those aged 65 and above. More than half (56%) of those who belong to, or were brought up in a religion never attend religious services or meetings. Just 14% attend weekly. Viewed in a temporal sense, one in three (31%) in 1983 did not belong to a religion, compared with one in two (50%) now. The largest decline has been in affiliation with the Church of England, which has halved since 1983 (from 40% to 20%).[33]

On the basis of these figures, the study draws an unambiguous conclusion: "Levels of religiosity have declined over the past three decades." Further, the study postulates that these levels of religiosity "are likely to decline further" and this "mainly as a result of generational replacement": "Nearly two thirds (64%) of those aged 18–24 do not belong to a religion, compared with 28% of those aged 65 and above." Thus the report concludes: "This

32. The British Social Attitudes Survey is administered periodically by NatCen, a large independent social science research organization. NatCen, "Losing Faith?"

33. NatCen, "Losing Faith?," 173.

change—which is likely to continue—can be explained by generational replacement, with older, more religious, generations dying out and being replaced by less religious generations."[34]

Other less scientifically reliable but still instructive surveys have shown an even more pronounced decline in English religiosity: A December 2016 YouGov poll of 1,595 adults conducted for *The Times* found that belief in God in Britain has dropped to only twenty-eight percent, with those affirming that they disbelieve in any god or higher power rising to thirty-eight percent. This data follows the same pattern as the British Attitudes Survey, with only twenty-five percent of those aged sixty-five or older affirming atheism, compared to forty-three percent of twenty-five to forty-nine year olds.[35] One result of this striking decline is that the Church of England, in its own informal studies, now expects its already low number of adherents to decline in half by 2030.[36]

In all, the state of religion is bleak in modern England. No doubt many sources are responsible for this. Yet, one factor has not been attended to: the influence of religious education on English religious culture. Hints at a causal connection are found in the cited 2010 Ofsted Report, which associates religious decline with the failure of religious education. Reflecting on the Report and their own research on religious instruction, James Conroy, David Lundie, and Vivienne Baumfield note that "everyday religious education is striated with failures of meaning that emanate from foundational, or constitutive confusions in the conduct of the subject that are deep seated. These constitutive failures, we propose, emerge out of epistemic and values confusions about the very purposes and meaning of religious education in a late industrial society."[37] The juxtaposition in the Ofsted Report of religious decline and religious education is highly suggestive yet not drawn with sufficient clarity. We wish to make the claim explicit: religious education has, we believe, been one factor in the decline of religiosity in contemporary England. Of course, we do not intend to be caricatured; the study of religion in contemporary life is too important to be dismissed by uncharitable exaggerations of our claim. We *do not say* that religious education is the only, or even the most, compelling force for secularization—only that it is a real and important one.

34. Ibid.

35. Coates and Burnes, "Belief in God Slumps After Turbulent Year."

36. *Independent*, UK, "Church of England Slowly Dying as Congregation Set to Halve over 30 Years."

37. Controy et al., "Failures of Meaning in Religious Education," 315.

This is an inference to be sure. Yet, it is an inference supported by the evidence. Since 1983—a time when the full thrust of transformed religious education began to take hold—the Church of England's membership has declined in half, and religious identity in general is found among only half of the population, down from the high eightieth percentile in the 1960s. The older seculars of today lived through the currically cataclysmic days of the religious education revolution. Further, English youth today have almost all had the deep confusion of the subject matter we traced above as their teaching standard. And they are hemorrhaging religiosity—with two-thirds of English youth now being non-observant. The remarkable number of atheists in general as well as the age distribution further corroborate the inference of a causal connection between contemporary religious education and religious disbelief: those sixty-five or older would have experienced a much more traditional form of religious instruction in their youth. Did not a wise Jesuit once say—let us paraphrase the hoary chestnut—that "if you allow me to influence a child's schooling, I can show you the man"? Religious education itself is likely a source of these declines.

Additional weight to this inference can be seen when we note that in the United States, which has to a profound extent very many of the same characteristics which in England are often seen as drivers of secularism—sexual liberation, LGBTQIA movements, extremist feminism, multicultural immigration, "new atheist" agitation, and rising consumerism—that is, the whole panoply of what Andrew Higgins of the *New York Times* calls "the tradition-crushing rush"[38] of so much in modern life[39]—there has not been anywhere near as sharp a decline in religious belief as witnessed in England. In the United States at most thirty to thirty-six percent of the young are without religion (and a good percentage of these have a "relationship" with God and not a "religion," or are "spiritual but not religious"), and decline in the general population has been much less stark.[40] What accounts for this surprising fact? We suspect it is in part due to the *absence* of state religious education: the very lack of state intervention in religious education might be one contributory factor to the vigor of religious life in America.

Distinguished British educational theorist L. Phillip Barnes, Professor of Religious Education at King's College, University of London agrees

38. Higgins, "In Expanding Russian Influence, Faith Combines with Firepower."

39. To be sure, there is sociological contestation as to whether there really is a divide between secular Europe and religious America. See Davie et al., *Religious America, Secular Europe?* Yet, we maintain that the social assessments they advance are overdrawn.

40. See Oppenheimer, "Examining the Growth of the Spiritual but Not Religious." See also Pew Research Center: Religion and Public Life," America's Changing Religious Landscape."

with our contention: he writes, "pupils [in England] are confronted with a range of religious possibilities from which they must choose; that many choose to be indifferent to religion [ ] later in life should not surprise us, given that education fails to engage them in rational [discussion] on the purported truth of religion and fails to involve them in discussion about the criteria that are relevant to [ ] religion."[41] We may not agree with Barnes on the precise reasons for why religious education stimulates religious indifference, but that religious education is causing changed religious behavior seems exactly on point. So also is the thought of philosopher of education Jim Mackenzie of the School of Education and Social Work at the University of Sydney. He too detects a causal linkage, a point he states approvingly in service of a tendentious conclusion: "a much greater proportion of adults in America regularly attend public worship than does so in [ ] Britain. Systematic Religious Education may be an effective way to discourage excessive piety in the general population."[42]

We conclude only that it seems strikingly naïve not to at least suspect that state religious education is a force for secularization, and to infer that the immunization of religion from state-controlled instruction is one of a number of important forces that shelters religious vitality. The evidence would seem to show that the Bible has thrived in America where religion is not (widely) taught in public schools, by contrast declining in England, where it is—declining not only in religious education, but in the national consciousness and personal confessional belief.

41. Barnes, Review of *Is Religious Education Possible?*, 69.
42. Mackenzie, Review of *Is Religious Education Possible?*, 792N1.

Chapter 8 —————————————————————

State Religious Education
and Global Civil Religion

IT IS POSSIBLE TO develop a counterargument to a core aspect of our argument against state religious education, namely our claim that religion is in decline in the Western world, and that that decline is in part due to contributions of state religious education itself. For it could be argued, and indeed it is being argued, that religion is not in fact in a state of considerable decline. In fact, some of the commentators most committed to this claim are in the field of religious education. This is especially so among continental European scholars of religious education. They note that across Europe there is an increase in state religious education. They further argue that this rise is itself indicative of what some call counter-secularization or desecularization: they assert that religious education has increased in Europe and that this increase evidences the resurgence of religion—that religious education has increased *because of* a broad resurgence in European religiosity. If true, this contention would constitute a serious challenge to our claim, since the British and continental European contexts are defined by quite similar cultural forces. Hence, to address our claim that religious education is actually harming religion, we need to broaden our focus to a study of the dynamics of religious education on the European continent.

In this chapter, we challenge a central presupposition underpinning the work of many leading researchers in European religious education who argue that the growing political interest in religious instruction is evidence of *counter*-secularization.[1] This chapter specifically examines these claims

1. This chapter is based largely on Gearon, "European Religious Education and

about counter-secularization through a critical review of the European Commission's largest ever funded research initiative on religion in education—an eight country study investigating whether religion in education is a source of conflict, or dialogue in a culturally and religiously plural continent—the Religion, Education, Dialogue and Conflict (REDCo) project.[2] A foundational claim of REDCo researchers is that current patterns in European religious education present decisive evidence of counter-secularization. Indeed, the project leader could not be clearer:

> In most European countries, we have assumed for a long time that increasing secularisation would lead to a gradual retreat of religion from public space. *This tendency has reversed itself in the course of the past decade as religion has returned to public attention.*[3]

This core supposition is open to serious questioning. Is any increase in religious education unambiguously a *volt face* from the secularization thesis, or just in fact its *new face*? Statements such as those of REDCo's leaders fail to reflect the inherent complexity and disagreement of what secularization is, or the manner in which it has and continues to occur. In this chapter, we develop an analysis of the convergence of European civil religion and European religious education, and argue that this convergence means that trends in European religious education are a useful way not of witnessing counter-secularization but of understanding a new and powerful agent of secularization's confirmation. The increase in religious education evidences not religion's marginalization in a classical sense but instead its incorporation into secular, political goals and ends, facilitated, consciously or otherwise, through education. In short, the *modus operandi* of REDCo is in its own terms oriented towards civil religion and thus to political, secular, even (though the empirical grounds of its effects are difficult to measure) secularizing goals, whether such ends are intended or not.

Hence, the increase in religious education does not undermine our claim that religion is in decline, and in part due to religious education itself, but, rather, this increase simply confirms it. Further, we argue that our conclusion demonstrates all the more the problem with state religious education that we addressed in the last chapter: not only does the increase in religious education bespeak the depth of secularization through the way religion is seized on to serve the state's security (or other) needs, this very process of

---

European Civil Religion."

2. Jackson, "Religion, Education, Dialogue and Conflict," 105–10.

3. Weisse, "Reflections of the REDCo Project," 111–25; emphasis added.

the state using religion for its objectives is itself a force that reduces the integrity of the teaching process and the accuracy of the religious educational content, which advances further the decline of religion in contemporary society. We here draw upon significant theorists of religious education—including Copley, Felderhof, and Wright—to argue in support of Barnes[4] that the current predominance of political and secularizing aims of religious education are a significant "misrepresentation" of religion within education.

Our analysis will undoubtedly be challenged. But some argument is needed to moderate the more extravagant counter-secularization claims of theorists and empirical researchers of European religious education, and to moderate too the worrying over-politicization of religious education in Europe.

God Is Back?

The intensified scholarly, political, and policy interest in religion in public life is evidenced by a vast multi-disciplinary literature[5] and is acutely apparent in education.[6] Such literature has prompted much debate over secularization, classically defined as the marginalization of religion from the public to the private sphere, "the process by which sectors of society and culture are removed from the domination of religious institutions and symbols."[7] In modern societies, Peter Berger claimed, consciousness itself becomes secularized.[8] Much recent debate on this topic has been quite high profile, for instance that between Jürgen Habermas and Cardinal Joseph Ratzinger, now Pope Emeritus Benedict XVI, and their public discussions on "the dialectics of secularization."[9]

While the use of dialectics in the debate between Habermas and Ratzinger refers to the critical interchange in a post-Enlightenment past and present between secularism and Christianity, "dialectic" has a wider

4. Barnes, "The Misrepresentation of Religion in Modern British (Religious) Education."

5. For example, Davis et al., *Theology and the Political: The New Debate*; Haynes, *The Handbook of Religion and Politics*; Haynes, *Religion and Politics*; and Trigg, *Religion in Public Life*.

6. See Arthur et al., *Education, Politics and Religion: Reconciling the Civil and the Sacred in Education*.

7. Berger, *The Sacred Canopy*, 107.

8. Berger, *A Rumor of Angels: Modern Society and the Rediscovery of the Supernatural*.

9. Habermas and Ratzinger, *The Dialectics of Secularization: On Reason and Religion*.

meaning in debates over secularization. It was Warner who challenged the linear (non-dialectical) model of secularization by classic secularization theories.[10] It is Warner who notes that the classic model is, or has been identified with Talcott Parsons, Robert Bellah, Peter Berger, Thomas Luckmann, Bryan Wilson, David Martin, and Richard Fenn, though each case presents theoretical variation on a theme, and, over the decades, some notable moves away from originally held positions. If Warner describes the "old paradigm" of secularization (represented by these latter theorists) as linear, there is, he claims, a "new paradigm" of secularization theory which gives more credence to a "dialectical" model, less easily identifiable as a straightforward, historically progressive path. Goldstein challenges this view, arguing strongly, and in our view convincingly, that the so-called "old paradigm" of secularization identified by Warner fails on two counts: one, it does not say fully what it means by linear; but two, it fails also to recognize the dialectics of the "old paradigm" represented by Parsons et al. Goldstein's argument is that secularization does not proceed in a smooth linear historical path but may stop and start, even temporarily halt. According to Goldstein's view, this would explain why secularization can (as in the present apparent resurgence of religion in global governance) occur simultaneously with periods of renewed sacralization.[11]

Goldstein's "Secularization Patterns in the Old Paradigm" is the finest summary of classical secularization and its changing nature today, and this chapter cannot do justice to the nuances of its wide treatment.[12] We can say that formerly ardent secularization theorists have moderated, or even reversed previously held intellectual positions. Berger is amongst the most prominent of these. Compare Berger's 1967 trenchant outline of the declining role of religion's social and political significance in *The Sacred Canopy* with his 1999 recantation in *The Desecularization of the World*, or his collaboration with Grace Davie in *Religious America, Secular Europe?*, challenging previously held assumptions of the European heartland of post-Enlightenment secularization[13]—the continent that produced Nietzsche, Marx, Freud, Durkheim, and a plethora of reductionist thinkers

10. Warner, "Work in Progress Toward a New Paradigm for the Sociological Study of Religion in the United States," 1044–93.

11. Goldstein, "Secualrization Patterns in the Old Paradigm." 157–78; see also Goldstein, "Patterns of Secularization and Religious Rationalization in Durkheim and Weber," *Implicit Religion*.

12. See Goldstein, "Secualrization Patterns in the Old Paradigm."

13. Berger, *Sacred Canopy*; Berger, *The Desecularization of the World: Resurgent Religion and World Politics*; and Davie et al., *Religious America, Secular Europe?*

on religion.[14] Though the Nietzschean claim that "God is Dead" still reverberates among die-hard secularization theorists who refuse to abandon the old sociological faith,[15] it has now become a commonplace espoused from education policy makers and theorists[16] to serious journalists that "God is Back."[17] Public debate as well as scholarly literature makes, then, a new claim: God is not dead, but secularization theory is. Stark puts it precisely in these terms: "Secularization R.I.P."[18] This chapter contests this conclusion. It has been claimed that attention to Islam in Europe, and the influence of Islam in public debate has prompted all major religious traditions to consider and re-evaluate their role in public life more generally. The prevalence of political theology has, in the Academy, given new life and vitality to theological debate.[19] It might here be argued that this gives considerable support to the idea that in fact "God is back." The question to be asked here then—if we concede that religions have become more prominent in public life—is this: "If God is back, on whose terms?" We contend that God is back, but in terms of political and not religious discourse, for the former (in arguments over citizenship, democracy, and human rights) predominantly frames the latter. This is acutely apparent in European religious education.

Studying European Religious Education

The REDCo project, financed by the European Commission between 2006 and 2009, has produced a significant number of research outputs, including twenty book-length volumes of findings, representing in its own word—"a necessary approach to address the core question laid out by the European Commission, how religions and values can contribute to dialogue or tension in Europe"—drawing together researchers in the humanities and social sciences "to gain better insight into how European citizens of different religious, cultural, and political backgrounds can live together and enter into dialogue of mutual respect and understanding, developing their respective

14. For a discussion of reductionist accounts in European religious history, see Pals, *Eight Theories of Religion*.

15. See for example Bruce, *God is Dead: Secularization in the West*; and Martin, *On Secularization: Towards a Revised General Theory*.

16. Cooling, *Doing God in Education*.

17. Micklethwait and Woolridge, *God is Back: How the Global Revival of Faith is Changing the World*.

18. Stark, "Secularization, RIP," 249–73.

19. See for example, Scott and Cavanaugh, *The Blackwell Companion of Political Theology*.

evolving positions . . . in the context of educational institutions." A core aim "was to look at the challenges facing religious education in the context of the current change in European societies, and its importance for dialogue and mutual understanding without disregarding potential problems": "Taking account of confrontational as well as dialogue potential, this allowed us to develop impulses for the future peaceful coexistence of people of different religions." The REDCo Project represents then in its own terms a "necessary approach to address the question, how religions and values can contribute to dialogue or tension in Europe," and "to gain better insight into how European citizens of different religious, cultural and political backgrounds can live together and enter into dialogue of mutual respect and understanding." The remit of REDCo is impressively wide, its recommendations addressed to: EU Institutions (Parliament, Commission, Council of Ministers), the Council of Europe, the United Nations (UNESCO, General Assembly, Alliance of Civilizations), national educational bodies of EU-member states, educational research associations, non-governmental organizations, religious organizations, and universities and schools within the European Union. The qualitative and quantitative research was carried out across eight countries: Germany, England, France, The Netherlands, Norway, Estonia, Russia, and Spain.[20]

Among key research findings of REDCo are an openness of students to learning about religion, and a respect for diversity of worldviews and religious pluralism (the "majority of students appreciated the religious heterogeneity in their societies.") The project noted, however, "a range of prejudices" and acknowledged the "most important source of information about religions and worldviews is generally the family, followed by the school." If, regardless of religious backgrounds, a majority of students "are interested in learning about religions in school" and there is openness "towards peers of different religious backgrounds," they still "tend to socialise with peers from the same background as themselves, even when they live in areas characterised by religious diversity." There was thus a disjuncture between, it is claimed, "a tolerant attitude" at the level of abstraction, and that on "a practical level." So, "tolerance expressed in classroom discussion is not always replicated in their daily life world."[21]

---

20 All quotations and project details, including lists of publications, can be found on REDCo's website. See also Jackson et al., *Religion and Education in Europe*; and Jackson, "Religion, Education, Dialogue and Conflict."

21. Weisse, *Religion in Education: Contribution to Dialogue Policy Recommendations of the REDCo Research Project*, 1–4; See also Dietz, "Invisibilizing or Ethnicizing Religious Diversity?," 103–32.

A key driver of REDCo is to support the recommendations of the Council of Europe, and the *Toledo Guiding Principles*. Readers unfamiliar with developments in European religious education might be surprised to know that the highly influential *Toledo Guiding Principles on Teaching about Religions and Beliefs in Public Schools* originate from a Cold War security organization called the Organisation for Security and Cooperation in Europe (OSCE).[22] This sharpening further of the political focus of religion in education to security concerns seems to leave the REDCo team unperturbed, and the status of the OSCE has itself been lauded in the context of religion and religious educations' new roles in international security. The following, cited *in extenso*, are the opening lines from one of the leading international journals which dedicated a special issue to the REDCo project:

> Especially in the years following the events of 9/11, 2001 in the USA, religion has become a major topic of public debate globally. In academic literature, there has been a growth in writing about the place of religion in the public sphere . . . and in policy development, at European and wider international levels, there has been close attention to education about religions and beliefs in schools. The Council of Europe completed its first ever project on the religious dimension of intercultural education, which includes a Recommendation by the Committee of Ministers—the Foreign Ministers of the 47 member states—that all young Europeans should learn about religious diversity [per the] Council of Europe, 2008. The Organisation for Security and Cooperation in Europe, the largest security organization in the world, published the *Toledo Guiding Principles on Teaching About Religions and Beliefs in Public Schools*, again arguing that education about the diversity of religions and beliefs in society should be a part of everyone's general education. The United Nations Alliance of Civilisations programme makes a similar recommendation through its education about religions and beliefs website (www.aocerb.org).[23]

Religious education in Europe has become, then (and we think this is incontestable), increasingly enmeshed with influential political agencies across a wide spectrum of geopolitical contexts. Such close and integral involvement with such political agencies will inevitably change the subject, and mould its interests to those political forces. REDCo, as an initiative, has in this regard then *itself* become politically significant. The project is

22. Organisation for Security and Co-operation in Europe, *Toledo Guiding Principles on Teaching about Religions and Beliefs in Public Schools*.

23. Jackson, "Religion, Education, Dialogue and Conflict," 105.

framed as providing clear evidence that religion has not been marginalized; that is, providing dis-confirmatory evidence of a key expectation of classical secularization theory.

Jean-Paul Willaime makes four general observations of religious education in Europe: (1) "School instruction about religious faith is a strong indicator of the way church-state and school-religion relations are constructed inside a given national framework" (examples cited are Greece, Italy, the UK, Germany, Ireland); (2) "However great the diversity of state-church and school-religion relations to the various European countries may be, and however many national approaches to the treatment of religion in education they may have, they are all confronted with similar challenges," including "secularization," the "lack of religious acculturation amongst school students and their loss of contact with religious life" and "an overall religious pluralisation"; (3) "There is also the need to strengthen the role of religious knowledge in public school education" mirroring "in spite of a high degree of difference which shows no sign of disappearing, there is a broad consensus in Europe of the need for instruction on religion in public schools"; (4) With the exception of France, "in practically all those countries, including those which joined the EU in 2004, there exist courses dedicated to the study of a religion or religious matters in general."[24]

Willaime, in sum, identifies three models of religious education in Europe: (1) "no religious instruction in schools"; (2) "confessional religious instruction"; (3) "non-confessional religious education."[25] There are three developments identified, which are shared with the REDCo project as a whole: (1) "A growing integration of religious education, be it confessional or not, with the overall educational goals of the school"; (2) "an increased openness, in different degrees, to the religious and philosophical plurality of European societies"; (3) that the latter developments "raise tensions and engender conflicts."[26]

Willaime and the REDCo Project here identify a pedagogical-political convergence: the *pedagogical* imperative of multi-faith teaching to address Europe's religious pluralism is also a *political* imperative to address the needs of peaceful democratic coexistence amid religious pluralism, a problem long familiar to political liberalism.[27] Willaime usefully frames this as a "double constraint": "a *sociological* one, in that the religious and philosophical pluralisation of European societies obliges them to include ever more

24. Willaime, "Different Models of Religion and Education in Europe," 57–59.

25. Ibid., 60.

26. Ibid.

27. See Rawls, *Political Liberalism*.

alternative religions and non-religious positions into their curricula, and a *legal* one, through the importance of the principle of non-discrimination on religious or philosophical grounds (as well as others such as gender or race) in international law, especially in the European Convention on Human Rights."[28] The pattern is not as one would expect homogenous. Each country of the study reflects not only the autonomy of each nation over its national education but a variety of responses to addressing religious pluralism.[29]

Whether we accept these accounts as evidence of counter-secularization or not, we can certainly note that there has been increased attention to teaching world religions in schools. Thus, within two generations, Europe has transformed close to two millennia of Christian identity into a plural, multi-faith orientation in its religious education systems. The project is not complete; there remain, for example, very many schools with a Christian foundation that are unlikely to adopt the trend toward uniformity of political-pedagogical purposes outlined by REDCo. But we need to be clear that what is meant by REDCo researchers by counter-secularization in Europe is thus really the *decline in Christian influence*. Take Knauth's summary of the German context:

> Up to the 1960s, religious education in public schools was taught in close cooperation with established churches. It was based on dogmatic and systematic theology and familiarized students with the Bible, the hymnbook, and central parts of church history. Its stated aim was to introduce the Gospel to the (mainly baptized) pupils as the liberating Word of God. Today, nearly 50 years later, religious education has opened itself to religious and cultural plurality It defines its purpose from its standing as a school subject, and therefore in pedagogical as well as theological terms. Every religious community which carries a share of responsibility for religious education in schools thus faces the challenge of interpreting its own religious tradition in a context of religious diversity and cultural heterogeneity.[30]

The REDCo findings here evidence a necessary marginalization of Christianity as a school subject in religious education. Indeed, as we shall

---

28. Willaime, "Different Models of Religion and Education in Europe," 60; emphasis in original.

29. The nations examined include France, Spain, Russia, Estonia, England, The Netherlands, Norway, and Germany.

30. Knauth, "Religious Education in Germany," 244.

argue, without achieving the removal of this Christian hegemony in religious education, *the civil religion cannot progress.*

Indeed, such developments are aligned specifically by another leading member of the REDCo project as precisely that of "civil religion." Notably, Jackson and O'Grady in "Religions and Education in England" conceive of religious education as the interface of "social plurality, civil religion and religious education pedagogy."[31] However, what is entailed by "civil religion" is not explored. The phrase "civil religion" appears in the title of the paper and in the conclusion but there is no definition or analysis, simply the closing intimation that: "It could be said that the particular approach to multiculturalism to be found in the syllabuses (rather than in current government rhetoric) reflects the particular history of civil religion in the UK, and Britain's particular history in becoming a multicultural society." It is thus not at all clear what is meant by "civil religion in the UK," though for REDCo researchers civil religion and counter-secularization are part of the same process of ensuring that European religious education mirrors political goals, especially that of *tolerance*, epitomized in the 1648 Treaty of Westphalia. In the aftermath of the post-Reformation wars of religion—a context which even a secular political philosopher like Rawls sees as critical to the rise of secular political authority[32]—"tolerance" is *the* key to the historical emergence of eighteenth-century civil religion. But further analysis of "civil religion" remains necessary. We believe that civil religion, when given this proper analysis, cannot be evidence of *counter*-secularization but only secularization's *confirmation.*

European Religious Education and European Civil Religion

Although its roots lie in classical Greek and Roman Antiquity,[33] the term civil religion was conceptualized with most prominence in the Enlightenment by Rousseau's *Social Contract.* Rousseau suggests that the deistic "dogmas of civil religion ought to be few, simple, and exactly worded, without explanation or commentary": "The existence of a mighty, intelligent and beneficent Divinity, possessed of foresight and providence, the life to come, the happiness of the just, the punishment of the wicked, the sanctity of the social contract and the laws: these are its positive dogmas." Its "negative

31. Jackson and O'Grady, "Religious Education in England: Social Plurality, Civil Religion and Religious Education Pedagogy," 181–202.

32. Rawls, *Political Liberalism*, xxii.

33. See Heater, *Citizenship: The Civic Ideal in World History, Politics and Education.*

dogmas I confine to one, intolerance." Rousseau rejects the notions of those "who distinguish civil from theological intolerance": "The two forms are inseparable. It is impossible to live at peace with those we regard as damned; to love them would be to hate God who punishes them: we positively must either reclaim or torment them. Wherever theological intolerance is admitted, it must inevitably have some civil effect—and as soon as it has such an effect, the Sovereign is no longer Sovereign even in the temporal sphere: thenceforth priests are the real masters, and kings only their ministers." Tolerance then "should be given to all religions that tolerate others, so long as their dogmas contain nothing contrary to the duties of citizenship." Though Rousseau preaches tolerance, he is less than sympathetic to Christianity: "Christianity preaches only servitude and dependence. Its spirit is so favourable to tyranny that it always profits by such a regime. True Christians are made to be slaves, and they know it and do not much mind: this short life counts for too little in their eyes."[34]

Bellah's "Civil Religion in America" reinvigorated this term, which had become neglected in mid-twentieth century sociological analysis.[35] But Bellah's use of the term differs from Rousseau's. In defining American civil religion, he uses President Kennedy's inaugural address as contemporary manifestation of a tradition that dates back to the American founding fathers. Bellah's analysis focuses not only on Kennedy's use of "God" in his inaugural address but similar uses of God in speeches by Lincoln, Jefferson, Franklin, and others. Thus, although American constitutional separation of church and state would forbid state favoritism of any particular denomination, civil religion is integral to American identity:

> What we have, then, from the earliest years of the republic is a collection of beliefs, symbols, and rituals with respect to sacred things and institutionalized in a collectivity. This religion—there seems no other word for it—while not antithetical to and indeed sharing much in common with Christianity, was neither sectarian nor in any specific sense Christian. At a time when the society was overwhelmingly Christian, it seems unlikely that this lack of Christian reference was meant to spare the feelings of the tiny non-Christian minority. Rather, the civil religion expressed what those who set the precedents felt were appropriate under the circumstances. It reflected their private as well as public views. Nor was the civil religion simply 'religion in general.' While generality was undoubtedly seen as a virtue by some . . . the civil religion was specific enough when it came

34. Rousseau, *The Social Contract*, 144.
35. See Bellah, "Civil Religion in America," 1–21.

to the topic of America. Precisely because of this specificity, the civil religion was saved from empty formalism and served as a genuine vehicle of national religious self-understanding.[36]

From the early 1830s, Tocqueville's *Democracy in America* makes similar observations, notably in Chapter XVII, in which he considers religion as "a political institution which powerfully contributes to the maintenance of a democratic republic among Americans." As Tocqueville states, "By the side of every religion is to be found a political opinion, which is connected with it by affinity."[37]

Bellah's civil religion can be distinguished from Rousseau's, above all in that Rousseau's conceptualization argues "there is and can be no longer an exclusive national religion." For Rousseau, it is shared humanity that matters. A year later, in a reprinted version of his 1967 paper, Bellah defends himself directly on this point, "against the accusation of supporting an idolatrous worship of the American nation." He counters: "I think it should be clear . . . that I conceive of the central tradition of the American civil religion not as a form of national self-worship but as the subordination of the nation to ethical principles that transcend it in terms of which it should be judged. I am convinced that every nation and every people come to some form of religious self-understanding whether the critics like it or not. Rather than simply denounce what seems in any case inevitable, it seems more responsible to seek within the civil religious tradition for those critical principles which undercut the ever-present danger of national self-idolization."[38]

These two forms of American and French (European) civil religion have deep and, as subsequent debates have illustrated, complex historical lineages. In Rousseau's case, civil religion replaces a Christianity which society has outgrown in its traditional forms; but this is not so in the American. Bellah is again useful here:

> . . . the civil religion was not, in the minds of Franklin, Washington, Jefferson, or other leaders, with the exception of a few radicals like Tom Paine, ever felt to be a substitute for Christianity. There was an implicit but quite clear division of function between the civil religion and Christianity.[39]

In contemporary America, President Obama has been the only United States president, or serious national candidate, formally to challenge the

36. Bellah, "Civil Religion in America," 1–2.

37. Tocqueville, *Democracy in America*, 118–19.

38. Bellah, *Beyond Belief*, 163–64.

39. Bellah, *The Sacred Canopy*, 7–8.

unstated common (vaguely) Christian heritage of America. For Obama, even the notionally Christian nature of American civil religion was rejected in widely reported statements in which he described America, in effect, as "not a Christian nation."[40] In Europe, such a proclamation about the continent's religiosity would not now be in the least problematic. Religious education of the kind advocated by REDCo and their political funders has helped facilitate this.

European Religious Education: Civil Religion and Secularization

Classic accounts of secularization come from disparate writings on religion from Comte, Durkheim, Marx, and Weber. These reductionist theorists of religion framed the terms of all later debate on secularization by not only explaining religion but in elaborating how religion could be explained away. Secularization theory—inherent in all reductionist theories of religion— was subsequently developed by such scholars as Luckmann,[41] Martin,[42] and Wilson.[43] There was nevertheless as much controversy among these theorists themselves as among their religious opponents. As one influential theorist commented: "Throughout the 1970s and 1980s, a controversy has raged among sociologists of religion around the question of secularization. One of the most puzzling aspects of the discussion is that sometimes the issue has seemed to be not so much whether secularization actually occurred, but whether or not 'secularization theory' itself exists."[44] The debate continues and nothing can be taken for granted, least of all something as multifaceted as religion and politics as it bears on education. REDCo researchers accept and *assume* counter-secularization through the evidence of religion's prominence in the public realm. The role of religious education here is to provide a facilitating framework in which disparate religious worldviews can live in harmony, a model which is seen in terms of civil religion. How-

40. On 28 June 2006, Senator Obama said the following: "Whatever we once were, we are no longer a Christian nation—or at least, not just. We are also a Jewish nation, a Muslim nation, a Buddhist nation, and a Hindu nation, and a nation of nonbelievers." Obama, "'Call to Renewal' Keynote Address." In Ankara Turkey, on 8 April 2009, President Obama said "we do not consider ourselves a Christian nation, or a Jewish nation, or a Muslim nation. We consider ourselves a nation of citizens who are bound by ideals and a set of values." See Obama, "We Do Not Consider Ourselves a Christian Nation."

41. Luckmann, *The Invisible Religion*.

42. Martin, *A General Theory of Secularization*.

43. Wilson, *Religion in Secular Society*.

44. Tschannen, "The Secularisation Paradigm," 395.

ever, examination of historical and contemporary understandings of civil religion supports the notion that rather than countering secularization civil religion is *integral* to it.

It was Richard Fenn who provided a concise framing of this idea in his paper on "The Relevance of Bellah's 'Civil Religion' Thesis to a Theory of Secularization."[45] Fenn develops this correlation in *Towards a Theory of Secularization*.[46] Segal identified five stages within Fenn's framework: "(1) the establishment of distinctively religious institutions like a priesthood, which thereby reduces other social institutions to merely secular ones; (2) the demand by minority groups for the demarcation of distinctively religious activities like marriage, which similarly leaves other social activities as merely secular ones; (3) the consequent forging of a common, civil religion as a means of overcoming the divisions thereby created; (4) the emergence of conflicting interpretations of that common religion by rival groups, whose self-serving, political motives call into question the objectivity and divinity of the common religion; and (5) the emergence of a clash between individual values and social ones, which individuals are thereby less willing to deem sacred."[47] The civil religion stage unifies (or attempts to unify) the differences created by increased plurality and diversity in modern societies.

Civil religion is "religion" in the Durkheimian sense of representing the most treasured values within a society, and that which helps at the same time to cohere societies through those values. It is this notion of civil religion and the concomitant values of democracy, citizenship, human rights, and above all tolerance, within the REDCo framework, that illustrates the politicization of religion in European religious education. Politicization of religion in European religious education is understood here as the incorporation of religion by secular politics for secular goals. Granted this position allows religions to *have* achieved greater public prominence. However, recalling Berger's classic definition of secularization above, incorporation of religion through education into a political sphere is on the terms of the political, not the religious. It is in no sense a reversal of religious power in the face of the political. It is this politicization which is critical (with civil religion) to understanding why current trends in religious education are anything but evidence of counter-secularization. In sum, the politicization of religion in education mirrors a *phase* of secularization through civil religion facilitated through European religious education itself.

45. Fenn, "The Relevance of Bellah's 'Civil Religion' Thesis to a Theory of Secularization, 502–11.

46. Fenn, *Towards a Theory of Secularization*.

47. Segal, *Toward a Theory of Secularization*, vol. 1.

Misrepresenting Religion in European Religious Education

The most significant challenge to this political trajectory in British religious education has come from L. Phillip Barnes. As we have referenced in earlier chapters, Barnes argues that "British religious education has misrepresented the nature of religion in efforts to commend itself as contributing to the social aims of education, as these are typically framed in liberal democratic societies."[48] Barnes argues that "current representations of religion in British religious education are limited in their capacity to challenge racism and religious intolerance, chiefly because they are conceptually ill equipped to develop respect for difference."[49] It is, Barnes states:

> . . . a tale of progress and the triumph of reason over unreason. In truth, as a number of recent writers have pointed out . . . the story is more controversial, convoluted and ideological, resulting in educational losses as well as educational gains. [In addition to] pedagogical concerns about the failure of some versions of post-confessional, multi-faith religious education to engage pupils' interest and the accusation that thematic teaching has the potential to confuse pupils, there is growing disquiet across a range of issues in religious education.[50]

Barnes summarizes his argument as follows: "British religious education has misrepresented the nature of religion in efforts to commend itself as contributing to the social aims of education, as these are typically framed in liberal democratic societies such as Britain in terms of furthering tolerance, respect for difference and social cohesion."[51]

Barnes's central thesis of the misrepresentation of religious education is, we believe, valid. Indeed, his thesis can be extended to the European context. For European religious education increasingly coheres with the political. This politicization of religion in education—civil religion—represents simply a more subtle development in secularization. The *politicization* of religion in education differs from religious education being concerned with politics. The politicization of religion in education implies not simply the focus of religion in education towards political ends, but, as the REDCo findings incline us to think, *a model of religion in education where political*

48. Barnes, "The Misrepresentation of Religion in modern British (Religious) Education," 395.

49. Ibid.395–96.

50. Ibid.

51. Ibid., 396.

ends are the predominant pedagogical goal. This view is likely to be contested. But to do so, European religious educators would have to provide convincing arguments of what goals *other* than these political goals *do* predominate.

Wright, Copley, and others (such as Felderhof, Thompson, and Torevel in 2007) have also critiqued the increasingly dominant political goals of religious education.[52] The common line of historical analysis is identification of the secular and secularizing legacy of the Enlightenment. Since the Enlightenment was fundamentally an antagonistic interplay between religious and newly emergent forms of political power, we make here the case for engagement with political theology to enrich debates about religion in education, especially around present themes of civil religion and secularization.

European Religious Education and Political Theology

Political theology, often referred to as public theology, is a form of intellectual discourse which, depending on your perspective, provides a theological interpretation of the political, or a political interpretation of the theological. Scott and Cavanaugh demonstrate the range of applications of political theology globally.[53] Though questions of church-state relations reach back to antiquity, Schmitt's *Political Theology* remains foundational to modern debate.[54] Indeed, Emden has commented that Carl Schmitt's *Political Theology: Four Chapters on the Concept of Sovereignty* has turned out to be one of the most important texts in modern political thought.[55] Yet, *Political Theology* (in the narrow sense of Schmitt's work) and political theology, in the wider sense of the modern field of enquiry which Schmitt so informed, is, in both senses, underused to address the questions of religion and politics in education.

Written at a time of crisis in German and European liberal democracy, *Political Theology* reframed a problem of the relationship of religious and political authority from antiquity into the context of modernity. Schmitt argued that "All significant concepts of the modern theory of the state are secularized theological concepts." That is, the theological has been transposed into the political. As Schmitt argues: " . . . not only because of their

---

52. See Wright, *Critical Religious Education, Multiculturalism and the Pursuit of Truth*; Copley, *Indoctrination, Education and God*; and Felderhof et al., *Inspiring Faith in Schools*.

53. Scott and Cavanaugh, *The Blackwell Companion of Political Theology*.

54. See Schmitt, *Political Theology: Four Chapters on the Concept of Sovereignty*.

55. Emden, *Carl Schmitt. Political Theology: Four Chapters on the Concept of Sovereignty*.

historic development—in which they were transferred from theology to the theory of the state, whereby, for example, the omnipotent God became the omnipotent lawgiver—but also because of their systematic structure, the idea of the modern constitutional state triumphed with deism [over] a [fuller] theology and metaphysics . . . "[56] Schmitt, above all theorists, demonstrates the way the political becomes theological.

The prescient timeliness of Schmitt's analysis of how this might lead to absolute power represented in the political realm (now that theology and metaphysics are displaced) was evidenced by the totalitarianism that emerged with his work. The theme of absolute secular power as totalitarian power was a theme taken up by mid-twentieth century political theorists such as Arendt, Aron, Friedrich, Brzezinski, Popper, Talmon, and the various writings of Eric Voegelin.[57] Each theorist in his own way showed how autocratic, dictatorial, and totalitarian systems replaced theology with similarly all-encompassing but secular ideologies, Latterly, figures as diverse as Bauman, Gray, and Wolin, coming from differing political standpoints, have all argued this too, none more pithily than Gray: "Modern politics is a chapter in the history of religions."[58]

REDCo research points precisely to this politicization of religion in *education*. Now, it could be contested, as Hull does, that religious education *needs* to be secular,[59] just as Taylor argues that modern democracies too need to be secular.[60] Taylor identifies three facets to this term,

> which we can class in the three categories of the French Revolutionary trinity [his language of course ironic]: 1. No one must be forced in the realm of religion or basic belief. This is what is defined as religious liberty, including of course, the freedom not to believe . . . 2. There must be equality between people of different faiths or basic belief; no religious outlook or (religious or areligious) Weltanschauung can enjoy a privileged status, let

56. Schmitt, *Political Theology*, 36.

57. See Arendt, *The Origins of Totalitarianism*; Aron, *The Opium of the Intellectuals*; Popper, *The Open Society and Its Enemies*; Talmon, *History of Totalitarian Democracy*; and the various writings of Eric Voegelin such as Hennington, *Modernity Without Restraint: The Political Religions, Collected Works of Eric Voegelin*, vol. 5. See also Burleigh, *Earthly Powers: Religion and Politics in Europe from the Enlightenment to the Great War* and Burleigh, *Sacred Causes: The Clash of Religion and Politics from the Great War to the War on Terror*.

58. Gray, *Black Mass*, 1; Bauman, *Modernity and the Holocaust*; and Wolin, *Democracy Inc.: Managed Democracy and the Specter of Inverted Totalitarianism*.

59. Hull, "The Blessings of Secularity: Religious Education in England and Wales," 51–58.

60. Taylor, "The Meaning of Secularism," 1. See also Taylor, *A Secular Age*.

alone be adopted by the state. Then 3. All spiritual families must be heard, included in the ongoing process of determining what the society is about (its political identity).[61]

This politically liberal position, according to Rawls, addresses two questions:

> The first question is: what is the most appropriate conception of justice for specifying the fair terms of social cooperation between citizens regarded as free and equal? . . . The second question is: what are the grounds of toleration understood in a general way, given the fact of reasonable pluralism as the inevitable result of the powers of human reason at work within enduring free institutions? Combining these two questions into one, we have: how is it possible for there to exist over time a just and stable society of free and equal citizens who still remain profoundly divided by religious, philosophical, and moral doctrines?[62]

Given this broad liberal political perspective (as defined by Rawls) in the light of democracies needing to be secular (as defined by Taylor), the incorporation of religion through education into the political sphere could be seen as a cooperative model, which creates a working space to allow the flourishing of religion itself, with education as an effective means of achieving this. However, even if this reasonable claim were accepted, it would still mean that religion in education receives its pedagogical rationale from political sources. Further, as Chaves argues, secularization can be characterised by a decline in religious authority.[63] Politicized religious education cannot be conceived here as evidence therefore of a reversal of religious vis-a-vis political authority. To present European religious education as counter to European secularization is thus misleading.

The Global Reach of European Religious Education

There is here a wider international dimension to this debate with which educators, and not simply religious educators, might usefully engage. For developments in European religious education are in line with numerous global, post-Cold War initiatives, which have emphasized the scope and need for political institutions to be supported by educational programs. The European initiatives discussed in this chapter can be contextualized as

61. Taylor, "The Meaning of Secularism," 1.

62. Rawls, *Political Liberalism*, 3–4; see also xxii–xxiv.

63. Chaves, "Secularization as Declining Religious Authority," 749–74.

part of the United Nations' post-Cold War International Decade of Human Rights Education (1995–2004), and subsequent World Programme for Human Rights Education (2005– and ongoing). UNESCO has played a major role here, including through a 60th Anniversary Commemoration of the Universal Declaration of Human Rights.[64]

What is *new* here is the incorporation of the role of religion and education into the political domain of facilitating values of democratic citizenship and human rights. This really began significant before 9/11, in the post-Iranian Revolution context of the United Nations' 1981 Declaration on the Elimination of Discrimination on the Basis of Religion or Belief, and the early 1990s creation of a United Nations Special Rapporteur for Freedom of Religion or Belief. Two months after 9/11, the then Rapporteur, Amor, produced "The Role of Religious Education in the Pursuit of Tolerance and Non-Discrimination" for the International Consultative Conference on School Education in Relation with Freedom of Religion and Belief, Tolerance and Non-Discrimination.[65] In the decade since Amor's statement, religion has come ever more to the forefront of national and international security.[66] One of the implications of this has been the securitization of religion in education—which we saw in the previous chapter—where religion in education is put not simply to political but security uses.

School education is here currently receiving high priority within the Office of the Special Rapporteur on Freedom of Religion or Belief. At the sixteenth session of the Human Rights Council, Agenda item 3 was the "Promotion and protection of all human rights, civil, political, economic, social and cultural rights, including the right to development." Bielefeldt, the present Rapporteur, reporting to the Human Rights Council, remarks: "The school constitutes by far the most important formal institution for the implementation of the right to education as it has been enshrined in international human rights documents, such as the Universal Declaration of Human Rights (art. 26), the International Covenant on Economic, Social and Cultural Rights (art. 13), and the Convention on the Rights of the Child (art. 28)." The Special Rapporteur refers to relevant international human rights documents, the elimination of stereotypes and prejudices, the issue of religious symbols in the school context, and religious instruction in schools. Concluding, the Special Rapporteur notes that "freedom of religion or belief

64. Gearon, "From Universal Declaration to World Program: 1948–2008: 60 Years of Human Rights Education."

65. Amor, "The Role of Religious Education in the Pursuit of Tolerance and Non-Discrimination."

66. Schmid, *The Routledge Handbook of Terrorism Research.* See also Seiple et al., *Routledge Handbook of Religion and Security: Theory and Practice.*

and school education is a multifaceted issue that entails significant opportunities as well as far-reaching challenges." He recommends that "States
should favourably consider a number of principles in this regard" and explicitly refers to "the final document adopted at the International Consultative Conference on School Education in relation to Freedom of Religion
or Belief, Tolerance and Non-discrimination . . . and to *the Toledo Guiding Principles on Teaching About Religions and Beliefs in Public Schools*."[67]
As noted, it is this latter document, originating from the OSCE, which is
having a profound effect on the nature, role, and political orientation of
European religious education.

To repeat, these developments in European religious education,
conceived as civil religion, can in no way be said to reflect counter-secularization for one major reason: the dominance of political objectives in
religious education is an example of the decline of religious authority not
its resurgence or new ascendancy. There is, in short, little that is *religious*
in these new models of civil religion. Developments in European religious
education merit weight, then, not as evidence for counter-secularization but
for secularization's advancement through shaping an emergent European
civil religion. Furthermore, the terms of civil religion conceived by REDCo
to address commonalities in political value (citizenship, democracy, human
rights) amid religious pluralism now have removed any reference whatsoever to "God," even in the more minimalist terms of Rousseau's deism: "God"
has, perhaps strangely, lost its definitional hold on religion more generally,
and it is difficult to see what is religious about REDCo's "civil religion," unless the deification is of democracy itself.

In short, we have attempted to open a new front in discussions of European religious education in this chapter. More work of course is needed
to do full justice to the variant readings of secularization theory and the
effects of secularization in education, politics, and more widely in public
life. Current, or at least emergent, policy in European religious education is
tending towards the bracketing out of the specific perspectives of religious
traditions, subsuming them within a common narrative of "civil religion."
We have characterized this as confirmation of rather countering secularization by arguing that this emergent civil religion (so prevalent in European
religious education) is in the terms of the political. Arguably, it is a variant
of what Milbank called "policing the sublime"[68] or, in educational terms,
what Barnes, Copley, and Wright, among others, has variously seen as the

---

67. United Nations Human Rights Council, Sixteenth Session, Agenda Item 3,
Report of the Special Rapporteur on Freedom of Religion or Belief, 1–19.

68. Milbank, *Theology and Social Theory*.

neutralizing of religion in the context of a liberal hegemony, where liberal politics is reflected in and by a liberal (religious) education. But liberal politics has not, it could be argued, (as classic secularization would suggest) removed religion from the public, it has simply altered it, transformed it to its own purposes. More widely then, to what extent does civil religion either remove, or reinforce religion in and from public life? It has the potential to do both. This is why the debate is a nuanced one, and we think important, as much for the future of religions themselves in relation to public life as to European religious education.

In conclusion, Grace Davie suggests that "it is most unlikely that grand theories (not least secularization theory) will help in our understanding of global civil religion, in that they are insufficiently flexible to deal with the new patterns and exchanges that are emerging."[69] We disagree. For we believe it is precisely in the terms of secularization by which we can understand not only the emergence of civil religion but its (seeming) continuation in and through European religious education. In all, then, the question to ask here, somewhat ironically, is whether religion is in danger of becoming no longer *marginalized* by politics but *subsumed by* it, *over*-politicized and *over*-integrated, even *reduced* to secular life? Liberal autocrats no longer ignore, or overlook, or mock religion, but *manipulate* and *re-define* it.[70]

To those so inclined, this acclimation remains merited: secularization *vivat*. Its substance seen in religious instruction voided of traditional content—in religious education of, by, and for the secular state.

---

69. Davie et al., *Religious America, Secular Europe?*, 472.

70. Arthur et al., *Education, Politics and Religion*, 92.

Chapter 9

An Open Conclusion
The Future of State Religious Education

OUR WORK HAS SOUGHT to provide a charitable critique of the movement for expanded biblical instruction in American public schools. We have not argued against this proposal on separationist grounds nor on the grounds of multicultural pedagogy. Instead, we have sought to highlight the harms to religious culture that expanded instruction on the Bible in public schools would likely engender. However, we must acknowledge that there is in fact a serious problem in the United States with religious illiteracy, as with growing biblical hostility. The Bible is a foundational text for American and Western civilization; its current low level of understanding constitutes a genuine educational scandal. We would indeed very much like to see an improvement in biblical literacy in the United States. And so indeed we would like to see increased knowledge in the United States of some of the perhaps now less well appreciated aspects of the Bible's legacy: how it inspired evangelicals, who took its words so very seriously to support the expansion of American democracy in the early nineteenth century;[1] how it fortified evangelical ministers

---

1. Richard Carwardine, for example, notes that the flowering of evangelical religiosity and the expansion of American democracy in the early nineteenth century were "not wholly independent events," as Bible-guided ministers and laymen injected a powerful influence on the growth and structure of "mass participatory politics," so much so that "it is doubtful if the extraordinary popular engagement in politics at this time—the greatest enthusiasm for politics the republic has ever seen—could have occurred had it not been for the integration of evangelicals and their organizational structures into the new order." Cardwardine, "Methodists, Politics, and the American Civil War," 176–77.

and missionaries to oppose the Indian Removal Act and its terrifying Trail of Tears;[2] how it inspired opposition to American nativism;[3] how it nurtured key aspects of the American feminist movement;[4] and how it galvanized vigorous resistance to American imperialism among leaders such as William Jennings Bryan.[5] There is, it would seem, so very much room for improvement.

Our initial response to the charge that our perspective robs students of an appropriate means to cultivate a much needed knowledge base is rather simple. Which is better, illiteracy or error? Illiteracy can be rectified; error, once rooted, is much harder to remove.

Our second response involves highlighting the distinctive and positive features of a program adopted in South Carolina in 2006, a program in public high schools whereby a student may choose to take and to receive full academic credit for a non-devotional course on the Bible taught by entities external to the public school system, a program often called a release time system. The South Carolina law represents a tremendous step forward, and we believe it deserves to be studied in great depth and potentially to be adopted across the country. The state of Ohio is currently considering adopting this distinctive program,[6] and other states would do well to consider the same.

To explore this promising development, we should first define what we *do not* mean by a release time system. Since 1914, students in American public schools have participated in voluntary devotional courses (off campus) during school hours.[7] When this practice was objected to on constitutional grounds in the early 1950s—part of the first wave of strict separationist agitation that would later see brief morning devotional Bible

---

2. Many Baptists, for example, "worked wholeheartedly and to the last ditch with the Cherokees against the removal effort" and were supported by their national mission board "which fully sympathized with their stand." McCoughlin, "Cherokees and Methodists: 1824–1834, *Church History*, 47.

3. See Quinn, "Expecting the Impossible? Abolitionist Appeals to the Irish in Antebellum America," 667–710. Especially impassioned in opposition to nativism were Unitarian minister Rev. George Bradburn (1806–1880) and Methodist minister and educational leader Alexander B. Longstreet (1790–1870).

4. See Dayton and Strong, *Rediscovering an Evangelical Heritage: A Tradition and Trajectory of Integrating Piety and Justice*, esp. chap. 8, "The Evangelical Roots of Feminism." And here also, as in so many similar areas, the work of evangelical leader Charles Grandison Finney looms large. See Hambrick-Stowe, *The Spirit of American Evangelicalism*.

5. See Kazin, *A Godly Hero: The Life of William Jennings Bryan*.

6. One important source can be found at releasetime.org.

7. Ibid.

readings, without comment, along with brief and vague prayers expelled from public schools—the Supreme Court upheld the devotional practice. In *Zorach v. Clauson,* Justice William O. Douglas wrote for the majority in upholding a New York release time program, and he did so on the sensible grounds that if the separation of church and state were so restrictive as to deny off-campus programs of this nature, then government and religion would be "aliens to each other—hostile, suspicious, and even unfriendly."[8] In fact, Douglas here repudiates the view of Sajo and a rising chorus of left-leaning secularists, underscoring how their views are foreign to American constitutional heritage.

However it is this kind of devotional release time program that we do not seek to examine.[9] Rather, the program established in 2006 in South Carolina is one for release time instruction in *non-devotional* coursework on the Bible.[10] The South Carolina law reads as follows:[11]

(A) A school district board of trustees may award high school students no more than two elective Carnegie units[12] for the completion of released time classes in religious instruction if:

  (1) for the purpose of awarding elective Carnegie units, the released time classes in religious instruction are evaluated on the basis of purely secular criteria that are substantially the same criteria used to evaluate similar classes at established private high schools for the purpose of determining whether a student transferring to a public high school from a private high school will be awarded elective [credits] for such classes. However, any criteria that released time classes must be taken at an accredited private school is not applicable for the purpose of awarding credits for released time classes; and

  (2) the decision to award elective Carnegie units is neutral as to, and does not involve any test for, religious content or denominational affiliation.

(B) For the purpose of subsection (A)(1), secular criteria may include, but are not limited to, the following:

---

8. 343 U.S. 306 (1952).

9. This is not to say that we necessarily oppose such a program.

10. See releasetime.org.

11. South Carolina Code: A322, R352, S148.

12. South Carolina, like many states, defines its educational course units as Carnegie Units.

(1) number of hours of classroom instruction time;

(2) review of the course syllabus which reflects the course requirements and materials used;

(3) methods of assessment used in the course; and

(4) whether the course was taught by a certified teacher.

This model deserves very careful study, and promises to allow educational reformers to achieve their objectives without exposing biblical instruction to a number of the problems we itemized above. There is a tremendous potential for these courses—which usually are taken in private schools—to experiment with pedagogies that develop instructional approaches to the Bible that minimize such problems as museumification and which reduce anti-religious bias. The law therefore represents a tremendous step forward.

No doubt questions still remain. The courses are subject to some measure of state review (as is fully appropriate), so the possibility of litigative overreach by anti-religious, or otherwise strict separationist activists demanding problematic impositions on the courses remains. However, the fact that in the program the teachers are not public school employees, and that the instruction is off campus serves vividly to underscore that of which Bible course advocates have long reminded their opponents: these courses are *elective* and not at all imposed. The physicality of having to remove oneself from the school, and enter a foreign space highlights the elective character of the courses by showcasing how conspicuously a student has to *opt in*. Plus the externality of the instruction underscores the degree to which these courses pose no risk of what some secularists consider the contagion of religion in public spaces, that is, the belief that if religion enters anywhere within the sanctuary of the secular state, such as the public schoolhouse, it will seep into all others. The removal of students to a separate location with separate faculty is a kind of secularist firewall. *In principle*, therefore, these courses should fare better against the litigative onslaught that no doubt would await them should they expand nationwide.

Indeed, the South Carolina credit-bearing Bible course release time program has already fared well in the federal courts. In *Moss v. Spartanburg County School District Seven*,[13] the U.S. Fourth Circuit Court of Appeals upheld the release time program, noting that it fell within the constitutionally protected right of parents to direct the upbringing of their children, and did not violate the non-establishment principle. The American Humanist Association and Americans United for the Separation of Church and State

13. 683 F. 3d 599 (4th Cir 2012).

appealed the decision but the Supreme Court did not grant certiorari and so the *Moss* decision remains good law.

Moreover, the release time program is promising also because private schools have a wealth of resources they can draw on to conduct meaningful non-devotional Bible coursework, including precisely the curricula developed by the NCBCPS, the Bible Literacy Project, and now the growing—and soon to be monumental—resources of the Museum of the Bible and its Green Scholars Program. As to the latter, the Museum of the Bible's educational outreach programs seek "to enhance collaborative learning through . . . [studying] the history, narrative, and impact of the Bible in an objective and descriptive manner."[14] With its commitment to excellent non-sectarian, non-devotional instruction, the Museum of the Bible provides an embarrassment of riches in terms of resource material for release time courses in private schools. The treasures designed for students at the high school level include:

> a new interactive Bible curriculum [that] allows students to travel beyond the classroom to create a meaningful learning experience. Consisting of 108 chapters over four volumes, the innovative content design engages the smartphone generation . . . the curriculum focuses on the history, narrative and impact of the Bible with hundreds of interactive media elements including virtual reality, animations, 3D models, interactive maps, gamified quizzes and more!
>
> History lessons examine the historical and archeological information fostering a better understanding of the Bible and its context. History lessons also benefit from drawing upon the 40,000 artifacts in the Museum Collection. Narrative lessons present significant concepts, events, and personalities of the Bible in an objective and descriptive way. The narrative lessons fit into the overall presentation of the Bible as a tool of cultural literacy and a primary force of Western Civilization. Impact lessons connect the influence of the Bible on societies and cultures over time. All lessons—history, narrative and impact—maintain religious neutrality to fully respect diverse religions and traditions associated with the Bible.[15]

Enriched by such increasingly impressive materials as those of the Museum of the Bible and the longer standing resource base of the BLP and the

14. Museum of the Bible, "Private School."
15. Museum of the Bible, "Curriculum."

NCBCPS, public school release time programs for non-devotional instruction of the Bible in private schools promise to provide genuine educational advances in American public schools.

However, this promising approach, to constitute a salve on the deep scars of biblical illiteracy would need at least two things to buttress it. First, it would need support in school districts across the country—outside conservative leaning states like South Carolina. Second, it would need to appeal to students and parents so that students would avail themselves of the opportunity.

In this context, we need to be sensitive to the driving forces contributing to rising religious and biblical illiteracy. No doubt the factors are vast. But one factor certainly is how the trope of the "strict separation of church and state" is being used by the secular left to attack religion by advancing the claim that separationism is deeply American, and that this deeply American principle is predicated on the uniquely poisonous tendency of religion to corrupt political and public life. Secularist advocate Brooke Allen writes in *The Nation* magazine of what she calls "Our Godless Constitution."[16] "Our Constitution makes no mention whatever of God." "The omission," she maintains, "was too obvious to have been anything but deliberate." From this Ms. Allen concludes, "the Founding Fathers were not religious men."[17] In turn, a sort of inverse originalism takes charge. Usually wary of originalist jurisprudence, the secular left in this area tends to wrap itself in the very garments in which it supposes the founding generation had so brilliantly been arrayed. For the founders, Allen states with confidence, "fought hard to erect a wall of separation between church and state." Why? Because, on this interpretation, the founders were consumed with a fear of the "corruption to which established priesthoods were liable."[18] And, the secularists have it, so must we. This move is made even more forcefully in a book-length treatment with the same title as that of Allen's (proving it *le mots juste* of the secular left). In the book, *The Godless Constitution,* Professor of Secular Studies Isaac Kramnick and Professor Laurence Moore argue that strict separationism is the original intent of the founders, and deserves to be seen as a "moral" commitment to which citizens in good conscience must remain ever committed.[19] Why? Because in their view, the founders saw religion,

16. Allen, "Our Godless Constitution."

17. Ibid.

18. Ibid.

19. Kramnick and Moore, *The Godless Constitution: A Moral Defense of the Secular State.*

when socially strong enough to influence the actions of the state, as a force destructive of the proper ends of government. And, once again, so must we.

This view that religion was seen by the sage founders as dangerous to the public and, for this very reason was deliberately excluded from governmental affairs, is a central motif of contemporary secularist advocacy. Such a view can over time be expected to cause an erosion of religious belief in some, perhaps even in many, and consequently a rise in biblical illiteracy and even biblical hostility. At least, this is the view of a number of recent scholars. Brendan Sweetman maintains that the strict separationist viewpoint inculcates the idea that "there is something wrong" with religious beliefs while instructing believers that "there is something wrong with them."[20] This view in turn, Robert Kraynack argues, "subverts the Christian faith by sapping its vital spiritual energies."[21] Liberalism based on strict separationism performs, Kraynack argues, a lobotomy on the higher spiritual instincts of man.[22] As a result of the (at least partial) public discrediting of Christianity caused by liberalism's separationist ideology, the idea of a Godless state serves to attack faith and to promote a "dogmatism" defined in large measure by adherence to reductive science, self-centered consumerism, and shallow careerism.

In response to this view, our arguments witness to a different reason for the non-establishment of religion: state incompetence.[23] State incompetence has been pointed to in various areas in this work, such as in the state's weakness in detecting motives preliminary to the determination of the enjoyment of a constitutional value, and in its tendency toward having its institutions securitized and unable to address phenomena on their own terms. In turn, our argument points to how it is in fact *good* not to have the state involved in religion. A constitution that does not have government directly aid religion should not be seen as a constitution opposed to religion. In fact, it is precisely one major way of *aiding* religion. We do not claim interpretive novelty here.[24] In fact, this view was made by many at the time

20. Sweetman, *Why Politics Needs Religion*, 14.

21. Kraynack, *Christian Faith and Modern Democracy*, 201–2.

22. Ibid., 270.

23. For one recent discussion of the importance of recognizing state incompetence in matters of religion, see Bradley, "Dueling Clios," 42–43.

24. Gedicks expresses this point by juxtaposing, correctly we believe, French Laicite and America's church/state doctrine: "Whereas 'religious freedom' in the United States typically suggests freedom of religion from state interference, in France Laicite often connotes the state's 'protecting citizens from the excesses of religion,' *and this makes all the difference*." Gedicks, "Religious Exemptions, Formal Neutrality, and Laicite," 476; emphasis added.

of the founding, and has been made by many throughout American history. Nevertheless, Andrew Koppelman is correct to note that "this rationale has been neglected in modern Establishment Clause theory."[25] Our argument against public schools teaching the Bible merely reiterates this idea in what we believe is an especially vivid manner. In turn, we hope it can reshape a culturally powerful paradigm about the reasons for the founding generation's so-called "Godless constitution." Perhaps we must speak, instead, of our *God-fearing* constitution. Did not the prophet Jeremiah remind us:

> you must not mention 'a message from the Lord' again, because each one's word becomes their own message. So you distort the words of the living God, the Lord Almighty.[26]

Nevertheless, there is by now a strong secular coalition which exerts considerable pressure on American political debate. We have noted its strength in terms of the likelihood of litigation over instructional approaches to the Bible that attempt to capture its living meaning. As a practical matter, for release time proposals such as those in South Carolina to have any likelihood of success outside of the conservative South, the secular forces in contemporary life must be contended with and, when appropriate, compromised with. In light of this fact, we argue that the best way to ensure that release time proposals are not crushed by the secular left is to seek overlapping accord with at least some of the strident secularists' key tenets. This will no doubt prove difficult given the hostility to religion surveyed above, but progress remains possible, as a kind of practical alliance might surface with at least some secularists in terms of a common appreciation of the weaknesses of the state as a moral tutor—as a paternalistic pedagogue of privileged values and principles.

With the goal only of opening avenues of future discussion, we propose at least considering the following, admittedly rather bold scenario. We are not committed to it. We *are* committed to exploring every possible option. In that spirit, we might remind ourselves that a key element in many forms of contemporary secularism is the theory of evolutionary naturalism.[27] As Richard Dawkins—a hero among so many secularists—averred: "Although atheism might have been *logically* tenable before Charles Darwin, Darwin made it possible to be an intellectually fulfilled atheist."[28] (The prevalence

25. Koppelman, "Corruption of Religion and the Establishment Clause," 1834.

26. Jer 23:36 (NIV).

27. By evolutionary naturalism, we mean not evolutionary science per se, but a philosophical conception that reduces all phenomena to the processes of evolutionary determination.

28. Dawkins, *The Blind Watchmaker*, 6; emphasis added.

of the ichthys transformed on car bumpers into a crouching reptile testifies to the common connection.) However, elements of evolutionary science have plausibly been interpreted by leading biologists, such as Dawkins and many others, as implying a very substantial degree of sexual differentiation between male and female humans. This in turn has placed evolutionary science in opposition to a number of theories common in more extreme forms of feminism, especially theories asserting complete gender interchangeablism, and denying any strong sense of sexual dimorphism.[29] Given the increasing social and political prowess of extreme forms of feminism, and their growing influence on educational elites, if evolutionary science were seen to bear in any negative way on current theories of the social construction of sexual dimorphism and the origins of gender identity, evolutionary science might come (perhaps only over a fairly lengthy period of time) to be condemned by many of the state's pedagogical bureaucrats: science could be sanctioned were it to enter the *sanctum sanctorum* of feminist theory. Yet, as we have seen, scientific naturalism with its commitment to Darwinian evolution is central to a great percentage of contemporary secular thought. It is worth asking whether an alliance allowing release time for biblical instruction might at some point in the future be forged with some secular opponents were support extended in turn for the biological sciences to be freed from the state's potential ring-fencing of privileged tropes and constructs. Perhaps, just perhaps, there is something in this idea worthy of deeper consideration.

In closing, the arguments in this book are constitutionally permissible and also could help religion in the concrete, first, by freeing it from state corruption and, second, by responding to those who have falsely seen in separationism something necessarily anti-religious. A corrected understanding on this score, and a lived embodiment of that understanding through release time programs could aid institutions other than the public schools to address the searing problems of biblical illiteracy, and biblical hostility.

---

29. The renowned philosopher and evolutionary naturalist Anthony Flew, writing well before his conversion later in life, put this point rather starkly: "to insist dogmatically, as many militant feminists in recent years have been insisting, that all or almost all observed differences between the abilities and inclinations of men and women are produced by differences in their social conditioning is, in effect, to put yourself in the position of refusing to accept that our species, like all other animal species, is the product of animal evolution." Flew, *Darwinian Evolution*, xii.

Bibliography

Ackroyd, Peter. *Newton.* London: Chatto and Windus, 2006.

Adams, Arlin M., and Charles J. Emmerich. "A Heritage of Religious Liberty." *University of Pennsylvania Law Review* 137 (1989) 1621–22.

Adamson, Fiona. "Islam in Europe: The Challenge of Institutionalization." Council for European Studies, 2006. http://councilforeuropeanstudies.org/files/Papers/Islam%20in%20Europe.pdf.

Adkins, Rodney C. "America Desperately Needs More STEM Students. Here's How to Get Them." *Forbes,* 9 July 2012. http://www.forbes.com/sites/forbesleadershipforum/2012/07/09/america-desperately-needs-more-stem-students-heres-how-to-get-them/#555740f828ea.

Administration for Children and Families. *Abstinence Report, 2011.* U.S. Department of Health and Human Services, 2011. http://acf.hhs.gov/programs/f 9 ysb/content/docs/20090226_abstinence.pdf.

al-Bukhari, Muhammad. *Sahih al-Bukhari.* Translated with introduction by Mushsin Khan, xxiv–xxv. Lahore, Pakistan: Kazi, 1979.

al-Farghani al-Marghinani, Burhan Uddin. *Al-Hidayah.* Vol 2. Translated by Imran Ahsan Khan Nyazee. Damascus, Syria: Al Ama, 2008.

al-Qayrawani, Ibn Abi Zayd, *The Epistle.* Translated by Leon Bercher. Algiers, 1960.

al-Mawardi, Abu'l Hasan. *al-Ahkam as-Sultaniyyah.* London: Ta-Ha, 1966.

Ali, Ayaan Hirsi. "A Problem from Heaven: Why the United States Should Back Islam's Reformation." *Foreign Affairs.* June 16, 2015. https://www.foreignaffairs.com/articles/2015-06-16/problem-heaven.

Allen, Brooke. "Our Godless Constitution." *The Nation,* 3 February, 2005. http://www.thenation.com/article/our-godless-constitution/.

American Academy of Religion. *Guidelines for Teaching About Religion in K-12 Public Schools in the United States.* AAR, May 2010. http://www.aarweb.org/Publications/Online_{ublications/Curriculum_Guidelines/AARK-12CurriculumGuidelines.pdf.

American Civil Liberties Union [ACLU]. *Anthony D. Romero, Executive Director.* http://www.aclu.org/anthony-d-romero-executive-director.

American Civil Rights Union. "ACLU Supports Smutty Photos of Teenagers as 'Free Speech.'" ACRU, 5 November 2009. http://theacru.org/acru/aclu_supports_smutty_photos_of_teenagers_as_free_speech/.

American College of Pediatricians. "Great News for Teen Pregnancy." 22 June, 2016. http://www.acpeds.org/great-news-for-teen-pregnancy-prevention.

Amor, A. *The Role of Religious Education in the Pursuit of Tolerance and Non-Discrimination.* Paper presented at the United Nations International Consultative Conference on School Education in Relation with Freedom of Religion and Belief, Tolerance and Non-Discrimination, 2011.

Anderson, Derek. "Characteristics of Atheist Pre-Service Elementary Teachers." *Secularism and Non-Religion*, 3 November 2015. http://www. secularismandnonreligion.org/article/10.5334/snr.bf/.

Andrae, Tor. *Muhammed: The Man and His Faith.* New York: Scribner's Sons, 1936.

Arendt, H. *The Origins of Totalitarianism.* New York: Schocken, 2004.

"Arizona Bible Course Bill to Teach Elective in Public Schools Becomes Law." *Huffington Post*, 19 April, 2012. http://www.huffingtonpost.com/2012/04/19/arizona-bible-course-bill_n_1437484.html.

Aron, R. *The Opium of the Intellectuals.* Translated by T. Kilmartin. New York: Doubleday, 1957.

Arthur, J. et al. *Education, Politics and Religion: Reconciling the Civil and the Sacred in Education.* London: Routledge, 2010.

Audi, Robert. *Epistemology: A Contemporary Introduction to the Theory of Knowledge.* London: Routledge, 2000.

———. "Natural Reason, Natural Rights, and Governmental Neutrality toward Religion." *Religion and Human Rights* 4 (2009) 158.

———. *Religious Commitment and Secular Reason.* Cambridge: Cambridge University Press, 2000.

Audi, Robert, and Nicholas Wolterstorff. *Religion in the Public Square: The Place of Religious Convictions in Political Debate.* Lanham, MD: Rowman and Littlefield, 1996.

Baker's Evangelical Dictionary of Biblical Theology. s.v. "atonement." 1996 ed. http:// www.biblestudytools.com/dictionary/atonement/.

Banks, Adelle M. "Hobby Lobby President's Bible Curriculum Shelved by Oklahoma School District." *The Washington Post*, 26 November, 2014. http://www. washingtonpost.com/national/religion/hobby-lobby-presidents-bible-curriculum-shelved-by-oklahoma-school-district/2014/11/26/b3bd2ce4-7590-11e4-8893-97bf0c02cc5f_story.html.

Barkey, David L. "Breaching the Wall: The Real World Impact of Town of Greece v. Galloway." 9 May, 2014. http://www.afj.org/blog/guest-blog-breaching-the-wall-the-real-world-impact-of-town-of-greece-v-galloway.

Barna Group. "National Christians Big Election Story." Barna Group, 1 Dec. 2016. http://www.barna.com/research/notional-christians-big-election-story-2016/.

Barnes, Albert. *An Inquiry into the Scriptural Views of Slavery.* Philadelphia: Parry and McMillan, 1857.

Barnes, L. Philip. "Michael Hand, 'Is Religious Education Possible?'" *Studies in Philosophy and Education* 27 (2007) 63–70.

———. "The Misrepresentation of Religion in Modern British (Religious) Education." *British Journal of Educational Studies* 54 (2006) 395–411

———. "What is Wrong with the Phenomenological Approach to Religious Education?" *Religious Education* 96 (2001) 445–61.

Bartkowski, John P. Review of *Christian America? What Evangelicals Really Want*, by Christian Smith, *Social Forces* 70 (2001) 1204–6.

Bates, D. "Christianity, Culture and Other Religions (Part 1): The Origins of the Study of World Religions in English Education." *British Journal of Religious Education* 17 (1994) 5–18.

Bauman, Z. *Modernity and the Holocaust.* Cambridge: Polity, 1991.

Beecher, Lyman. "An Address of the Charitable Society for the Education of Indigent Pious Young Men, for the Ministry of the Gospel," 1816. https://babel.hathitrust.org/cgi/pt?id=chi.51314719;view=1up;seq=7.

———. s.v. "Beecher, Lyman (1775–1863)." http://www.encyclopedia.com/topic/Lyman_Beecher.aspx.

———. "Lyman Beecher: Revivalist Who Moved with the Times." Christian History Series, *Christianity Today.* http://www.christianitytoday.com/history/people/pastorsandpreachers/lyman-beecher.html.

Behe, Michael J. *Darwin's Black Box: The Biochemical Challenge to Evolution.* New York: Free, 1996.

Bellah, R. *Beyond Belief.* Berkeley: University of California Press, 1968.

———. "Civil Religion in America." *Daedalus* 96 (1967) 1–21.

Benard, Cheryl. "Moderate Islam Isn't Working." *The National Interest,* 20 December, 2015. http://nationalinterest.org/feature/moderate-islam-isnt-working-14693.

Berg, Thomas. "Secular Purpose, Accommodations, and Why Religion is Special (Enough): A Response to Micah Schwartzmann, 'What if Religion Is Not Special?'" *University of Chicago Law Review, Dialogue* 80 (2013) 24–42.

Berger, P. *The Desecularization of the World: Resurgent Religion and World Politics.* Grand Rapids: Eerdmans, 1999.

———. *A Rumor of Angels: Modern Society and the Rediscovery of the Supernatural.* Garden City, NY: Doubleday, 1970.

———. *The Sacred Canopy.* New York: Doubleday, 1967.

Bible Literacy Project. *The Bible and Its Influence.* http://www.bibleliteracy.org.

Bishop, George F. et al., "American Public Opinion and the 'Culture War' Politics of Teaching Human Evolution." In *Curriculum and the Culture Wars: Debating the Bible's Place in Public Schools,* edited by Melissa Deckman and Joseph Prud'homme, 85–118. Washington College Studies in Religion, Politics, and Culture 3. New York: Lang, 2014.

Bivins, Jason. *Religion of Fear: The Politics of Horror in Conservative Evangelicalism.* New York: Oxford University Press, 2008.

Black, Nathan. "Report: Over 350 Public Schools Teaching Bible." *The Christian Post,* 29 Sept. 2009. http://www.christianpost.com/news/report-over-350-public-schools-teaching-the-bible-41129/.

Boghossian, Peter. *A Manual for Creating Atheists.* Foreword by Michael Shermer. Chicago: Pitchstone, 2013.

Boomsma, Diederik, and Jonathan Price. "Western Suttee: Against a Right to Be Killed." *National Review* 63, no. 10 (2011) 28–30.

Boston, Robert. "The Religious Right's New Tactics for Invading Public Schools." Americans United for Separation of Church and State, 3 Oct. 2007. http://www.alternet.org/authors/rob-boston.

Bradley, Gerard V. "Dueling Clios: Stevens and Scalia on the Original Meaning of the Establishment Clause." In *Challenges to Religious Liberty in the Twenty-First Century,* edited by Gerard V. Bradley, 25–48. New York: Cambridge University Press, 2012.

Bragg, Melvyn. *The Book of Books*. London: Hodder and Stoughton, 2011.

Brighouse, Harry. *On Education*. London: Routledge, 2006.

British Journal of Educational Studies. *The Spens Report on Secondary Education*. London: HMSO, 1938.

Brockman, David. "Expert Details Importance of Teaching Religion in Public Schools." *Tennessean*, 10 February, 2016. http://www.tennessean.com/story/news/education/2016/02/10/expert-details-importance-teaching-religion-public-schools/80072576/.

Brooks, David. "A Matter of Faith." *New York Times*, 22 June, 2014.

Brown, Amanda Colleen. "Losing My Religion: The Controversy over Bible Courses in Public Schools." *Baylor Law Review* 59 (2007) 193–240.

Brown, Callum G. *The Death of Christian Britain: Understanding Secularisation, 1800–2000*. London: Routledge, 2001.

Brown, Emma. "GOP Platform Encourages Teaching about the Bible in Public Schools." *The Washington Post*, 14 July, 2016. http://www.washingtonpost.com/news/education/wp/2016/07/14/gop-platform-encourages-teaching-about-the-bible-in-public-schools/.

Bruce, S. *God Is Dead: Secularization in the West*. Oxford: Blackwell, 2002.

Burgess, Kaya. "Migrants Put their Faith in Britain." *The Times*, 28 March, 2016.

Burleigh, M. *Earthly Powers: Religion and Politics in Europe from the Enlightenment to the Great War*. London: Harper Perennial, 2006.

Burleigh, M. *Sacred Causes: The Clash of Religion and Politics from the Great War to the War on Terror*. London: HarperCollins, 2007.

Butler-Sloss, Rt. Hon. Baroness. *Living with Difference: Report of the Commission on Religion and Belief in British Public Life*. Cambridge: Woolf Institute, 7 Dec. 2015. http://corablivingwithdifference.files.wordpress.com/2015/12/living-with-difference-online.pdf.

Buunk, Bram P., and Pieternel Dijkstra. "Evidence from a Homosexual Sample for a Sex-Specific Rival-Oriented Mechanism: Jealousy as a Function of a Rival's Physical Attractiveness and Dominance." *Personal Relationships: The Journal of the International Association for Relationship Research* 8, no. 4 (2001) 391–406.

Byrd, James P. *Sacred Scripture, Sacred War: The Bible and the American Revolution*. Oxford: Oxford University Press, 2013.

Callan, Eamon. "Justice and Denominational Schooling." *Canadian Journal of Education* 13 (1988) 367–83.

Campbell, G. *Bible: The Story of the King James Version*. Oxford: Oxford University Press, 2010.

Cardwardine, Richard. "Methodists, Politics, and the American Civil War." In *Religion and American Politics: From the Colonial Period to the Present*, edited by Mark A. Noll and Luke E. Harlow, 169–200. New York: Oxford University Press, 2007.

Carpenter, Janis E. "Calderon's Painter, Gadamer's Spectator: Extending the Realm of Play." *Coastline Journal*, August 2010. http://coastlinejournal.org/2010/08/07/.

Caussade, Jean-Pierre de. *L'abandon à la Divine Providence*. (*Abandonment to Divine Providence* or *The Sacrament of the Present Moment*. Paris, 1966.

Centers for Disease Control and Prevention. *Youth Risk Behavior Survey: 1991–2015*. http://www.cdc.gov/healthyyouth/data/yrbs/pdf/trends/2015_us_sexual_trend_yrbs.pdf.

Centers for Disease Control and Prevention. *Sexual Identity, Sex of Sexual Contacts, and Health-Related Behaviors among Students Grades 9–12—United States and Selected Sites*. Morbidity and Mortality Weekly Report, 22 June, 2016. http://www.cdc.gov/mmwr/volumes/65/ss/pdfs/ss6509.pdf.

Chancey, Mark A. "Bible Bills, Bible Curricula, and Controversies of Biblical Proportions: Legislative Efforts to Promote Bible Courses in Public Schools." *Religion and Education* 34 (2007) 1–20.

———. "Sectarian Elements in Public School Bible Courses: Lessons from the Lone Star State." *Journal of Church and State* 49 (2007) 719–42.

———. "A Textbook Example of the Christian Right: The National Council on Bible Curriculum in Public Schools." *Journal of the American Academy of Religion* 75 (2007) 554–81.

———. "Writing & Religion II: Texas Public School Bible Courses in 2011–2012." The Texas Freedom Network, 11 Dec. 2013. http://religionandpolitics.org/2014/01/07/how-should-we-teach-the-bible-in-public-schools/.

Chappell, David L. *A Stone of Hope: Prophetic Religion and the Death of Jim Crow*. Chapel Hill: University of North Carolina Press, 2004.

Charter, M., and C. Erricker. *Does Religious Education Have a Future?* Oxford: Routledge, 2012.

Chaves, M. "Secularization as Declining Religious Authority." *Social Forces* 72 (1994) 749–74.

Chesebrough, David B. *Clergy Dissent in the Old South: 1830–1865*. Carbondale: Southern Illinois Press, 1996.

Chesterton, G. K. *The Everlasting Man*. 1925. http://gutenberg.net.au/ebooks01/0100311.txt.

Christianity Today. "Hobby Lobby's Bible Course Cancelled by Oklahoma School District." *Christianity Today*, 29 Nov. 2014. http://www.christiantoday.com/article/hobby.lobbys.bible.course.cancelled.by.oklahoma.school.district/43668.htm.

———. "Lyman Beecher: Revivalist Who Moved with the Times." Christian History Series, *Christianity Today*. http://www.christianitytoday.com/history/people/pastorsandpreachers/lyman-beecher.html.

Clarke, Paul. "Religion, Public Education and the Charter: Where Do We Go Now?" *McGill Journal of Education* 40 (2005) 351–81.

Coates, Sam, and Kaya Burnes. "Belief in God Slumps After Turbulent Year." *The Times*, 23 December, 2016.

Collins, Damian. "Culture, Religion, and Curriculum: Lessons from the 'Three Books' Controversy in Surrey, BC." *Canadian Geographer* 50 (2006) 342–57.

Committee of Enquiry into the Education of Children from Ethnic Minority Groups. *Education for All*. London: Her Majesty's Stationery Office, March 1985. http://www.educationengland.org.uk/documents/swann/.

Conn, Joseph L. "Church Stetson's Trojan Horse?" *Church and State,* January, 2006.

Controy, James C., et al. "Failures of Meaning in Religious Education." *Journal of Beliefs and Values* 33 (2012) 309–23.

Cooling, T. *Doing God in Education*. London: THEOS, 2009.

Copley, T. *Indoctrination, Education and God*. London: SPCK, 2005.

———. *Teaching Religion*. 2nd ed. Exeter: Exeter University Press, 2008.

Copley, T., et al. *On the Side of the Angels: The Third Report of the Biblos Project*. Exeter: University of Exeter, 2004.

Corbin, Clark. "Otter Vetoes Bible-in-Schools Bill." *Idaho Ed News*, 4 May, 2016. http://www.idahoednews.org/news/otter-vetoes-bible-schools-bill/.

Cox, Edwin. "Changes in Attitudes towards Religious Education and the Bible among Sixth Form Boys and Girls." *British Journal of Educational Psychology* 41 (1971) 328–41.

Cox, James. *A Guide to the Phenomenology of Religion: Key Figures, Formative Influences and Subsequent Debates*. London: Continuum, 2006.

———. *An Introduction to the Phenomenology of Religion*. London: Continuum, 2010.

Crawford, M., and G. Rossiter. "The Secular Spirituality of Youth: Implications for Religious Education." *British Journal of Religious Education* 18 (1996) 133–43.

Darwin, Charles. *Evolutionary Writings, Including Autobiographies*. Oxford: Oxford World's Classics, 2008.

Davie, G., et al. *Religious America, Secular Europe?* Aldershot: Ashgate, 2008.

Davis, C., et al., eds. *Theology and the Political: The New Debate*. Durham, NC: Duke University Press, 2005.

Dawkins, Richard. *The Blind Watchmaker*. New York: Norton, 1986.

———. *The God Delusion*. New York: Bantam, 2006.

———. *The Greatest Show on Earth*. London: Transworld, 2007.

Dawood, N. J., trans. *The Koran: With Parellel Arabic Text*. New York, Penguin, 2014.

Dayton, Donald W., and Douglas M. Strong. *Rediscovering an Evangelical Heritage: A Tradition and Trajectory of Integrating Piety and Justice*. Grand Rapids: Baker Academic, 2014.

Deckman, Melissa. "Religious Literacy in Public Schools: Teaching the Bible in America's Classrooms." In *Curriculum and the Culture Wars: Debating the Bible's Place in Public Schools*, edited by Melissa Deckman and Joseph Prud'homme, 31–47. Washington College Studies in Religion, Politics, and Culture 3. New York: Lang, 2014.

DelFattore, Joan. *The Fourth R: Conflicts over Religion in America's Public Schools*. New Haven: Yale University Press, 2004.

dePauley, William C. *The Candle of the Lord: Studies in the Cambridge Platonists*. New York: MacMillan, 1937.

Dietz, G. "Invisibilizing or Ethnicizing Religious Diversity?" In *Religion and Education in Europe: Developments, Contexts and Debates*, edited by Jackson et al., 103–32. Munster: Waxmann, 2007.

Dover, Alison G. "Teaching for Social Justice and the Common Core: Justice-Oriented Curriculum for Language Arts and Literacy." *Journal of Adolescent and Adult Literacy* 59 (2016) 517–27. http://onlinelibrary.wiley.com/doi/10.1002/jaal.488/full.

Downey, Roma, and Mark Burnett. "Why Public Schools Should Teach the Bible." *The Wall Street Journal*, 1 March, 2013.

Dreisbach, Daniel L. "A Handbook for Republican Citizenship? The Founders Debate the Bible's Use in Schools." In *Curriculum and the Culture Wars: Debating the Bible's Place in Public Schools*, edited by Melissa Deckman and Joseph Prud'homme, 3:7–29. New York: Lang, 2014.

———. *Reading the Bible with the Founding Fathers*. New York: Oxford University Press, 2017.

Education for Liberation Network. *EdLib Lab database*. http://www.edliberation.org/resources/lab.

Edwards Jr., Jonathan. *The Injustice and Impolicy of the Slave Trade and the Slavery of the Africans: Illustrated in a Sermon Preached before the Connecticut Society for the Promotion of Freedom, and for the Relief of Persons Unlawfully Holden in Bondage,* 15 September, 1791. New Haven: New Haven Anti-Slavery Society, 1833.

Edwards, Jonathan. *The Works of Jonathan Edwards.* Vol. 24, *Blank Bible.* New Haven: Yale University Press, 2006.

Emden, Christian J. Review of *Political Theology: Four Chapters on the Concept of Sovereignty,* by Carl Schmitt. H-Net Reviews., Oct. 2006. http://www.h-net.org/reviews/showpdf.php?id=12384.

Engelhardt, Craig. "The Necessary Role of Religion in Civic Education." In *The Role of Religion in 21st-Century Public Schools,* edited by Steven P. Jones and Eric C. Sheffield, 163–86. New York: Lang, 2009.

Engler, John. "STEM Education Is Key to U.S.'s Economic Future." *U.S. News,* 15 June, 2012. thttp://www.usnews.com/opinion/articles/2012/06/15/stem-education-is-the-key-to-the-uss-economic-future.

Evans, Carolyn. "Religious Education in Public Schools: An International Human Rights Perspective." *Human Rights Law Review* 8 (2008) 449–73.

"Faith and Wellbeing." Is There a God? http://www.is-there-a-god.info/life/faithandwellbeing.shtml.

Feistritzer, C. E., et al. *Profile of Teachers in the US, 2011.* Washington, DC: National Center for Education Information, 2011.

Felderhof, M. et al., eds. *Inspiring Faith in Schools.* Aldershot, UK: Ashgate, 2007.

Feldman, Noah. *Divided by God: America's Church State Problem—and What We Should Do about It.* New York: Farrar, Straus and Giroux, 2005.

Fenn, R. "The Relevance of Bellah's 'Civil Religion' Thesis to a Theory of Secularization." *Social Science History* 1 (1977) 502–11.

———. *Towards a Theory of Secularization.* Storrs, CT: Society for Scientific Study of Religion, 1979.

Findlay, James F., Jr. *Church People in the Struggle: The National Council of Churches and the Black Freedom Movement, 1950–1970.* New York: Oxford University Press, 1993.

Flew, Anthony. *Darwinian Evolution.* 2nd ed. New Brunswick, NJ: Transaction, 1997.

Fraser, James W. *Between Church and State: Religion and Public Education in a Multicultural America.* New York: St. Martin's, 1999.

Freedom from Religion Foundation. "Our Legal Work." https://ffrf.org/legal/.

———. *Year In Review Annual Report, 2011.* http://ffrf.org/uploads/files/2011yearinreview.pdf.

Friends of Darwin. http://www.friendsofdarwin.com.

Froese, Paul. *The Plot to Kill God: Findings from the Soviet Experiment in Secularization.* Berkeley: University of California Press, 2008.

Fuller, Lon. *The Morality of Law.* 2nd ed. New Haven: Yale University Press, 1969.

Fuller, Richard. *Domestic Slavery Considered as a Scriptural Institution.* New York: Colby, 1845.

Gadamer, Hans-Georg. *Truth and Method.* New York: Continuum, 2004.

Garnett, Richard W. "A Quiet Faith? Taxes, Politics, and the Privatization of Religion." *Boston College Law Review* 42 (2001) 771–803.

Garry, Patrick M. "The Cultural Hostility to Religion." *Modern Age: A Quarterly Journal* 47 (2005) 121–31.

Garvey, John H. "Free Exercise and the Values of Religious Liberty." *Connecticut Law Review* 18 (1986) 779–802.

Gearon, Liam. "The Counter Terrorist Classroom: Countering Extremism through (Religious) Education?" *Tony Blair Faith Foundation*, 6 May 2015. http:// tonyblairfaithfoundation.org/foundation/news/counter-terrorist-classroom-countering-extremism-through-religious-education.

———. "The Counter Terrorist Classroom: Religion, Education, and Security." *Religious Education* 108 (2013) 129–47.

———. "European Religious Education and European Civil Religion." *British Journal of Educational Studies* 60 (2012) 151–69.

———. "From Universal Declaration to World Program: 1948–2008: 60 Years of Human Rights Education." In *Contemporary Issues in Human Rights Education*, edited by UNESCO, 39–98. Paris: UNESCO, 2011. http://unesdoc.unesco.org/ images/0021/002108/210895e.pdf.

———. *On Holy Ground: The Theory and Practice of Religious Education.* New York: Routledge, 2014.

———. "The King James Bible and the Politics of Religious Education: Secular State and Sacred Scripture." *Religious Education* 108 (2013) 9–27.

Gedicks, Frederick M. "Public Life and Hostility to Religion." *Virginia Law Review* 78 (1992) 671–96.

———. "Religious Exemptions, Formal Neutrality, and Laicite." *Indiana Journal of Global Legal Studies* 13 (2006) 473–92.

———. *The Rhetoric of Church and State: A Critical Analysis of Religious Clause Jurisprudence.* Durham, NC: Duke University Press, 1995.

Genovese, Eugene, and Elizabeth Fox-Genovese. *The Mind of the Master Class: History and Faith in the Southern Slaveholders' Worldview.* Cambridge: Cambridge University Press, 2005.

Georgia. "Georgia State Bill 79: Section One of An Act to Amend Part 2 of Article 6 of Chapter 2 of Title 20 of the Official Code of Georgia Annotated." June 2005. http:// www1.legis.ga.gov/legis/2005_06/pdf/sb79.pdf.

Giarelli, James. Foreword to *In the Name of Morality: Character Education and Political Control*, by Tianlong Yu, New York: Lang, 2004.

Gillard, Derek. *Education in England: The History of Our Schools.* Education in England, 2011. http://www.educationengland.org.uk/.

Glenn, Charles L. "Disestablishing Our Secular Schools." *First Things*, January 2012. http://www.firstthings.com/article/2012/01/disestablishing-our-secular-schools.

Glynn, Patrick. *God: The Evidence, The Reconciliation of Faith and Reason in a Post-Secular World.* New York: Three Rivers Press of Random House, 1999.

Goldman, R. J. *Readiness for Religion: A Developmental Basis for Religious Education.* London: Routledge, 1965.

———. *Religious Thinking from Childhood to Adolescence.* London: Routledge, 1964.

Goldstein, Warren S. First published online: January 1, 2009 "Patterns of Secularization and Religious Rationalization." *Implicit Religion* 12 (1999), 2.

———. "Secularization Patterns in the Old Paradigm." *Sociology of Religion* 70 (2009): 157–78.

Goodheart, Lawrence B. *Abolitionist, Actuary, Atheist: Elizur Wright and the Reform Impulse.* Kent, OH: Kent State University Press, 1990.

Goodlad, John C. "Education and Community." In *Democracy, Education, and the Schools*, edited by Roger Stone, 92. San Francisco: Jossey-Bass, 1996.

Gray, J. *Black Mass.* London: Penguin, 2007.

Green, William H. *The Higher Criticism of the Pentateuch.* New York: Scribner's Sons, 1906.

Greenawalt, Kent. *Does the Bible Belong in Public Schools.* Princeton: Princeton University Press, 2005.

Greene, Richard A. "Religious Belief is Human Nature, Huge New Study Claims." *CNN*, 12 May 2011. http://religion.blogs.cnn.com/2011/05/12/religious-belief-is-human-nature-huge-new-study-claims/.

Greggs, Thomas. "Religionless Christianity in a Complexly Religious and Secular World: Thinking Through and Beyond Bonhoeffer." In *Religion, Religionlessness and Contemporary Western Culture*, edited by Ralf K. Wustenberg and Stephen J. Plant, 1:111–25. Frankfurt: Lang, 2008.

Grimmitt, M., ed. *Pedagogies of Religious Education.* Great Wakering, UK: McCrimmons, 2010.

Gryboski, Michael. "Arkansas Public School District to Offer Controversial Bible Class Next Fall." *The Christian Post*, 20 January 2016. http://www.christianpost.com/news/arkansas-bible-class-public-education-act-1440-westside-consolidated-school-district-fall-2016-2017-155475/.

Guelzo, Allen. Interviewed and quoted in Bruce Feiler, *America's Prophet: Moses and the American Story*, 163. New York: HarperCollins, 2009.

Gutierrez, Bridget. "Legislature 2006: Senate Approves Bible Classes in Public Schools." *Atlanta Journal-Constitution*, 4 February 2006.

Haake, Kathryn. "GOP Idaho Governor Vetoes 'Unconstitutional' Bill to Teach Bible in Public Schools." *Talking Points Memo*, 6 April 2016. http://talkingpointsmemo.com/news/idaho-governor-vetoes-unconstitutional-bill-teach-bible-public-schools.

Haas, Guenther. "The Kingdom and Slavery: A Test Case for Social Ethics." *Calvin Theological Journal* 28 (1993) 74–89.

Habermas, J., and J. Card. Ratzinger. *The Dialectics of Secularization: On Reason and Religion.* Edited by Florian Schuller. Translated by Brian McNeil. San Francisco: Ignatius, 2007.

Hagee, John. Letter to Representative Scott Benson and the Alabama State Legislature. *Bible in Schools*, 12 March 2006. http://.bibleinschools.net/images/pdf/John_Hagee_Letter03—12—06.pdf.

Hague, William. *Christianity and Slavery: A Review of Doctors Fuller and Wayland, On Domestic Slavery.* Boston: Gould, Kendall and Lincoln, 1847.

Halford, Joan Montgomery. "Longing for the Sacred in Schools: A Conversation with Nell Noddings." *Educational Leadership* 56 (1998–1999) 28–32.

Hambrick-Stowe, Charles E. *The Spirit of American Evangelicalism.* Grand Rapids: Eerdmans, 1996.

Hamburger, Philip. *Separation of Church and State.* Cambridge, MA: Harvard University Press, 2002.

Hamlin, H., and H. W. Jones, eds. *The King James Bible After Four Hundred Years: Literary, Linguistic, and Cultural Influences.* Cambridge: Cambridge University Press, 2010.

Hand, M. *Is Religious Education Possible? A Philosophical Investigation*. London: Continuum, 2006.

———. "A Response to Philip Barnes." *Studies in Philosophy and Education* 27 (2007) 71–75.

Hansen, Susan B. *Religion and Reaction: The Secular Political Challenge to the Religious Right*. Lanham, MD: Rowman and Littlefield, 2011.

Hanson, B. Smidt. "Phenomenology of Religion: A Bridge between the Scholarly Study of Religion and Religious Education." *British Journal of Religious Education* 6 (1983) 14–19.

Hart, H. L. A. *The Concept of Law*. Oxford: Clarendon, 1997.

Hart, Levi. *Liberty Described and Recommended*. In a sermon, preached to the Corporation of Freemen in Farmington, at their meeting on Tuesday, September 20, 1774, and published at their desire. Farmington: Corporation of Freemen, 1794.

Harte, Julia, et al. "U.S. Eyes Ways to Toughen Fight against Domestic Extremists." *Reuters*, 4 February, 2016. http://ca.news.yahoo.com/u-eyes-ways-toughen-fight-against-domestic-extremists-060402478.html.

Hartog, Jonathan Den. *Politics and Piety: Federalist Politics and Religious Struggle in the New American Nation*. Charlottesville: University of Virginia Press, 2015.

Harvard Divinity School. *Religious Literacy Project*. http:www.hds.harvard.edu/faculty-research/programs-and-centers/religious-literacy-project.

———. *Study about Religion in the Schools*. H-STARS: Harvard Studies in Teaching about Religion in Schools. 2005. http://www.extension.harvard.edu/degrees-certificates/professional-certificates/religious-studies-education-certificate.

Hasan al-Mawardi, Abu'l. *al-Ahkam as-Sultaniyyah*. London: Ta-Ha, 1966.

Haynes, J., ed. *The Handbook of Religion and Politics*. London: Routledge, 2008.

———. *Religion and Politics*. 4 vols. London: Routledge, 2009.

Heater, D. *Citizenship: The Civic Ideal in World History, Politics and Education*. Manchester: Manchester University Press, 2004.

M. Hennington, ed. *Modernity without Restraint: The Political Religions, Collected Works of Eric Voegelin*. Vol. 5. Columbia: University of Missouri Press, 1999.

Higgins, Andrew. "In Expanding Russian Influence, Faith Combines with Firepower." *New York Times*, 13 September 2016. http://www.nytimes.com/2016/09/14/world/europe/russia-orthodox-church.html?_r=0.

Hill News. "Hillary Clinton's Attack Dog David Brock Forming Koch Like Donor Network with George Soros and Others." *The Hill News*. http://thehillnews.net/news/Hillary-Clinton-attack-dog-David-Brock-forming-Koch-like-donor-network-with-George-Soros-&-others.

Holifield, E. Brooks. *Theology in America: Christian Thought from the Age of the Puritans to the Civil War*. New Haven: Yale University Press, 2003.

Holzer, Shannon. *Competing Schemas within the American Liberal Democracy: An Interdisciplinary Analysis of Differing Perceptions of Church and State*. Vol. 8. New York: Lang, 2016.

Howe, Daniel Walker. "The Evangelical Movement and Political Culture in the North during the Second Party System." *The Journal of American History* 77 (1991) 1216–39.

Hull, J. "The Blessings of Secularity: Religious Education in England and Wales." *Journal of Religious Education* 51 (2003) 51–58.

Hull, J. M. "From Christian Nurture to Religious Education." *Religious Education* 73 (1978) 124–43.

Hurd, Elizabeth S. *Beyond Religious Freedom: The New Global Politics of Religion.* Princeton: Princeton University Press, 2015.

———. "How International Relations Got Religion, and Got It Wrong." *The Washington Post*, 9 July 2015. http://www.washingtonpost.com/blogs/monkey-cage/wp/2015/07/09/how-international-relations-got-religion-and-got-it-wrong/.

Huxley, Thomas. "The School Boards." *Contemporary Review* 16 (1870) 1–15.

Hyde, K. E. *Religion in Childhood and Adolescence: A Comprehensive Review of the Research.* Birmingham: Religious Education, 1990.

Ibn Abi Zayd al-Qayrawani. *The Epistle.* Translated by Leon Bercher. 5th ed. Algiers: Biblioteque arab-francaise, 1960.

Ibrahim, Raymond. "Obama: Get off Your 'High Horse' and Stop Criticizing Islamic Terror." *The Christian Post*, 10 February 2015. http://www.christianpost.com/news/obama-get-off-your-high-horse-and-stop-criticizing-islamic-terror-133845/.

Independent, UK. "Church of England Slowly Dying as Congregation Set to Halve over 30 Years." *Independent*, 18 February 2016. http://www.independent.co.uk/news/uk/church-of-england-slowly-dying-as-congregation-set-to-halve-over-30-years-a6881641.html.

Indiana University. *Prayer at College Events.* 3 May 2013. http://www.indiana.edu/~vpgc/docs/LegalUpdates/PrayerAtCollegeEvents_2013-5-3.pdf.

Jackson, R. "Religion, Education, Dialogue and Conflict." *British Journal of Religious Education* 33 (2011) 105–10.

———. *Rethinking Religious Education and Plurality: Issues in Diversity and Pedagogy.* London: Routledge, 2004.

Jackson, R., and K. O'Grady. "Religious Education in England: Social Plurality, Civil Religion and Religious Education Pedagogy." In *Religion and Education in Europe: Developments, Contexts and Debates*, edited by R. Jackson, S. Miedema, W. Weisse, and J.-P. Willaime, 181–202. Munster: Waxmann, 2007.

Jackson, R., et al. *Materials Used to Teach about World Religions in Schools in England.* London: Department for Children, Schools and Families, 2010.

Jackson, R., et al., eds. *Religion and Education in Europe: Developments, Contexts and Debates.* Munster: Waxmann, 2007.

Jensen, Jim. "The Civic and Community Engagement of Religiously Active Americans." 31 December 2011. http://www.pewinternet.org/Reports/2011/Social-side-of-religion.aspx.

Jeynes, William H. "Are America's Public Educational Institutions Anti-Religious?" *Education* 119 (1998) 172–75.

———. *A Call for Character Education and Prayer in the Schools.* Santa Barbara: Prager/ABC-CLIO, 2010.

Johnson, Luke T. "Textbook Case: A Bible Curriculum for Public Schools." *Christian Century* 123 (2006) 34–37.

Kahan, Dan M., et al. "Motivated Numeracy and Enlightened Self-Government." *The Cultural Cognition Project.* http://www.culturalcognition.net/kahan/.

Kaufmann, Eric. "The Future Will Be More Religious and Conservative Than You Think." *The American,* 8 May 2012. http://www.aei.org/publication/the-future-will-be-more-religious-and-conservative-than-you-think/.

———. *Shall the Religious Inherit the Earth? Demography and Politics in the 21st Century.* London: Profile, 2010.

Kazin, Michael. *A Godly Hero: The Life of William Jennings Bryan.* New York: Anchor, 2007.

"Kentucky Public Schools Create Bible Course as an Elective." *CBN News*, 2 March 2016. http://www1.cbn.com/cbnnews/us/2016/march/kentucky-public-schools-create-bible-course-as-an-elective.

Kerry, John. *Address to Rice University.* 26 April 2016. http://www.state.gov/secretary/remarks/2016/04/256618.htm.

Khaldun, Ibn. *The Muqaddimah [Prolegomenon]: An Introduction to History.* Translated by Franz Rosenthal. Edited by N. J. Dawood. Princeton: Princeton University Press, 1967.

Khan, Mariam. "Donald Trump's National Security Adviser Mike Flynn Has Called Islam a 'Cancer.'" *ABCNEWS*, 18 November 2016. http://abcnews.go.com/Politics/donald-trump-national-security-adviser-mike-flynn-called/story?id=43575658.

Kids without God. http://kidswithoutgod.com/.

Kim, Christine. "Family Fact of the Week: The Abstinent Majority." *The Daily Signal*, 5 July 2012. http://dailysignal.com/2012/07/05/family-facts-of-week-the-abstinent-majority/.

King James Bible Online. "Congress Further Decreed Its Gratitude for the Influence the King James Version Has Bestowed Upon the United States." 12 April 2011. http://www.kingjamesbibleonline.org/King-James-Bible-News/.

Kitchen, Kenneth. *On the Reliability of the Old Testament.* Grand Rapids: Eerdmans, 2003.

Klein, Rebecca. "Hobby Lobby Leaders Hope to Spread Bible Course to Thousands of Schools." *Huffington Post*, 18 April 2014. http://www.huffingtonpost.com/2014/04/18/hobby-lobby-bible-course_n_5174686.html.

Knauth, T. "Religious Education in Germany." In *Religion and Education in Europe: Developments, Contexts and Debates,* edited by R. Jackson et al., 244. Munster: Waxmann, 2007.

Knight, Frances. *The Church in the Nineteenth Century.* London: Tauris, 2008.

Koppelman, Andrew. "Corruption of Religion and the Establishment Clause." *William and Mary Law Review* 50 (2009) 1831–1935.

———. *Defending American Religious Neutrality.* Cambridge, MA: Harvard University Press, 2013.

———. "Secular Purpose." *Virginia Law Review* 88 (2002) 87–166.

———. "Secular Purpose." March 1998. http://lists.ucla.edu/pipermail/religionlaw/1998-March/011848.html

Korach, William, and William A. Saxton, "Corrections to Islam-biased Content in Florida's K-12 Textbooks." *Citizens for National Security*, 11 February 2012. http://education-curriculum-reform-government-schools.org/w/wp-content/uploads/2012/02/Textbook-Corrections-Final-2.0.pdf.

Kramnick, Isaac, and Laurence Moore. *The Godless Constitution: A Moral Defense of the Secular State.* New York: Norton, 2005.

Kraynack, Robert P. *Christian Faith and Modern Democracy: God and Politics in the Fallen World.* Notre Dame: University of Notre Dame Press, 2001.

Lack, Caleb, and Jacques Rousseau. *Critical Thinking, Science, and Pseudoscience: Why We Can't Trust Our Brains.* Heidelberg: Springer, 2016.

Lacorne, Denis. *Religion in America: A Political History.* New York: Columbia, 2011.

Lagniappe Weekly. "The Legacy of Wallace v. Jaffree and the Separation of Church and State." *Lagniappe Weekly*, 3 December 2014. http://www.lagniappemobile.com/cover-story-legacy-wallace-v-jaffree-separation-church-state/.

Laughland, John. "European Integration." *The Monist* 92 (2009). http://www.marxists,org/archive/marx/works/1883/death/dersoz1.htm.

Lawler, Peter Augustine. *Aliens in America: The Strange Truth about Our Souls.* Wilmington, DE: ISI, 2002.

Leachman, Michael et al. "Most States Have Cut School Funding, and Some Continue Cutting." *Center for Budget Priorities and Policy*, 25 January 2016. http://www.cbpp.org/research/state-budget-and-tax/most-states-have-cut-school-funding-and-some-continue-cutting.

Legutko, Ryszard. *The Demon in Democracy: Totalitarian Temptations in Free Societies.* Translated by Teresa Adelson. New York: Encounter, 2016.

Leiter, Brian. *Brian Leiter's Nietzsche Blog: Thinking Out Loud about Nietzsche's Philosophy.* http://brianleiternietzsche.blogspot.com/. Accessed 22 November, 2017.

———. *Why Tolerate Religion?* Princeton: Princeton University, 2012.

Libresco, Leah. "Trump is Driving Catholic Voters toward Clinton." http://www.fivethirtyeight.com, 27 July, 2016.

Lincoln, Abraham. First Inaugural Address in March of 1861. *Dred Scott v. Sandford*, 60 U.S. 393 (1857). http://avalon.law.yale.edu/19th_century/lincoln1.asp.

———. "Reply to Delegation of Baptists on May 30, 1864." In *Collected Works of Abraham Lincoln*, edited by Roy P. Basler, 8:368. New Brunswick, NJ: Rutgers University Press, 1953.

———. Second Inaugural Address. Saturday, March 4, 1865. http://avalon.law.yale.edu/19th_century/lincoln2.asp.

Linker, Damon. "How Donald Trump's Strongman Act Won Over Evangelicals." *The Week*, 4 August 2016. http://theweek.com/articles/640247/how-donald-trumps-strongman-act-won-over-evangelicals.

Livingston, David. *Darwin's Forgotten Defenders: The Encounter between Evangelical and Evolutionary Thought.* Vancouver: Regent College Publishing, 1984.

Locke, John. *Some Thoughts Concerning Education.* In *Philosophy of Education: The Essential Texts*, edited by S. M. Cahn, 179–99. London: Routledge, 2009.

Loukes, H. *Readiness for Religion.* Wallingford, PA: Pendle Hill, 1963.

———. *Teenage Religion.* London: SCM, 1961.

Luckmann, T. *The Invisible Religion.* New York: Macmillan, 1966.

Lynn, Barry W. "Studying the Bible in Public Schools: Sounds Good in Theory, But. . ." In *Curriculum and the Culture Wars: Debating the Bible's Place in Public Schools*, edited by Melissa Deckman and Joseph Prud'homme, 3:49–55. New York: Lang, 2014.

MacCulloch, Diarmaid. *All Things Made New: Writings on the Reformation.* London: Lane, 2016.

Mackenzie, Jim. Review of *Is Religious Education Possible? A Philosophical Investigation*, by Michel Hand. *Educational Philosophy and Theory* 31 (2007) 787–94.

Maddox, Marion. "Religion, Secularism and the Promise of Public Theology." *International Journal of Public Theology* 1 (2007) 82–100.

Madison, James. *Federalist* no. 48. http://avalon.law.yale.edu/subject_menus/fed.asp.

Marsden, George. "Religion, Politics, and the Search for an American Consensus." In *Religion and American Politics from the Colonial Period to the Present*, edited by Mark A. Noll and Luke A. Harlow, 465. Oxford University Press, 2007.

Martin, D. *A General Theory of Secularization*. Oxford: Blackwell, 1978.

———. *On Secularization: Towards a Revised General Theory*. New York: Routledge, 2005.

McCarthy, Andrew C. "The Problem with Islam is Aggressive Scripture, not Aggressive 'Traditionalism.'" *National Review Online*, 16 January 2016. http://www.nationalreview.com/article/429871/islams-problem-aggressive-scripture-not-aggressive-traditionalism.

McConnell, Michael W. Review of *Why Tolerate Religion?* by Brian Leiter. *Yale Law Journal* 123 (2013) 81. http://www.yalelawjournal.org/review/why-protect-religious-freedom#_ftnref24.

McCoughlin, William. "Cherokees and Methodists: 1824–1834." *Church History* 50 (1981) 44–63.

McKenzie, Steven L. Review of *The Bible and Its Influence, Society of Biblical Literature Forum*, by Cullen Schippe and Chuck Stetson. *SBL Forum*, November 2005. http://www.sbl-site.org/publications/article.aspxarticleId=465.

McLoughlin, William, ed. *The American Evangelicals, 1800–1900: An Anthology*. New York: Harper, 1968.

Meier, John P. "Why Get to Know the Historical Jesus?" *US Catholic*, July 2008. http://www.uscatholic.org/church/2008/07/why-get-know-historical-jesus#sthash.nAAqwBQu.dpuf.

Metaxas, Eric. "Man Does Not Live by Math Alone: Education Is More than STEM." *CNS News*, 13 April 2016. http://www.cnsnews.com/commentary/eric-metaxas/man-does-not-live-math-alone-education-more-stem#.Vw60Q4JZoYk.gmail.

Micklethwait, J., and A. Woolridge. *God Is Back: How the Global Revival of Faith Is Changing the World*. London: Penguin, 2009.

Milbank, John. *Theology and Social Theory: Beyond Secular Reason*. Oxford: Blackwell, 1993.

Miller, S. J. "Cultivating a Disposition for Sociospatial Justice in English Teacher Preparation." *Teacher Education and Practice* 27 (2014) 44–74.

Mohler, Albert. "Moral Argument in Modern Times: A Conversation with Robert P. George." 24 January 2011. http://www.albertmohler.com/2011/01/24/moral-argument-in-modern-times-a-conversation-with-robert-p-george-2/.

Moore, Diane. *Overcoming Religious Illiteracy: A Cultural Studies Approach to the Study of Religion in Secondary Schools*. New York: Palgrave MacMillan, 2007.

———. "Teaching about the Bible in Public Schools: A Religious Studies Framework." In *Curriculum and the Culture Wars: Debating the Bible's Place in Public Schools*, edited by Melissa Deckman and Joseph Prud'homme, 3:77. New York: Lang, 2014.

Morgan, M. L., ed. *Classics of Moral and Political Philosophy*. 4th ed. Indianapolis: Hackett, 2005.

Moss, Candida R., and Joel S. Baden. *Bible Nation: The United States of Hobby Lobby*. Princeton: Princeton University Press, 2017.

Museum of the Bible. *2015 Annual Report*. https://www.museumofthebible.org/2015AnnualReport/#vision.

———. *Homeschool Curriculum*. http://www.museumofthebible.org/curriculum.

———. *Museum of the Bible Curriculum. Vol. 1. Private School Edition.* http://www.museumofthebible.org/private-school.

———. *The Scholars Initiative.* Oklahoma City and Washington, DC: Museum of the Bible. https://www.museumofthebible.org/scholars-initiative

NatCen. "Losing Faith?" British Social Attitudes Survey, 173–84. http://www.bsa.natcen.ac.uk/media/38958/bsa28_12religion.pdf.

National Abstinence Education Association. *Abstinence Works.* http://www.thenaea.org/docs/Abstinence_Works.pdf.

National Council of Teachers of English. "Beliefs about Social Justice in English Education." Conference on English Education Executive Committee, 2009. www.ncte.org/cee/positions/socialjustice.

National Council on Bible Curriculum in Public Schools. "Alabama Adopts New Textbook for Academic Study of the Bible." Greensboro, NC: Author, 20 November 2016. http://bibleinschools.net/News/Alabama-Adopts-New-Textbook-for-Academic-Study-of-the-Bible.php.

———. *The Bible in History and Literature.* http//www.bibleinschools.net/.

Netushtan, Yossi. *Intolerant Religion in a Tolerant Liberal Democracy.* Oxford: Hart, 2015.

Nicolson, A. *When God Spoke English: The Making of the KJV.* London: Harper, 2011.

Noddings, Nell. *Critical Lessons: What Our Schools Should Teach.* Cambridge: Cambridge University Press, 2006.

———. *Educating for Intelligent Belief or Unbelief.* New York: Teachers College Press, 1993.

———. "Public Schooling, Democracy, and Religious Dissent." In *Developing Democratic Character in Young People*, edited by Roger Soder et al., 152–63. San Francisco: Josey Bass, 2001.

———. "Understanding Unbelief as Part of Religious Education." In *The Role of Religion in 21st Century Public Schools*, edited by Steven P. Jones and Eric C. Sheffield, 19–33. New York: Lang, 2009.

Noll, Mark. *America's God: From Jonathan Edwards to Abraham Lincoln.* New York: Oxford University Press, 2002.

———. *In the Beginning Was the Word: The Bible in American Public Life, 1492–1783.* New York: Oxford University Press, 2015.

———. *The Civil War as a Theological Crisis.* Chapel Hill: University of North Carolina Press, 2006.

Obama, Barak. "Call to Renewal Keynote Address." *YouTube.* Washington, DC, 28 June, 2006.

———. "We Do Not Consider Ourselves a Christian Nation." Lifesite News, 8 April, 2009. http://www.lifesitenews.com/news/obama-we-do-not-consider-ourselves-a-christian-nation.

Oberoi, Sidharth. "The Economic Impact of Early Exposure to STEM Education." Center for Economic Development, 21 June 2016. http://www.ced.org/blog/entry/the-economic-impact-of-early-exposure-to-stem-education.

Ofsted Report. *Transforming Religious Education.* London: Her Majesty's Stationery Office, 2010.

Oppenheimer, Mark. "Examining the Growth of the Spiritual but Not Religious." *New York Times*, 18 July 2014. http://www.nytimes.com/2014/07/19/us/examining-the-growth-of-the-spiritual-but-not-religious.html?_r=0.

Organisation for Security and Co-operation in Europe. *Toledo Guiding Principles on Teaching about Religions and Beliefs in Public Schools*. OSLO Coalition, 27 November 2017. http://www.oslocoalition.org/toledo_guidelines.pdf.

Osborne, Jeff. "Study: Belton ISD's Bible Literature Course Breaks Federal Commandments." *Temple Daily Telegram*, 17 November 2013. http://www.tdtnews.com/news/school_news/article_35e588a8-4c65-55a4-82b3-718d4d9dca06.html.

Padgett, Alan G., ed. *Reason and the Christian Religion: Essays in Honour of Richard Swinburne*. Clarendon: Oxford University Press, 1994.

Pals, D. L. *Eight Theories of Religion*. 2nd ed. Oxford: Oxford University Press, 2008.

Paulson, Michael S. "God Is Great, Garvey Is Good: Making Sense of Religious Freedom." *Notre Dame Law Review* 72 (1997) 1597–1626.

Perry, Michael. "Herein on/of the Nonestablishment of Religion." *Philosophy and Social Criticism* 25 (2009) 105.

———. *Morality, Politics and the Law: A Bicentennial Essay*. New York: Oxford University Press, 1988.

———. "Why Religion in Politics Does Not Violate *La Conception Americaine de la Laicite*." *Indiana Journal of Global Legal Studies* 13 (2006) 543–60.

Peters, Rudolph. *Jihad in Classical and Modern Islam*. Princeton: Wiener, 1996.

Pew Research Center: Religion and Public Life. "America's Changing Religious Landscape." Pew Forum, 12 May 2015. http://www.pewforum.org/2015/05/12/americas-changing-religious-landscape/.

Popper, K. *The Open Society and Its Enemies*. London: Routledge, 1946.

Porterfield, Amanda. *Conceived in Doubt: Religion and Politics in the New American Nation*. Chicago: University of Chicago Press, 2012.

Prendergast, Monica. "Playing Attention: Contemporary Aesthetics and Performing Arts Audience." *The Journal of Aesthetic Education* 38 (2004) 36–51.

Prothero, Stephen. *Religious Literacy: What Every American Needs to Know—And Doesn't*. San Francisco: Harper, 2007.

Prud'homme, Joseph. "Conclusion." In *Religion, Religionlessness and Contemporary Western Culture*, edited by Ralf K. Wustenberg and Stephen J. Plant, 1:177–203. Frankfurt: Lang, 2008.

———. "Conclusion." In *Curriculum and the Culture Wars: Debating the Bible's Place in Public Schools*, edited by Melissa Deckman and Joseph Prud'homme, 185–92. Washington College Studies in Religion, Politics, and Culture 3. New York: Lang, 2014.

———. "Evangelical Ministers in the Antebellum South and Guilt over Slavery: The Incoherence of Evangelical Pro-Slavery." In *Faith and Politics in America from Jamestown to the Civil War, Major Concepts in Politics and Political Theory*, edited by Joseph Prud'homme, 29:205–58. New York: Lang, 2011.

Qualifications and Curriculum Authority. *Religious Education in English Schools*. London: Department for Children, Schools and Families, 2010.

Querry, K., and Lorne Fultonberg. "208 Oklahoma City Teaching Positions Will Be Cut Because of 'Catastrophic Budget Crisis.'" *KFOR-TV*, 23 March 2016. http://kfor.com/2016/03/23/208-oklahoma-city-classroom-teaching-positions-will-be-affected-by-catastrophic-budget-crisis/.

Quinn, John. "Expecting the Impossible? Abolitionist Appeals to the Irish in Antebellum America." *New England Quarterly* 82 (2009) 667–710.

———. "Three Cheers for the Abolitionist Pope." In *Civil War as Theological Crisis*, 131. Chapel Hill: University of North Carolina Press, 2006.

Randall, David. "The Disappearing Continent: A Critique of the Revised Advanced Placement European History Examination." National Association of Scholars, 2016. https://www.nas.org/images/documents/NAS_apeh_complete.pdf.

Ratzinger, Cardinal Joseph. *Truth and Tolerance: Christian Belief and World Religions.* San Francisco: Ignatius, 2004.

Ravitch, Diane. *The Great School Wars.* New York: Basic, 1974.

Rawls, J. *Political Liberalism.* Expanded ed. New York: Columbia University Press, 2005.

REDco. July 2009. http://www.redco.uni-hamburg.de/web/3480/3481/index.html.

Released Time. http://www.releasedtime.org/stateinfo/8-states/72-state272a.

Richard, David A. J. *Fundamentalism in American Religion and Law: Obama's Challenge to Patriarchy's Threat to Democracy.* Cambridge: Cambridge University Press, 2010.

Richter, Kent. *Religion: A Study in Beauty, Truth and Goodness.* New York: Oxford University Press, 2016.

Rom, Mark C. "Below the (Bible) Belt: Religion and Sexuality Education in American Public Schools." In *Curriculum and the Culture Wars: Debating the Bible's Place in Public Schools*, edited by Melissa Deckman and Joseph Prud'homme, 3:140. New York: Lang, 2014.

Rosenblith, Suzanne, and Beatrice Bailey. "Cultivating a Religiously Literate Society: Challenges and Possibilities for America's Public Schools." *Religious Education* 103 (2008) 145–61.

Rousseau, J. J. *The Social Contract.* London: Penguin, 1968.

Sajo, Andras, ed. "From Militant Democracy to the Preventive State?" *Cardozo Law Review* 27 (2006) 2255–94.

———. "Preliminaries to a Concept of Constitutional Secularism." *International Journal of Constitutional Law* 6 (2008) 605–29. http://icon.oxfordjournals.org/content/6/3–4/605.

———. "Militant Democracy and Transition toward Democracy." In *Militant Democracy*, edited by Andras Sajo, 209–30. Utrecht: Eleven, 2004.

Schall, S. J., and James V. "Realism and Islam." *Catholic World Report*, 17 April 2016. http://www.catholicworldreport.com/Item/4731/realism_and_islam.aspx?utm_content=bufferaabf4&utm_medium=social&utm_source=twitter.com&utm_campaign=buffer.

Schapiro, Jeff. "Atheist Richard Dawkins Supports Bibles in Schools." *Christian Post*, 21 May 2012. http://www.christianpost.com/news/atheist-richard-dwakins-supports-bibles-in-schools-75290.

Scheffbuch, Winrich. *Christians under the Hammer and Sickle: A Documentary Study of What is Happening and Has Happened to Christians in the Soviet Union.* Translated by Mark Noll. Grand Rapids: Zondervan, 1974.

Schmid, A. P., ed. *The Routledge Handbook of Terrorism Research.* London: Routledge, 2011.

Schmitt, C. *Political Theology: Four Chapters on the Concept of Sovereignty.* Translated by G. Schwab. Chicago: Chicago University Press, 2005.

Schools Council. *Working Paper 36: Religious Education in Secondary Schools.* London: Evans/Mthuen, 1971.

Schools Curriculum and Assessment Authority [SCAA]. *Model Syllabuses for Religious Education.* London: SCAA, 1994.

Schoville, Keith N. *Biblical Archaeology in Focus.* Grand Rapids: Baker Book House, 1978.

Schwartzman, Micah. "What If Religion Is Not Special?" *University of Chicago Law Review* 79 (2012) 1351–1427.

Schweitzer, Albert. *The Quest of the Historical Jesus.* Translated and edited by John Bowden. 2nd ed. Minneapolis: Fortress, 2010.

Scott, P., and W. T. Cavanaugh. *The Blackwell Companion of Political Theology.* Oxford: Wiley-Blackwell, 2004.

Segal, R. *Toward a Theory of Secularization.* Edited by Richard K. Fenn. Society for the Scientific Study of Religion Monograph 1. Storrs, CT: Society for the Scientific Study of Religion, 1979.

Seiple, C. et al., eds. *Routledge Handbook of Religion and Security: Theory and Practice.* London: Routledge, 2011.

Shanks, Caroline L. "The Biblical Anti-Slavery Argument of the Decade 1830–1840." *Journal of Negro History* 15 (1931) 132–57.

Sheldon, Garrett. "Religion in the Thought of James Madison." In *Faith and Politics in America from Jamestown to the Civil War,* edited by Joseph Prud'homme, 100–101. New York: Lang, 2011.

Sherry, Suzanna. "Enlightening the Religion Clauses." *Journal of Contemporary Legal Issues* 7 (1996) 473–95.

———. "Responsible Republicanism: Educating for Citizenship." *University of Chicago Law Review* 62 (1995) 131–208.

———. "The Sleep of Reason." *Georgetown Law Journal* 84 (1996) 453–84.

Silk, Mark, and Andrew Walsh. *One Nation, Divisible: How Regional Religious Differences Shape American Politics.* Lanham: Rowman and Littlefield, 2008.

Smart, Ninian. "The Comparative Study of Religions and the Schools." *Religious Education* 64 (1969) 26–30.

———. "Guest Editorial." *Learning for Living* 11 (1972) 5.

Smith, Brittany. "Project 2026 Launched to Restore Christian Values." *Christian Post,* 4 January, 2012.

Smith, Christian. *Christian America? What Evangelicals Really Want.* Berkeley: University of California Press, 2000.

Snay, Mitchell. *Gospel of Disunion: Religion and Separatism in the Antebellum South.* Chapel Hill: University of North Carolina Press, 1997.

Society of Biblical Literature. "Bible Electives." http://www.sbl-site.org.

South Carolina State House. "Code: A322, R352, S148, 2005–2006." http://www.scstatehouse.gov/sess116_2005-2006/bills/148.htm.

———. "South Carolina A102, R155, S726 [2]: An Act to Amend Chapter 29." Title 59 Code of Laws of South Carolina, 2007. http://www.scstatehouse.gov/sess117_2007_2008/bills/726.htm.

Stanton, Glenn T. "CDC Study Says Teen Virgins Are Healthier." *Federalist,* 29 November 2016. http://thefederalist.com/2016/11/29/cdc-study-says-teen-virgins-healthier/.

Stark, Rodney. "Secularization, RIP." *Sociology of Religion* 60 (1999) 249–73.

———. *The Triumph of Faith: Why the World is More Religious Than Ever.* Wilmington, DE: ISI, 2015.

Stern, Madeleine. *Patriarch: A Biography of Stephen Pearl Andrews.* Austin: University of Texas Press, 1968.

Stone, Lyman. "Roy Moore Had Lowest White Evangelical Support of Any Alabama Republican in the 21st Century." *The Federalist*, December 13, 2017. http://thefederalist.com/2017/12/13/roy-moore-lowest-white-evangelical-support-alabama-republican-21st-century/. Accessed Dec. 19, 2018.

Sunderland, LaRoy. *The Testimony of God against Slavery, or a Collection of Passages from the Bible Which Show the Sin of Holding Property in Men.* Boston: Webster and Southard, 1835.

Sweetman, Brendan. *Why Politics Needs Religion: The Place of Religious Arguments in the Public Square.* Downers Grove, IL: InterVarsity, 2006.

Takaki, Ronald. *A Pro-slavery Crusade: The Agitation to Reopen the African Slave Trade.* New York: Free, 1971.

Talmon, J. L. *History of Totalitarian Democracy.* London: Secker & Warburg, 1952.

Tarr, Alan G. "Church and State in the States." *Washington Law Review* 64 (1989) 73–110.

Taylor, C. "The Meaning of Secularism." *Hedgehog Review* 12 (2010) 1.

———. *A Secular Age.* Cambridge, MA: Harvard University Press, 2007.

Texas Freedom Network. *Religious Right in Texas.* http://tfn.org/mission.

———. *The Bible and Public Schools: Report on the National Council on Bible Curriculum in Public Schools.* Austin: Texas Freedom Network, 2005.

The Koran with Parallel Arabic Text. Translated by N. J. Dawood. New York: Penguin, 2014.

Thomas, Merrilyn. Review of *Religion and the Cold War* by Diane Kirby. *Reviews in History*, review 362. http:www.history.ac.uk/reviews/review362.

Thompson, Andrew. *Slavery Not Sanctioned, But Condemned, by Christianity.* Edinburgh, 1829.

Thompson, Joseph P. *Christianity and Emancipation; or, the Teachings and the Influence of the Bible against Slavery.* New York: Randolph, 1863.

Tobin, Gary A., and Dennis R. Ybarra. *Trouble with Textbooks: Distorting History and Religion.* Rowman and Littlefield, 2008.

Tocqueville, Alexis de. *Democracy in America.* Translated by H. Rowe. 1835. Repr., London: Wordsworth, 1998.

———. *Democracy in America.* Translated by Harvey C. Mansfield and Delba Winthrop. Chicago: University of Chicago Press, 2000.

Trigg, Roger. *Equality, Freedom, and Religion.* Oxford: Oxford University Press, 2012.

———. *Religion in Public Life: Must Faith be Privatized?* Oxford: Oxford University Press, 2007.

Tschannen, O. "The Secularisation Paradigm." *Journal for the Scientific Study of Religion* 30 (1991) 395–415.

U.S. News/Raytheon. STEM Index reports. 20 November 2015. http://www.usnews.com/news/stem-index/articles/2015/11/20/op-ed-students-need-stem-education-for-21st-century-economy

United Nations Alliance of Civilisations. http://www.aocerb.org.

United Nations Human Rights Council. Sixteenth Session, Agenda Item 3, Report of the Special Rapporteur on Freedom of Religion or Belief, Heiner Bielefeldt, United Nations General Assembly document A/HRC/16/53, 1–19, 2010.

Uskel, Edip. *Manifesto for Islamic Reform.* Breinigsville, PA: Brainbow, 2009.

van Biema, David. "The Case for Teaching the Bible." *Time* 22 March 2007. http://www.time.com/time/magazine/article/0,9171,1601845—4,00.html.

———. "Hobby Lobby's Steve Green Launches Public School Bible Course." *Baptist Standard*, 21 April 2014. http://www.baptiststandard.com/news/national/16354-hobby-lobby-s-steve-green-launches-public-school-bible-curriculu.

Vatican Archives. "Catechism of the Catholic Church." http://www.vatican.va/archive/ccc_css/archive/catechism/p1s1c2a2.htm

Vitz, Paul C. *Censorship: Evidence of Bias in our Children's Textbooks.* Ann Arbor, MI: Servant, 1986.

Vlach, Michael J. "Americans and the Bible: Ownership, Reading, Study and Knowledge in the United States." http://www.theologicalstudies.org/page/page/1572910.htm.

Vogue, Ariane de. "Supreme Court Lets Full Travel Ban Take Effect." *CNN*, Dec. 5, 2017. http://www.cnn.com/2017/12/04/politics/supreme-court-travel-ban/index.html. Accessed December 19, 2017.

Wachlin, Marie. "What Do High School Teachers Think Students Need to Know about the Bible?" In *The Bible Literacy Report: What Do American Teens Need to Know and What Do They Know?*, edited by Marie Wachlin and Byron R. Johnson, 8–21. New York: Bible Literacy Project, 2005.

Warner, R. S. "Work in Progress Toward a New Paradigm for the Sociological Study of Religion in the United States." *American Journal of Sociology* 98 (1993) 1044–93.

Watson, J. "Can Children and Young People Learn from Atheism for Spiritual Development? A Response to the National Framework for Religious Education." *British Journal of Religious Education* 30 (2008) 49–58.

———. "Including Secular Philosophies such as Humanism in Locally Agreed Syllabuses for Religious Education." *British Journal of Religious Education* 32 (2010) 5–18.

Wayland. Francis. "Correspondence with Richard Fuller." In *Domestic Slavery Considered as a Scriptural Institution*, reviewed and corrected by Richard Fuller and Francis Wayland, 2–125. New York: Colby, 1845.

Webb, Stephen. "The Supreme Court and the Pedagogy of Religious Studies: Constitutional Parameters for the Teaching of Religion in Public Schools." *Journal of the American Academy of Religion* 70 (2002) 135–57.

Webster, Noah, Jr. *A Collection of Essays and Fugitive Writings: On Moral, Historical, Political and Literary Subjects.* Boston: Thomas and Andrews, 1790.

———. *A Grammatical Institute of the English Language, In Three Parts.* Part I. Hartford: Hutson and Goodwin, 1783.

———. *A Grammatical Institute of the English Language, In Three Parts.* Part III. Hartford: Barlow and Babcock, 1785.

Weisse, W. "Reflections of the REDCo Project." *British Journal of Religious Education* 33 (2011) 111–25.

———. *Religion in Education: Contribution to Dialogue Policy Recommendations of the REDCo Research Project.* Hamburg, 2009. http://www.redco.uni-hamburg.de/cosmea/core/corebase/mediabase/awr/redco/research_findings/REDCo_policy_rec_eng.pdf.

Weithman, Paul, ed. *Religion and Contemporary Liberalism.* Notre Dame: University of Notre Dame Press, 1997.

Westmoreland, Charles R. "*Wallace v. Jaffree* (1985)." In *Encyclopedia of Alabama*, 11 May 2010. http://www.encyclopediaofalabama.org/article/h-1623.

Willaime, Jean-Paul. "Different Models of Religion and Education in Europe." In *Religion and Education in Europe: Developments, Contexts and Debates*, edited by R. Jackson et al., 57–66. Munster: Waxmann, 2007.

Wills, Garry. *Head and Heart: A History of Christianity in America*. New York: Penguin, 2007.

Wilson, B. R. *Religion in Secular Society*. London: Watts, 1966.

Wilson, D. *The People's Bible*. Oxford: Lion Hudson, 2011.

Wolin, S. *Democracy Inc.: Managed Democracy and the Specter of Inverted Totalitarianism*. Princeton: Princeton University Press, 2008.

Wright, A. *Critical Religious Education, Multiculturalism and the Pursuit of Truth*. Cardiff: University of Wales Press, 2007.

Wright, Susan. "Nearly 100 Evangelical Leaders Draft a Petition to Denounce Trump." *RedState*, 7 October 2016. http:// www.redstate.com.

Wyatt-Brown, Bertram. "Church, Honor, and Secession." In *Religion and the American Civil War*, edited by Randall M. Miller et al., 91. New York: Oxford University Press, 1998.

Yu, Tianlog. *In the Name of Morality: Character Education and Political Control*. New York: Lang, 2004.

Zimmerman, Jonathan. "Anti-Blasphemy Laws Have a History in America." *Newsworks*, 9 October 2012. http://www.newsworks.org/index.php/local/thats-history/45356-anti-blasphemy-laws-have-a-history-in-america.

Zuckerman, Philip. *Living the Secular Life*. New York: Penguin, 2015.

Index